DEATH THERAPY!

DEATH THERAPY!

Benefitting From Near-Death Experiences
Without the Inconvenience of Dying

Michael K. Crossley, M.D.

MCP BOOKS

MCP Books
2301 Lucien Way #415
Maitland, FL 32751
407.339.4217
www.millcitypress.net

Unless otherwise indicated, Scripture quotations taken from the King James Version (KJV) – *public domain.*

Printed in the United States of America.

ISBN-13: 9781545644171

Contents

Introduction

I STOLE THE TITLE TO THIS BOOK.
It came from one of my favourite movies: *What About Bob?*[1]

Bob Wiley is plagued by multiple phobias. He's worn out every psychiatrist who's tried to help him. The story opens with Bob's current psychiatrist (apparently on the verge of insanity himself), ecstatic at finally pawning off his nemesis on an unsuspecting colleague, Dr. Leo Marvin. His jubilation is an ominous harbinger of the mayhem that Bob is about to inflict on his new healer.

Just one session with the brilliant Dr. Marvin convinces Bob that he's finally found someone who can help him. As the therapy session ends, however, Dr. Marvin drops a bombshell on Bob when he informs him he's leaving town immediately for a month's vacation. But he hands Bob a copy of his new book, *Baby Steps*, along with the assurance that it contains the solutions to all of Bob's problems and that it will sustain him until he returns. Dr.

---

[1] *What About Bob?* is a 1991 comedy by Touchstone Pictures, directed by Frank Oz, starring Bill Murray, Richard Dreyfuss, and others.

Marvin then skips off happily to his vacation home on Lake Winnipesaukee.

Bob, unable to face a whole month without his new-found saviour, immediately catches a bus to the lake. Furious at the invasion of his closely-guarded privacy, Dr. Marvin deploys every legitimate weapon in the psychiatrist's arsenal to fend off his annoying new patient, unaware that Bob is human superglue—not easily dislodged. Bob stays, and slowly but surely, ingratiates himself with the Marvin family, to the utter chagrin of the quirky doctor.

A series of crushing blows to Dr. Marvin's pride (inflicted unwittingly by the affable but lethal Bob) leads the increasingly deranged psychiatrist to conclude that Bob has to go, one way or another. He hatches a fool-proof plot to get rid of Bob: *death therapy!* He breaks into the local store, steals twenty pounds of black powder, takes Bob into the woods, ties him up with rope, and hangs the canisters of gunpowder around Bob's neck with detonator and timer attached.

Bob, confused but intrigued, questions the doctor about this rather unusual departure from protocol:

Bob: "What are we up to?"

Dr. Marvin: *"Death therapy*, Bob! It's a guaranteed cure!"

His job done, the now completely unhinged psychiatrist dances off, exclaiming, *"Free! Free!"* leaving Bob alone in the woods to contemplate his fate.

Bob, however, still enamoured with his brilliant mentor and obediently "baby-stepping" forward with irrepressible optimism, manages to find higher purpose in the strange exercise. He reasons:

*"This is tricky. I'm all tied up... Yeah, you're saying I'm all tied up inside... and these phony bombs mean that... if I don't untie myself inside... the emotional knots... I'm going to explode! Yeah, it's so simple... yet so brilliant! Okay, Dr. M, I get it! Baby step: **untie your knots!**"*

The scene shifts from the woods to the Marvins' home on the lake. Having somehow extricated himself from the sticky situation in the woods, Bob is now exiting the house, bearing Dr. M's birthday cake and singing: "Leo Marvin's a genius! Your death therapy cured me, you genius!"

Struggling to recover from the shock of seeing Bob alive and free, the psychiatrist asks anxiously: "The bags I put around your neck, Bob, where are they?"

"In the house... why?"

The camera pans to the Marvins' beautiful lakeside home—which promptly disintegrates in a massive explosion.

The film ends with the title card:

Bob went back to school and became a psychologist.
*He then wrote a huge bestseller: "**Death Therapy**."*
Leo is suing him for the rights.

Death Therapy

Well, happily, *What About Bob?* is fiction. The movie isn't based on a true story and *Death Therapy* was never written!

So, I'm using the title.

Lest you get the wrong impression, let me say at the outset that I'm not advocating tying someone up and hanging gunpowder around his neck as a means of overcoming hang-ups! It clearly worked for Bob, but may not pass muster in the real world.

What I *am* suggesting, is that if we were to discover what really happens to us when we die, then that precious perspective could have a profound effect on the way we live. If we could somehow learn what characteristics count the most on the other side, perhaps we could start developing those character traits now while we still have the opportunity to make some changes. That's what *Death Therapy* is all about: learning to live better by gaining a clearer understanding of death.

The problem has been that, until recently, the knowledge just hasn't been there, at least not in abundance. From the beginning of time, death has remained life's greatest mystery—the last frontier. It's the road we simply can't take—a dead end (pun intended).

There is, of course, the possibility of inducing one's own death in hopes of glimpsing the afterlife and being resuscitated before too much damage is done. That's the premise of the movie *Flatliners*,[2] but outside of Hollywood, few would be foolhardy enough to try it.

All that changed in the middle of the twentieth century with the advent of CPR.[3] For the first time in history, people were being brought back from cardiac arrest

---

[2] *Flatliners* is a 1990 science fiction/drama by Columbia Pictures, directed by Joel Schumacher, starring Kiefer Sutherland, Kevin Bacon, Julia Roberts, and others. A sequel is planned for release in 2017.

[3] CPR: Cardiopulmonary resuscitation.

in significant numbers, and a fortuitous by-product of these resuscitations (in addition to lives being saved!), was that for some patients, the experience turned out to be more than just an interruption in wakefulness—much, much more. While cardiac monitors recorded prolonged periods of "flatline," the individual's awareness of consciousness continued to skip along merrily as though nothing had happened. Many were brought back to life utterly convinced that they had remained very much "alive" throughout the ordeal.

And it wasn't just that consciousness had endured. The very essence of who the person was had instantly relocated from the failing physical body into a spectacular spiritual one in an almost seamless transition.

Furthermore, in many cases, this sleek new version of the individual went on to take an extended peek behind the "curtain" of death. Little by little, stories began to emerge of a world of sublime peace and indescribable beauty. Near-death survivors were returning to life in large numbers, utterly convinced that death is not the end of existence. Many would even claim to have felt far more alive in that world than in this.

Resuscitation from death is not an entirely new phenomenon, of course—there are sporadic anecdotal accounts throughout history. But the sheer volume of people now coming back from the brink of death with incredible tales to tell is nothing short of a revolution. It jump-started a wave of interest in death that would become a tsunami.

It was a young, aspiring doctor by the name of Raymond Moody who first realized that these descriptions of an afterlife were more than just the idiosyncratic fantasies of a few individuals. There were too many near-death survivors telling the same story. Their consistency convinced Moody that this phenomenon was real, and that something new and exciting was afoot.

He collected over one hundred near-death accounts, compared them side by side, and compiled them in a book. When he published *Life After Life* in 1975, it could be argued that the concept of consciousness surviving death was no longer a matter of faith. Moody introduced us to a phrase that would become part of the public lexicon: *near-death experience* or *NDE*.

Life After Life ignited the fire.

Dr. Moody's publication gave thousands of people the courage to come forward with near-death accounts of their own. Emboldened by the knowledge that they were not alone in their brush with death, they came out of the woodwork in droves—many with stories of stunning detail and compelling consistency. They spoke of emerging from a dark tunnel into a world of indescribable beauty, of being enveloped in a light that overwhelmed them with feelings of love and joy.

Family and friends (even pets) were there to welcome the traveller home. Their joy at the reunion was unrestrained. Many met a "being of light" who emanated love and compassion and sometimes granted them a comprehensive review of their life.

The news that the person must return to life is often received with profound dismay. So enamoured is the traveller with this glorious new world that the desire to stay often trumps the thought of leaving loved ones behind. It's hard to imagine, but even mothers can instantly stop worrying about leaving their little children. They just know they'll be okay.

But this is not their time. Most are resigned to that fact, and so they return to their former lives, bolstered by the knowledge that there is still much work for them to do.

Re-entry into the physical body is a rather unwelcome return to reality. Many comment that they were just getting used to this wonderful new "body" and were ready to take it out for a spin. I suppose it would be a little like having to leave the sleek Ferrari in the showroom and skulk home in the battered piece of junk you drove up in.

Sceptics have tried to explain away near-death experiences by offering multiple alternative explanations: the throes of a dying brain, anoxia, temporal lobe seizures, drug effects, etc., etc. They point out that an LSD trip can produce similar results.

While none of these mechanisms come close to approximating the complexity of the near-death experience, the one thing they *really* can't do is produce a lasting change in the life of the survivor.

NDEs change lives.

Survivors come back to Earth determined to live a better life and to make the most of the time they have left. For the most part, returnees are more loving, kind, forgiving, patient, and more inclined to look for the good in people. They have a newfound thirst for knowledge. Almost all lose their fear of death.

The changes "NDEers" make are real and lasting—this wasn't a trip to Disneyland. You come home from Disneyland a little poorer and totally unable to get that irritating "It's a Small World" song out of your head, but otherwise unchanged. NDEs are different. This was a visit to the afterlife and a brush with The Divine. You don't come back from something like that unchanged. Most survivors would say that their NDE was *the* defining moment of their lives.

Here's the thing, however: as wonderful as these experiences are, they've only been "enjoyed" by a small percentage of the population (about 5 percent of Americans actually, which still represents millions of people). That leaves the rest of us in the dark, and with one-in-twenty odds, it isn't likely that you or I will ever have the chance to join this privileged fraternity for whom knowledge of the afterlife is no longer a matter of faith. That is our reality.

But we don't have to remain in the dark!

As I was reading account after account of the dramatic and positive changes that accompany the NDE, I realized that these incredible stories were beginning to have a very real impact on me, too. By coming to understand what's really important in the next life, I discovered that my own values were changing. It was becoming a little easier to love people and to treat them with respect. It was easier to forgive them. My tolerance for different viewpoints was growing. In short, I felt that I was subtly changing for the better just by reading about the near-death experiences of others. The changes weren't as abrupt or as dramatic, but they were real, nonetheless.

And that's when I had an epiphany:

Nothing changes a person quite like dying—but, I don't have to die to learn from those who have!

If they can come back from such a trauma, radically changed for the better, maybe I could make some lasting changes in my life without having to go through the inconvenience of dying! That's the essence of *Death Therapy*—living better by learning from those who've died and come back.

Where else can you find such a treasure trove of useful knowledge? What could add more meaning to life than understanding what really happens to us when we die? The near-death phenomenon may be one of the greatest untapped therapies available to us in life, and the beauty of it is that we can participate while we're still breathing!

What qualifications do I have for writing this book? None whatever. I have not had a near-death experience (nor do I want one!), and even though I've resuscitated a lot of people in my profession as an ER doctor, I've never personally known anyone who's had an NDE.

But why let ignorance get in the way?

Actually, it occurred to me that my ignorance may even be a plus. While most books on NDEs are written either by people who've actually had an experience or by those who've interviewed them, this book makes no such claims of legitimacy. In fact, I've deliberately avoided seeking out near-death experiencers in order to maintain a sort of "purity of ignorance."

Since 95 percent of us are ignorant on the subject, this book is directed to the great unwashed majority who, like me, may never have a close encounter with death, but are open to learning from those who have. It's written in the hope that I can encourage you to learn more about near-death and reap the benefits this knowledge can bring. My aspiration is that as you delve into these first-hand accounts of people who've visited the next life, you'll feel the sincerity and power of their words and, like me, be prompted to make some changes.

We don't have to wait until we die to unlock death's secrets. We can enjoy a little glimpse of it now.

So, join me in therapy... *Death Therapy, Bob! It's a guaranteed cure!*

Chapter 1

Life After Life

Pippin: *I didn't think it would end this way.*
Gandalf: *End? No, the journey doesn't end here. Death is just another path, one that we all must take. The grey rain-curtain of this world rolls back, and all turns to silver glass, and then you see it.*
Pippin: *What? Gandalf? See what?*
Gandalf: *White shores, and beyond, a far green country under a swift sunrise.*
Pippin: *Well, that isn't so bad.*
Gandalf: *No. No, it isn't.*
　　　　　　—J. R. Tolkien, *The Lord of the Rings*

"Momma always said dyin' was a part of life. I sure wish it wasn't."　　—Forrest Gump[4]

---

[4] *Forrest Gump* is a 1994 comedy/drama by Paramount Pictures, directed by Robert Zemeckis, starring Tom Hanks, Robin Wright, and others. It is based on the 1986 novel of the same name by Winston Groom.

"To the well-organized mind, death is but the next great adventure."
—Albus Dumbledore in
Harry Potter and the Sorcerer's Stone[5]

Consistency and Real Estate

Mac and Dick McDonald operated a successful drive-in restaurant in San Bernardino, California, from 1940 to 1948. It had twenty-five items on the menu and was named "McDonald's Bar-B-Que." As was the custom at the time, the customer remained in the car, and carhops delivered the food to him or her.

Despite the venue's popularity, the brothers decided to shut the restaurant down temporarily and try something new. They reduced the menu to six items (hamburger, cheeseburger, potato chips, coffee, soft drinks, and apple pie), streamlined the production process, eliminated the carhops, and introduced the revolutionary practice of having the customer come to the window to order his or her own food. When they reopened the restaurant two months later, it was under a new name, simply: "McDonald's."

In addition to simplifying the menu and the name, the brothers focused on producing quality hamburgers that were exactly alike every time.

Over time, McDonald's was transformed from a single, sit-down diner into a fast-food "chain" consisting of three

---

[5] *Harry Potter and the Sorcerer's Stone* (originally *Harry Potter and the Philosopher's Stone*) is the first novel in the Harry Potter series and J. K. Rowling's debut novel, first published in 1997 by Bloomsbury.

local restaurants. Customers still had the option of dining inside the restaurant, but everything about the experience screamed: *hurry up and leave!* The heating was turned off and seats were fixed in an upright position so that customers would be hunched over their food, prompting them to eat faster. Drinks were served in cone-shaped cups, forcing the customers to hold their drink whilst eating, further shortening the dining process. Then, of course, there was that hideous yellow and red decor, which was calculated to induce migraines, seizures, or nervous breakdowns if endured for longer than fifteen minutes at a stretch. McDonald's was all about efficiency and volume, and their *"no loitering"* policy ensured that no one gummed up the works.

But they did make great hamburgers, and they did it with a consistency and efficiency previously unseen in the restaurant business.

Meanwhile, on the other side of the country, a man by the name of Ray Kroc was eking out a living hawking Multimixer brand milkshake machines. When Kroc learned that the McDonald brothers were using eight of his Multimixers in a single restaurant he set out for San Bernardino to find out why. He was astonished by the innovative brilliance of the McDonald's operation. It didn't take him long to realize that their model was the future of the fast-food industry and he requested the opportunity to start franchising McDonald's nationwide. The brothers were sceptical that their self-service approach would work in colder, wetter climates, but reluctantly agreed to allow

Kroc to set up restaurants in return for half a percent of gross sales.

Ray Kroc worked tirelessly to build McDonald's into a national chain. It was not without its share of growing pains, however. As innovative as the concept was, Kroc knew it wouldn't succeed unless he could achieve uniformity in quality and service throughout the company. He discovered a solution that would ensure the rapid growth of the chain while still retaining control over the franchisees. The parent company started buying land and leasing it to the franchisee, thus keeping the franchisee beholden to the corporation. The success of this strategy led to those golden arches being found on every major intersection of the civilized world (and much of the uncivilized world), and the McDonald's corporation becoming the single largest owner of real estate on the planet. Kroc would later famously say: "I'm not in the hamburger business. My business is real estate."

As in most ventures where big money is involved, friction developed between the partners. Kroc wanted to grow rapidly, but was handcuffed by the brothers' insistence on keeping a tight lid on operations. They eventually agreed to part ways, Kroc buying the McDonald brothers out for $2.7 million, and making a handshake commitment to pay them 1.9 percent in royalties (the altruistic brothers feeling that 2 percent sounded greedy).

At closing, the brothers refused to transfer the San Bernardino restaurant to Kroc because they wanted to donate it to the founding employees. This so incensed Kroc that he later refused to honour the royalty agreement. Not content with this slight (which would cost the brothers hundreds of millions in future earnings), Kroc further rubbed salt into the wound by opening a new McDonald's across the street from the original, to force it out of business. He even required Mac and Dick McDonald to rename the original restaurant since they'd neglected to retain the rights to their own surname.

McDonald's enjoyed spectacular growth through the '70s. It survived the brutal "Burger Wars" of the early '80s (including Wendy's vaunted "Where's the beef?" campaign). McDonald's even got into higher education, opening four "Hamburger Universities" and granting over forty-thousand coveted "Bachelor of Hamburgerology" degrees.

They expanded rapidly overseas but ran into problems as the brand came to be viewed by some as the face of American imperialism. In the new millennium, the public began to demand healthier foods, forcing McDonald's to phase out the "Super Size" concept and bring in such healthy options as (*gasp!*) fruits, salads, and Chicken McNuggets that were actually made of chicken.

The decor was redesigned. Gone were the harsh yellows and hard plastic of the "no loitering" era, replaced with soothing earth tones and padded seating.

Some fun McDonald's trivia:
- 1 percent of the world's population eats at McDonald's every day.
- McDonald's sells over seventy-five hamburgers a second.
- The McDonald's "economy" is bigger than Ecuador's.

- The golden arches are more recognizable world-wide than the Christian cross.
- Chicken McNuggets used to be made from a pink goo that looked more like ice cream than chicken.
- The Queen of England owns a McDonald's down the street from Buckingham Palace.

Mac and Dick McDonald's innovations revolutionized the fast-food industry, but if it had not been for the vision and ambition of Ray Kroc, their little chain would likely have remained a household name only in San Bernardino and the surrounding area. Kroc took a kernel of an idea and grew it into a multinational behemoth. Between Ray Kroc and the brothers, the McDonald's Corporation became what is arguably the most successful business enterprise in history.

The McDonald's of the Afterlife

Don't panic at the heading! I'm not suggesting that McDonald's reach extends into the afterlife. No one has seen those golden arches in heaven, at least not that I'm aware of.

(As for hell, who knows? I'm sure Lucifer has considered it. It's difficult to imagine a more diabolical punishment than an eternity of only Chicken McNuggets and Big Macs, and besides, hell may be the last place still available for franchises.)

No, the point is, that what McDonald's did for the fast-food industry, Raymond Moody's Life After Life did for the near-death experience—it put it on the map. Raymond

Kroc brought McDonald's out of obscurity and made it a household name. Raymond Moody did the same for the NDE. And while the term "near-death experience" may not be as ubiquitous as "McDonald's," its day is coming. No one escapes death: someday everyone will book a table at that great "restaurant in the sky," and that's an inevitability even McDonald's can't claim.

When Life After Life hit the bookstores in 1975, it was a game-changer. It came at a time when the belief in the survival of the soul was slowly being relegated to the realm of religion and anecdote. In an increasingly secular world, science wasn't willing to give much credence to the possibility of an afterlife.

Life After Life changed all that.

The book was, in some ways, quite simple. Moody merely catalogued multiple accounts of visits to the next world and compared them side by side. As elementary as Life After Life was, it caught the imagination of the public and thrust the tantalizing possibility of a glorious afterlife firmly onto the public radar. With so many credible witnesses, it was no longer as easy to dismiss the possibility of life after death as merely the ethereal whim of religionists and philosophers.

Moody's work certainly wasn't proof of an afterlife, but by the same token, his assertions weren't easy to ignore. Multiple highly-consistent, first-hand accounts of a life beyond this life could hardly be taken lightly. Moody introduced the public to what may be the most exciting phenomenon of the modern era: the near-death experience (NDE).

The term may have been new, but the concept wasn't. Isolated accounts of NDEs had been described for centuries. Perhaps the oldest surviving account in Western literature is Plato's account of Er, a soldier who returned to life twelve days after being abandoned for dead on a funeral pyre—with a remarkable tale to tell. The Tibetan Book of the Dead, the Bible, and the Koran all likewise contain detailed stories of life after death. None of them would seem too out of place in a modern book about NDEs.

But these accounts were anecdotal and sporadic at best. Life After Life was different.

Moody compiled a large collection of near-death accounts side-by-side and analysed them for common themes. The consistency he found was compelling. He concluded that these were honest, rational people who were simply reporting what they saw, apparently without any ulterior motive or desire for personal gain. Their stories weren't the elaborate constructs of a dying brain or an overenthusiastic imagination. The place they were describing was real.

Consciousness continues! There *is* a life after this life!

What was it that got Raymond Moody interested in death in the first place? Death isn't a subject many of us like to contemplate and it's generally the last thing on the mind of a young college student. A chance meeting with a professor of psychiatry at the University of Virginia changed all that.

Young Raymond was struck by the warmth and candour of the kindly professor and was surprised to discover that Dr. George Ritchie had died and been revived not just once, but twice, and that he had experienced remarkable out-of-body journeys both times. Moody was fascinated. As interesting as it was, however, it was just one man's story and the young undergrad simply filed it away and didn't think much more about it.

Years later, after earning a PhD, Dr. Moody found himself teaching philosophy in North Carolina. One day, he was approached by a young student who wanted to discuss the question of the immortality of the soul. The student was interested because he had a grandmother who had "died" during an operation and upon resuscitation had recounted an amazing out-of-body experience. Dr. Moody was intrigued when the young man relayed a sequence of events that sounded eerily similar to the tale told by his psychiatry professor many years earlier. It evoked some powerful memories.

Moody was hooked!

Without overtly referencing these two encounters, Dr. Moody began introducing the topic of survival of biological death in his philosophy lectures. To his amazement, he found that in almost every class, at least one student would approach him and volunteer a near-death experience. What really caught his attention were the striking similarities of the stories. With remarkable consistency, his students all described the same series of events.

By 1972, Dr. Moody had accumulated a sizable collection of first-hand accounts and began giving lectures on the subject. Attendees were fascinated, and invariably someone would approach him afterward, anxious to share his or her own near-death story. He carefully interviewed each one and rapidly accumulated over 150 well-documented accounts. He whittled the pool down and made the stories the core of his book.

Dr. Moody constructed a prototypical "ideal" or "complete" model of the NDE that incorporated all the elements of the phenomenon in the order in which they typically occur:

> *"A man is dying and, as he reaches the point of greatest physical distress, he hears himself pronounced dead by his doctor. He begins to hear an uncomfortable noise, a loud ringing or buzzing, and at the same time feels himself moving very rapidly through a long dark tunnel. After this, he suddenly finds himself outside of his own physical body, but still in the immediate physical environment, and he sees his own body from a distance, as though he is a spectator. He watches the resuscitation attempt from this unusual vantage point and is in a state of emotional upheaval.*

> *"After a while, he collects himself and becomes more accustomed to his odd condition. He notices that he still has a 'body,' but one of a very different nature and with very different powers from the physical body he has left behind. Soon other things begin to happen. Others come to meet and to help him. He glimpses the spirits of relatives and friends who have already died, and a loving warm spirit of a kind he has never encountered before—a*

being of light—appears before him. This being asks him a question, nonverbally, to make him evaluate his life and helps him along by showing him a panoramic, instantaneous playback of the major events of his life. At some point he finds himself approaching some sort of barrier or border, apparently representing the limit between earthly life and the next life. Yet, he finds that he must go back to the Earth, that the time for his death has not yet come. At this point he resists, for by now he is taken up with his experiences in the afterlife and does not want to return. He is overwhelmed by intense feelings of joy, love, and peace. Despite his attitude, though, he somehow reunites with his physical body and lives.

"Later he tries to tell others, but he has trouble doing so. In the first place, he can find no human words adequate to describe these unearthly episodes. He also finds that others scoff, so he stops telling other people. Still, the experience affects his life profoundly, especially his views about death and its relationship to life." (*Life After Life*, pp. 21–23)

The term "model" has to be used with some caution. Although a definite pattern emerges in regard to the process of dying, it's unusual to find any one story that could be described as the "typical" NDE. People are unique, and just as our perspective of this world is very much coloured by our background and conditioning, it appears that NDEs are no different. To illustrate: two tourists can visit Paris for the first time. One returns raving about the stunning beauty of the architecture, the other rants about the stunning rudeness of the waiters. They both visited Paris, but each had a different experience.

But Dr. Moody's model was sound. Every element in his prototypical NDE appeared in multiple accounts. He was clearly on to something.

The actual words of the survivors are what make Life After Life so compelling. These people are trusting us with the most intimate and sacred experience of their lives and one can't read their words without feeling a profound sense of awe.

Here are some excerpts from Life After Life, broken down according to the "typical" sequence of Moody's model:

1) The realization that one has died

> *"At the point of injury there was a momentary flash of pain, but then all the pain vanished. I had the feeling of floating in a dark space... I remember thinking, 'I must be dead.'"* (*Life After Life*, pp. 28–29)

> *"Oh, I'm dead! How lovely!"* (Ibid, p. 41)

What a remarkable thing! The most fateful moment of your life, the moment your worst fear (death) has become a reality, and people describe it like they've just arrived at Grandma's. Perhaps it's because we still have a body, and the new body looks so much like the old one that many of the newly-deceased have trouble realizing they've actually died!

> *"I still felt an entire body form, legs, arms, everything—even while I was weightless."* (Ibid, p. 50)

> *"I could feel my body, and it was whole. I know that. I felt whole, and I felt that all of me was there, though it wasn't."* (Ibid, p. 53)

2) Feelings of warmth and comfort

> *"The day was bitterly cold, yet while I was in that blackness all I felt was warmth and the most extreme comfort I have ever experienced."* (Ibid, pp. 28–29)

> *"I began to experience the most wonderful feelings. I couldn't feel a thing in the world except peace, comfort, ease—just quietness. I felt that all my troubles were gone, and I thought to myself, 'Well how quiet and peaceful, and I don't hurt at all.'"* (Ibid, p. 29)

Stress and anxiety are constant companions in today's frenetic world. Happily, just as we are *entering* death's door, it appears that these unwelcome guests are *shown* the door.

3) Meeting friends and relatives

"I realized that all these people were there, almost in multitudes it seems, hovering around the ceiling of the room. They were all people I had known in my past life, but who had passed on before. I recognized my grandmother and a girl I had known when I was in school, and many other relatives and friends... They all seemed pleased. It was a very happy occasion, and I felt that they had come to protect or to guide me. It was almost as if I were coming home, and they were there to greet me or to welcome me. All this time, I had the feeling of everything light and beautiful. It was a beautiful and glorious moment." (Ibid, pp. 55–56)

"It seemed as if I were on a ship or a small vessel sailing to the other side of a large body of water. On the distant shore, I could see all of my loved ones who had died—my mother, my father, my sister, and others. I could see them, could see their faces, just as they were when I knew them on Earth. They seemed to be beckoning me to come on over, and all the while I was saying, 'No, no, I'm not ready to join you. I don't want to die. I'm not ready to go...'" (Ibid, pp. 74–75)

There's a saying in life: *You can choose your friends, but you can't choose your family.* Apparently, it's just as applicable in death. So be nice to your family. They're not going away!

4) **The light**

> *"I floated right straight on through the screen, just as though it weren't there, and up into this pure, crystal clear light, an illuminating white light. It was beautiful and so bright, so radiant, but it didn't hurt my eyes. It's not the kind of light you can describe on Earth. I didn't actually see a person in this light, and yet it has a special identity, it definitely does. It is a light of perfect understanding and perfect love."* (Ibid, pp. 62–63)

Absent any other element of the near-death experience, just the light itself brings feelings of incredible peace and joy to the individual:

> *"A brilliant white light appeared to me. The light was so bright that I could not see through it, but going up into its presence was so calming and so wonderful. There is just no experience on Earth like it... the most wonderful feelings came over me—feelings of peace, tranquility, a vanishing of all worries."* (Ibid, p. 75)

> *"The whole thing was permeated with the most gorgeous light—a living, golden yellow glow,*

a pale colour, not like the harsh gold colour we know on Earth...

"It was such a wonderful, joyous feeling; there are just no words in human language to describe it." (Ibid, pp. 75–76)

5) Beings of light

Not everyone sees a being of light, but many do. NDEers often have difficulty distinguishing between the light itself and the source of the light, but even when they don't actually see an individual, there's a feeling that some*one* is in the light. That someone radiates pure love:

"I definitely felt the presence of a very powerful, completely loving being there with me all through this experience." (Ibid, p. 70)

"The love which came from it is just unimaginable, indescribable. It was a fun person to be with! And it had a sense of humor, too—definitely!" (Ibid, p. 64)

6) The life review

The interview we've been anticipating for a lifetime! The moment when we account for everything we've done in life. The experience usually occurs in the presence of a being of light and begins with a simple question:

"The first thing he said to me was... if I was ready to die, or what I had done with my life that I wanted to show him." (Ibid, p. 61)

Talk about a loaded question! How could we possibly come up with an answer that would impress a being made of light? It would be like trying to one-up Neil Armstrong (first man on the moon) in an "epic journeys" contest: *"Well, I once drove all the way to Alaska and back!"*

Happily, impressing the being of light doesn't appear to be the object of the interview:

"Incidentally, all insist that this question, ultimate and profound as it may be in its emotional impact, is not at all asked in condemnation. The being, all seem to agree, does not direct the question to them to accuse or to threaten them, for they still feel the total love and acceptance coming from the light, no matter what their answer may be. Rather, the point of the question seems to be to make them think about their lives, to draw them out." (Ibid, pp. 61–62)

The comprehensive review of our lives is a remarkable thing. Time doesn't exist in that dimension, so when you hear people say, "My whole life flashed before my eyes," they really mean it. A lifetime can be condensed into a millisecond:

"I can't exactly describe it to you, but it was just all there. It was just all there at once, I mean, not one thing at a time, blinking off and on, but it was everything, everything at one time." (Ibid, p. 69)

[From a Vietnam veteran]: *"I was hit with six rounds of machine gun fire, and as it happened I wasn't upset at all. In my mind, I actually felt relieved when I was wounded. I felt completely at ease, and it was not frightening.*

"At the point of impact, my life began to become a picture in front of me, and it seemed that I could go back to the time when I was still a baby, and the pictures seemed to progress through my whole life.

"I could remember everything; everything was so vivid. It was so clear in front of me. It shot right by me from the earliest things I can remember right on up to the present, and it all happened within a short time. And it was not anything bad at all; I went through it with no regrets, no derogatory feelings about myself at all." (Ibid, pp. 70–71)

7) Reluctance to return

"After I came back, I cried off and on for about a week because I had to live in this world after

seeing that one. I didn't want to come back." (Ibid, p. 84)

"I never wanted to leave the presence of this being." (Ibid, p. 77)

We cling to life tenaciously now, but once we've caught a glimpse of what comes next, the desire to remain on this earth won't be nearly as strong. Almost all are ready to move on. For perspective, imagine having to go back to school after you've already graduated!

8) A changed life

This is the acid test of the veracity of the NDE: Does it change lives?[6]

"Since then it has been on my mind constantly what I have done with my life, and what I will do with my life. My past life—I'm satisfied with it. I don't think the world owes me anything... But since I died, all of a sudden, right after my experience, I started wondering whether I had been doing the things I had done because they were good, or because they were good for me...

---

[6] Acid test: In the late eighteenth century, gold prospectors used nitric acid to distinguish gold from base metal. Less valuable metals dissolved more readily than gold. Hence, to determine if a find was really gold, it was subjected to the "acid test."

"I try to do things that have more meaning, and that makes my mind and soul feel better. And I try not to be biased, and not to judge people. I want to do things because they are good, not because they are good to me. And it seems that the understanding I have of things now is so much better. I feel that this is because of what happened to me, because of the places I went and the things I saw in this experience." (Ibid, p. 90)

"It made life much more precious to me." (Ibid, p. 90)

9) Loss of the fear of death

Another universal theme. The very name *near-death* **experience** implies that life goes on, that death is not the end. Also, for most, death turned out to be the antithesis of fear.

"I was only a child when it happened, only ten, but now, my entire life through, I am thoroughly convinced that there is life after death, without a shadow of a doubt, and I am not afraid to die. I am not. Some people I have known are so afraid, so scared. I always smile to myself when I hear people doubt that there is an afterlife, or say, 'When you're dead, you're gone.' I think to myself, 'They really don't know.'

"*I've had many things happen to me in my life. In business, I've had a gun pulled on me and put to my temple. And it didn't frighten me very much, because I thought, 'Well, if I really die, if they really kill me, I know I'll still live somewhere.'*" (Ibid, pp. 94–95)

"*When I was a little boy I used to dread dying. I used to wake up at night crying and having a fit...*

"*But since this experience, I don't fear death. Those feelings vanished. I don't feel bad at funerals anymore. I kind of rejoice at them, because I know what the dead person has been through.*

"*I believe that the Lord may have sent this experience to me because of the way I felt about death.*" (Ibid, p. 95)

"*Now, I am not afraid to die. It's not that I have a death wish, or want to die right now. I don't want to be living over there on the other side right now, because I'm supposed to be living here. The reason why I'm not afraid to die, though, is that I know where I'm going when I leave here, because I've been there before.*" (Ibid, pp. 95–96)

"Some say that we are not using the word "death" because we are trying to escape from it. That's not true in my case. After you've once had the experience that I had, you know in your heart that there's no such thing as death. You just graduate from one thing to another— like from grammar school to high school to college." (Ibid, p. 97)

"Life is like imprisonment. In this state, we just can't understand what prisons these bodies are. Death is such a release—like an escape from prison. That's the best thing I can think of to compare it to." (Ibid, p. 97)

There are many, many more touching stories recounted in Life After Life, but that was a little taste of the phenomenon that fired Raymond Moody's imagination. This was heady stuff!

Dr. Moody summarized his journey of discovery with this personal observation:

"It might be more appropriate to ask, not what conclusions I have drawn on the basis of my study, but rather how the study has affected me personally. In response I can only say: There is something very persuasive about seeing a person describe his experience which cannot easily be conveyed in writing. Their near-death experiences were very real events to these people, and through my association

*with them the experiences have become real
events to me."* (Ibid, p. 183)

Life After Life wasn't a scientific study by any means,
but the stories were compelling. I remember reading it
with wonder as a teenager.

If the book was fascinating to those of us who *hadn't*
experienced a brush with death, Life After Life was to
have a profound but unanticipated effect on the small but
growing minority of people who *had*. With the publication of multiple credible stories of encounters with the
next world, other survivors of near death awoke to the
realization that their experiences were not as unique as
they once thought. It gave many the courage to "come out
of the closet."

Why hadn't they come forward sooner? Actually, many
had, or at least had tried. But attempts to share their experiences had, too often, been met with scepticism or, at best,
a tolerant shrug of the shoulders. The reaction was fairly
predictable: interesting story, but just too fantastic to take
seriously. The stories were so far removed from everyday
life that it was difficult for any but the most open-minded
to lend them any credence. Anyone with a scientific background found it especially difficult to view the phenomenon with anything but profound disbelief.

But things were different now.

Here was a published collection of stories, volunteered
by people who appeared to be just as rational as you and
me (well, me at least; I'm not sure about you!); and as fascinating a read as Life After Life was to the average person,
it must have been especially poignant to those who'd had

an experience of their own. Thousands of other near-death survivors read the book and suddenly realized: *I'm not alone!* For years they'd kept the most profound event of their life a secret, fearful that they'd be labelled a quack if they tried to share it. Not anymore. Life After Life mirrored in every relevant detail their own experience.

Out of the woodwork they came.

And if the flow began as a trickle, it would soon become a torrent. It turned out that thousands (if not millions) of very ordinary people had experienced some sort of encounter with death. A 1992 Gallup poll estimated that as many as thirteen million people in the United States alone had experienced an NDE.[7] That was one in twenty, or 5 percent of the population at the time.

A revolution was born!

More books began to appear. They generally fell into one of two categories. The first group consisted of the researchers, the majority of whom were doctors (MDs or PhDs). Inspired by Life After Life and discovering that many of the patients they were treating had experienced a similar encounter with death, they began cataloguing and publishing their own collection of stories.

The second class of books were the autobiographies of individuals who were near-death survivors themselves. Some of their experiences were so deep and profound that they felt they merited a book of their own.

The theme common to both classes of books were the changes in the lives of all involved, both researcher and experiencer. Neither group would ever quite be the same

---

[7] This poll was mentioned in the Introduction of *Coming Back to Life: The After-Effects of the Near-Death Experience* by P. M. H. Atwater.

after their encounter. For some, learning about death (whether first- or second-hand), would result in a complete turnaround in the course of their lives.

A few examples:

In 1978 Dr. Maurice Rawlings, a cardiologist from Chattanooga, Tennessee, published Beyond Death's Door. The circumstances that led to the book were fascinating:

Dr. Rawlings was performing a routine cardiac stress test on a forty-eight-year-old mail carrier. During the test the patient had a cardiac arrest and CPR was started. He went in and out of consciousness, reviving during chest compressions and "dying" again when compressions were stopped.

> *"Each time he regained heartbeat and respiration, the patient screamed, 'I am in hell!' He was terrified and pleaded with me to help him... He said, 'Don't you understand? I am in hell. Each time you quit I go back to hell! Don't let me go back to hell!'"* (Beyond Death's Door, p. 19)

Happily, his life was saved. Dr. Rawlings approached him a couple of days later very curious to learn about hell. The patient's reply: "What hell? I don't recall any hell!"

He had no unpleasant memories. Instead he described a highly pleasurable encounter with loved ones in a beautiful valley bathed in brilliant light!

This incident raises all kinds of questions which we'll wrestle with later, but the impact on the cardiologist was profound. A self-professed "lukewarm" Christian prior to the incident, Dr. Rawlings would become a devout believer and an avid student of the near-death phenomenon.

Dr. Kenneth Ring, a psychologist, wondered about the cosmic implications of the explosion in interest in this new field of study and published his conclusions in his 1985 book: Heading Toward Omega: In Search of the Meaning of the Near-Death Experience.

Postulating that we are nearing the end of an era in human development (*Omega* being the last letter in the Greek alphabet), Dr. Ring suggested the fascinating possibility that the NDE movement might represent:

> *"An evolutionary thrust toward higher consciousness for humanity at large..."* (Heading Toward Omega, p. 255)

In other words, is the arrival of the near-death revolution all part of an evolutionary process that will prepare mankind for a quantum leap in spirituality? A little grandiose maybe, but if true, it would elevate the NDE phenomenon to more than just an interesting field of study. Maybe a new generation of "Death Therapists" are just what this decaying world needs. At the very least, it would be difficult to claim that the contributions of near-death survivors to the moral fibre of our society have been anything but positive.

Death doesn't spare the young, and it soon became evident that children were having near-death experiences, too. This opened up an interesting new avenue of research and posed some provocative questions: Do children have the same experience as adults? Do they have life reviews? Are there toys in heaven? Are there special angels assigned to two-year-olds, and if so, is this a form of penance for those angels?

Dr. Melvin Morse, a practicing paediatrician from Seattle, Washington, became interested in NDEs when his young patients began volunteering their own stories. In 1990, he published a book, Closer to the Light: Learning from the Near-Death Experiences of Children.

He realized that children had a lot to add to the growing pool of knowledge about death. Blessed with the virtues of honesty and innocence, and approaching their experience without having lived long enough to develop too many prejudices, the NDEs of children may be the most reliable of all. Children simply report what they see.

It turns out that childhood NDEs are not much different than adults', just that the experience seems to be tailored to the child's age and maturity. Life reviews are rare in children (probably because there isn't much life to review), and interestingly, children tend to encounter more dead pets than dead people. Perhaps this is because they are more likely to have lost a pet than a friend or family member (or, maybe there are just more pets in heaven than people—which wouldn't be hard to believe given what Mark Twain and others have said on the subject![8]). Like adults', children's NDEs are overwhelmingly positive. More about that later.

---

[8] A few examples:
- Mark Twain: "Heaven goes by favor. If it went by merit, you would stay out and your dog would go in."

Childhood NDEs would become a lifetime passion for Dr. Morse.

Most of the criticism of NDEs and the theories that sprang from them came from the scientific community. They centred around the fact that the whole thing was, almost entirely, subjective. In an age when new theories receive little credence unless they can be backed up with empirical proof, the whole near-death phenomenon is a little too pie-in-the-sky for some. If it doesn't conform to the rigid confines of Newtonian physics, anything "other-worldly" is automatically relegated to the realm of "fringe science." Never mind that quantum theory is challenging the whole premise that what we now view as "reality" in the Newtonian world may be anything *but* real—sceptics still want hard proof.

Along came a cardiologist—Dr. Pim van Lommel.

Dr. van Lommel grew up in the ultra-secular society of the Netherlands, where more than half the population: *"...is relatively confident that death is the end of everything."* (Consciousness Beyond Life, p. 57)

His cultural bias toward nihilism was further reinforced by the cold, hard conditioning of a medical education. In his words:

- James Thurber: "If I have any beliefs about immortality, it is that certain dogs I have known will go to heaven, and very, very few persons."
- Robert Lewis Stevenson: "You think dogs will not be in heaven? I tell you, they will be there long before any of us."
- *All Dogs Go to Heaven* was a title of a 1989 animated comedy/drama by Goldcrest Films International, directed by Don Bluth and Gary Goldman, starring Dom DeLuise, Burt Reynolds, and others.

"I grew up in an academic environment where I was taught that there is a reductionist and materialist explanation for everything. And up until that point, I had always accepted this as indisputably true." (Ibid, p. viii)

But the dispassionate scientist in him was to take a broadside from the very passionate claims of his patients. Despite being under heavy anaesthesia, and with sophisticated instruments showing they were clinically dead, some of his patients were later able to accurately describe the goings-on in the operating suite. As a cardiologist, Dr. van Lommel was taught (as are most doctors), that when cardiac activity ceases, so does consciousness. And yet, here were his patients describing a state of vivid consciousness while their brains were clearly not functioning.

The "evidence" of a wakeful state in the heart lab may have been what got the doctor curious, but it was his patients' further out-of-body excursions that really got his attention. Many travelled far beyond the confines of the lab, returning from the netherworlds (to the Netherlands!) with the utter conviction that consciousness endures in another dimension.

Van Lommel tried to keep it scientific. He embarked on a semi-prospective study to verify the accuracy of his patients' claims. He placed markers on top of the lights in the operating theatres that only someone floating high in the room could see, and later asked his patients if they experienced anything out of the ordinary during their procedure. Some did. He conducted standardized interviews with NDEers immediately after the experience, and then again years later to see if their stories changed. They didn't. His study probably wasn't objective enough to satisfy a purist, but it was a valiant attempt to bring the study of NDEs out of the realm of subjectivity and inject a measure of science. Regardless, the consistency of his findings and the remarkable changes in the lives of his patients were enough to convert this pragmatist into a passionate believer in the reality of life after death. He even drew on the growing fund of knowledge of quantum theory to "prove" that consciousness beyond life is not only possible, but highly plausible.

This is something that is important to note about the NDE researchers. Most didn't start out as believers in life after death. Rather, many began their journey with serious doubts about the possibility of anything existing beyond the known physical world. Either their experience, the experiences of others, or just the sheer weight of "evidence," changed them from sceptic to believer. Such is the power of the NDE.

What of the experiencers themselves?

So far, we've cited a few of the books written by the "experts" in the field of near-death studies, but what of the individuals who had their own experience and felt it significant enough to write a book? There are many, but I'll mention just two. Again, both are medical doctors.

In 1999, Dr. Mary Neal, an orthopaedist from Jackson Hole, Wyoming, was kayaking in South America with friends. She went underwater in powerful rapids and her kayak became lodged between two rocks. Unable to free herself from the kayak or the kayak from the rocks, she remained submerged for about fifteen minutes. It takes about five minutes of no oxygen to the brain for irreversible damage to occur. Before her body eventually freed itself from the kayak, Dr. Neal's spirit freed itself from her body and "went to heaven." Whilst there, she had experiences that would change her forever. She wrote a book and titled it To Heaven and Back.

> *"[I] encountered a group of fifteen to twenty souls (human spirits sent by God), who greeted me with the most overwhelming joy I have ever experienced and could ever imagine. It was joy at an unadulterated core level... I knew each of them well, knew they were from God, and knew that I had known them for an eternity."* (To Heaven and Back, pp. 68–69)

While her very much alive, spiritual self was experiencing this joyful welcoming party, Dr. Neal's lifeless body was finally pulled out of the water and desperate resuscitative measures were started. With unrestricted spiritual vision, she was able to observe both worlds with pristine clarity. Caught between two worlds, and with the connection to the physical world not yet completely severed, Dr. Neal was able to gaze down on her earthly companions' frantic efforts to coax her limp body back to life. With each desperate plea for her to breathe, the doctor's compassion for her friends' despair compelled her to keep briefly "jumping" back into her body to take a breath.

But all this time, her spirit was being drawn deeper into this beautiful new world:

"My companions and I began to glide along a path, and I knew that I was going home. We were returning to God and we were all very excited...

"We were traveling down a path that led to a great and brilliant hall, larger and more beautiful than anything I can conceive of seeing on Earth. It was radiating a brilliance of all colors and beauty.

"I felt my soul being pulled toward the entry and, as I approached, I physically absorbed its radiance and felt the pure, complete, and utterly unconditional absolute love that ema-nated from the hall. It was the most beautiful and alluring thing I had ever seen or experi-enced. I knew with a profound certainty that it represented the last branch point of life, the gate through which each human being must pass. It was clear that this hall is the place where each of us is given the opportu-nity to review our lives and our choices, and where we are each given a final opportunity to choose God or to turn away—for eternity. I felt ready to enter the hall and was filled with an intense longing to be reunited with God. (Ibid, pp. 72–74)

That reunion would have to wait. Against all odds, Dr. Neal was revived on the bank of the river. Even more improbably, she would eventually go on to make a complete recovery—messed-up knees and back maybe, but not a trace of brain damage.

Dr. Neal was a Christian before her NDE, but would still undergo a profound spiritual transformation as a result of the experience. The turnaround may not have been as dramatic as that of a secularist like Dr. van Lommel, but Mary Neal was changed nonetheless. She describes it this way:

> *"Before my near-death experience, I was a Christian and believed that the Bible was the absolute and historically accurate Word of God. I was not, however, what anyone would call deeply spiritual or deeply religious and had no preconceived notions about life after death. My experience changed me profoundly in both spiritual and religious ways. I now know the promises of God to be true, that there is life after death, and our spiritual life is eternal."* (Ibid, p. 218)

In order for her body to free itself from the kayak, Dr. Neal's knees had to bend completely backwards—frontwards actually (anyway, not the way they're supposed to bend!). She watched the destruction of her knees through spiritual eyes and with the detached curiosity of an orthopaedic surgeon. She knew exactly which ligaments were snapping and when. Weird!

Dr. Neal (the bone doctor) got to watch her knees being destroyed through the eyes of an expert. In another strange twist of irony, Dr. Eben Alexander (a brain doctor) bagged a front-row seat to the destruction of his brain by a particularly aggressive bacteria. It put him in a coma for a week. When he finally recovered, Dr. Alexander, a practicing neurosurgeon, would have the unique opportunity of examining the course of his illness through the lens of one who has a comprehensive understanding of the brain.

Dr. Alexander's NDE is remarkable in two respects:

First, his recovery can only be described as a miracle. His brain and spinal fluid were infected with a nasty strain of E. coli, which attacked quickly and ruthlessly. By the time he got to the hospital, the cortex of his brain was literally bathed in pus. He would spend a week in a coma. The chances of surviving the illness, let alone coming out of it without permanent brain damage, were slim to none. Yet, survive he did, and with no significant physical after-effects.

Second, Dr. Alexander's neurosurgical background gave him an understanding of his experience that few could match. In a rare instance of serendipity, he was not just a practicing neurosurgeon, but also an avid student of the science of consciousness. Years of education and research into the brain had granted him a perspective on his NDE that is truly unique. Following his recovery, he was able to look at his illness with the clarity and objectivity of a professional. It quickly became obvious to him that he should not be alive, and if his survival was remarkable, the fact that he still had a functioning brain was nothing short of a miracle.

Dr. Alexander wasn't much of a believer before his NDE. While he attended church sporadically, his focus was his work, and like many doctors, his passion for medicine didn't allow much room for spirituality. So, if his patients made bizarre, otherworldly claims it would have been especially easy for a neurosurgeon like him to dismiss their ramblings as merely the complex idiosyncrasies of a malfunctioning brain. The possibility that lucidity could continue without a functioning brain would never have entered the mind of this very practical neurosurgeon.

Yet here he was, confronted with irrefutable evidence that, while his own brain had shut down for a full week, the conscious part of him remained very much alive. And during that week, he had visited a world which he would later describe as infinitely more real than this one. His experience couldn't be attributed to seizures, drugs, hallucinations, or vivid dreams. He had gone to heaven and nothing could convince him otherwise.

Dr. Eben Alexander has become an avid advocate for the legitimacy of the near-death experience and the certainty that consciousness continues after death.

Well, that's a little taste of this exciting new phenomenon known as the near-death experience. These few examples are just the tip of the iceberg, but hopefully they're sufficient to whet the appetite. NDEs are real—they change lives.

I haven't come close to seeing the life after this life and neither have I met anyone who has. However, I have felt the sincerity of the words of these believers, and their passion has changed me, too.

There *is* a life after this life, Bob. And learning about it can radically affect the quality of both that life and this. The benefits don't have to be restricted to those who've "seen" it. You and I can participate, too.

That's the beauty of *Death Therapy*. It's cheap therapy for the masses, and it's a guaranteed cure!

Chapter 2

Love

"I went skydiving,
I went Rocky Mountain climbing,
I went 2.7 seconds on a bull named Fumanchu,
And I loved deeper,
And I spoke sweeter,
And I gave forgiveness I'd been denying...
Someday I hope you get the chance,
To live like you were dying."
—Tim McGraw, "Live Like You Were Dying."[9]

"All you need is love"
—The Beatles[10]

---

[9] "Live Like You Were Dying" was released by country music artist Tim McGraw on August 24, 2004. It was number one on the Billboard country music charts for seven weeks and won a Grammy Award for Best Male Country Vocal Performance. The music video that accompanied the song prominently featured McGraw's father, former baseball player Tug McGraw, who had recently died of brain cancer.

[10] "All You Need Is Love" is a song by the Beatles, released July 1967, written by John Lennon.

ILOVED VISITING MY GRANDPARENTS when I was a boy. Grandparents are wonderful: lots of love, very little discipline. However, visits were not without their share of drama. This was England in the '60s, and neither set of grandparents ever really got over the trauma of the War or the Depression. They'd known deprivation, hunger, and the anxiety of an uncertain future. Some of the fallout from all that found expression when we came to visit.

Cleanliness always seemed to be an issue. Apparently, my parents lacked the wherewithal to take proper care of me, and so Grandma felt the need to make sure I never left her house without a thorough cleaning. The area of greatest concern seemed to be the parts behind my ears. I was constantly being quizzed about this area, which was apparently nothing more than a breeding ground for an assortment of bacteria. Without vigorous scrubbing, dire illness evidently ensued. This seemed a little strange to me because of all my body parts that were prone to come in contact with dirt, the behind-the-ears bits seemed to be as well protected as anywhere. Nevertheless, I dutifully cleaned them, and Grandma's worst fears were never realized.

Baths were quite an adventure. The thinking seemed to be that if the bathwater wasn't close to scalding, then it didn't do any good. I'd come out of the tub steaming like an overcooked lobster, and lest any doubt remained as to my sterility, vigorous scrubbing with a towel impregnated with gravel would complete the task (the gravel may have just been my imagination). Apparently, the idea was that whatever hardy creatures weren't incinerated by the scalding bathwater would certainly be removed by the gravel towel—along with several layers of skin. Those pesky bugs behind the ears? Gone!

This all probably stemmed from the fact that daily baths weren't an option for my grandparents, so when you did bathe you had to make sure it counted. For at least a week following a bath at Grandma's (along with clean underwear, because you never knew when you'd be in an accident), I'd be in a constant state of readiness for emergency surgery; no scrubbing required.

The science behind all this was a little suspect, but no one could question the motivation: my grandparents loved their grandson. Their job was to keep me alive, since my parents clearly weren't up to the task.

I wasn't the only one who ended up on the receiving end of folklore. My parents paid a price, too. While my grandparents handled some post-war technology with aplomb, with others they didn't do so well. This was never more apparent than in the case of non-stick pans. Teflon was entirely too much for my grandmother.

How could you trust a pan that didn't require lubrication with a big slab of lard? Not to worry, the Teflon coating on my mother's brand-new pans was no match for a wire brush and some elbow grease.[11] The original metal surface was restored to pristine splendour in no time. Problem solved.

My mother wasn't too thrilled, of course, but to Grandma it was a labour of love. You had to protect your progeny from sinister technology.

---

[11] Discovered in 1938 and patented by DuPont Co. in 1941. The "Teflon" name was patented in 1945.

Some breakthroughs were received with enthusiasm. My grandfather thought that sliced bread was the most wonderful thing since, well...sliced bread. But, as miraculous as those perfectly cut slices were, he wasn't about to squander precious butter on them. Butter was a scarce commodity during the war and those lessons in austerity weren't easily forgotten. Many times, I'd watch him take a big knob of butter, spread it thickly over the first slice of bread, then scrape all of it off, leaving only a microscopic film. He'd then move the knob to the next slice and repeat the process until the whole loaf was buttered. An amazing lesson in economy!

Of course, you barely knew the bread had any butter on it but, on the bright side, you never had to worry about your cholesterol.

The "buttered" bread was generally served with a delicacy such as tongue or black pudding. Again, this was probably a holdover from the war when it was a sin to waste any edible part of the animal ("edible" being a relative term). Cows' tongue has the consistency of rubber and tastes about like you'd expect tongue to taste (pardon the pun). Black pudding (congealed pigs' blood in the form of a sausage) is—well, use your imagination.

In my youthful opinion (and at the risk of offending a whole generation of Englishmen), tongue and black pudding were two of the reasons why British cuisine had long been considered to be the worst on the planet. It did not, however, justify former French president Jacques Chirac firing this cheap shot across the bow of British culinary pride: *"One cannot trust people whose cuisine is so bad!"*

I'm not sure how a nation's food choices relate to trust, but I suppose Jacques is entitled to his opinion.

(Parenthetically—and at the risk of offending a whole generation of Frenchmen—at the time of writing, the cruise ship we're on is about to dock in Cannes, France. In honour of the occasion, I managed to force down a lone *escargot* for dinner. [Actually, it went down rather easily—too easily!] I was struck with the irony of the world's fascination for French cuisine when their idea of culinary delights are snails and frogs' legs!

And in defence of British food, let me just offer two unassailable counterarguments: fish 'n' chips, and Cadbury's chocolate. End of discussion. Eat that, Jacques!)

Anyway, I digress. Getting back to the tongue and black pudding (though I'd rather not): again, it was done out of love. Believe it or not, tongue actually cost more than the standard parts of the cow, so in my grandparents' minds, they were treating us to a rare delicacy.

What does all this have to do with near-death experiences?

Not a lot, but it has everything to do with love. I just loved my grandparents, idiosyncrasies and all, and had no doubt that they loved me. Adversity may have instilled in them some strange notions in the realms of health and technology, but they'd learned, for the most part, that life is about people and how to show love for them. Hopefully, for all of us, as the years advance, so should our ability to love.

These memories serve to highlight the two attributes that NDEs teach us are prized most highly in the next life: love and knowledge. And even then, while knowledge is important, it's only really helpful if it teaches us how to love.

To put it more explicitly, you could fail in just about every other facet of life, but if you can learn to really love people you'd probably still be in great shape in the next life.

The near-death experience utterly overwhelms the senses. Like the jolt astronauts experience when powerful rockets blast them out of Earth's atmosphere, the entry into the next world is so exhilarating and profound that any previous life event seems positively banal by comparison. The relative dreariness of this world just can't prepare the traveller for the splendour of the next.

The NDE is a multifaceted gem, breathtaking from any angle, but there is one aspect of the experience that eclipses all the rest and which really rocks the world of the new arrival: it's the stunning discovery that we are loved more deeply than we can possibly imagine.

It isn't just an awareness that deeper love is possible, it's an introduction to the existence of *unconditional* love—something that is in very short supply in this world of ours. NDEers have been known to say things like, *"I hadn't known love like this was possible!"* (Return from Tomorrow, p. 54)

Before I started getting interested in the near-death literature, I believed in the reality of a loving God. I *felt* his love. I don't know where it came from, I just believed. In my Protestant upbringing, I was taught that Jesus was the personification of God's love. I read about his life and teachings and felt they demonstrated a genuine love for people, especially the downtrodden.

But it was more of an abstract belief than a concrete assurance—and there were reasons for doubt.

For one, the God of the Old Testament didn't seem to mesh with the God of the New. He seemed to be quite vengeful at times, even cruel. He appeared a little too eager to smite the wicked for such minor infractions as, say, being a Canaanite. He just seemed to really relish the opportunity to uncork the divine wrath!

Church didn't help much. I was taught that, while God is generally kind, he has also prepared a miserable hell ready to swallow those who failed to measure up to his exacting standards; and while churchgoers like me were offered the hope of escape, pity the fool who was less diligent in his devotion. He might as well just book passage to purgatory and be done with it. God apparently had no qualms about consigning a goodly portion of his creations to an eternity of suffering. Sundays seemed to be a test of devotion in those days: maintain a passing grade, or else!

While the odds didn't look too good for mankind in general, at least regular church attendance kept *me* on the right side of the equation. Still, somehow, lost in all this was the love of God.

World conditions didn't help. I saw evil in the world and pondered the question most ask at some point in their lives: Why would a loving God permit such things to happen? That stumbling block hit closer to home when I had to face my own little allotment of suffering.

I suppose I just wondered why God couldn't be a little kinder to his creatures here below.

Time and experience have a way of softening a person, however, and some undeniable brushes with the divine eventually convinced me that there is a God in heaven who really cares about his children (even the Canaanites!).

All this was before I started getting interested in the subject of near-death.

As I began to delve into the literature, what I wasn't prepared for was the sheer depth of emotion that pours from near-death survivors as they try to describe the love that envelops them the moment they enter the light. They struggle to know how to convey the sensation of suddenly being made aware that they are loved, absolutely and unconditionally. Love instantly ceases to be an abstract principle for them. It overwhelms them and becomes a consummate reality. They can't find enough superlatives to do justice to the love they feel.

Some have tried:

> *"The love that was emanating from the light is by far the most difficult aspect of my experience to relate to others. I feel so inadequate to speak of this love. Not because I am not a scholar, a theologian, a scientist or someone who can dissect it and analyze it. I am limited simply by being human! It was not a human kind of love. It does not lie within the framework of our human experiences. Therefore, it defies human explanation. I can only say that it is because of this love that was channeled to me that I am able to remain strong and*

travel down life's highway knowing that a great truth has occurred.

"I wanted to remain in the presence of this light forever!" (Heading Toward Omega, pp. 223–225)

"'I was there. I was on the other side.' For a long time that was all I could say. I still get tears in my eyes thinking about the experience. Too much! It's simply too much for human words. The other dimension, I call it now, where there's no distinction between good and evil, and time and place don't exist. And an immense, intense pure love compared to which love in our human dimension pales into insignificance, a mere shadow of what it could be. It exposes the lie we live in in our dimension. Our words, which are so limited, can't describe it. Everything I saw was suffused with an indescribable love... The frustrations at not being able to put it into human words is immense.

"I regret that words cannot do my experience justice. I must admit that human language is woefully inadequate for conveying the full extent, the depth, and the other dimension I've seen. In fact, no pen can describe what I went through." (Consciousness Beyond Life, p. 18)

"Love is the major impression I still retain. In heaven there is light, peace, music, beauty and joyful activity, but above all there is love and within this love I felt more truly alive than I have ever done before." (Return from Death, p. 53)

"There was the warmest, most wonderful love. Love all around me... I felt light-good-happy-joy-at ease. Forever—eternal love. Time meant nothing. Just being. Love. Pure love. Love." (Heading Toward Omega, p. 55)

There is a term for this inability to adequately describe something: *ineffable*. It means "incapable of being expressed or described in words." Our lexicon simply isn't sophisticated enough, and besides, most near-death survivors are not poets or writers anyway. Some do better than others, but the reality is that no one really has the vocabulary. There just isn't an adequate frame of reference.

"What the light communicates to you is a feeling of true, pure love. You experience this for the first time ever. You can't compare it to the love of your wife, or the love of your children. Even if all those things were combined you cannot compare it to the feeling you get from this light." (Return from Death, p. 54)

It's a love that almost assaults the senses:

"It was a dynamic light, not like a spotlight. It was an incredible energy—a light you wouldn't believe. I almost floated in it. It was feeding my consciousness feelings of unconditional love, complete safety, and complete, total perfection... It just powed into you. My consciousness was going out and getting larger and taking in more; I expanded and more and more came in. It was such rapture, such bliss.

"As the light continued to surround me and engulf me, my consciousness expanded and admitted more and more of what the light embraces: peace and unconditional love."
(The Return from Silence, p. 122)

Most NDE investigators are not near-death survivors themselves and have not had the opportunity of experiencing this love first-hand. But they do have the benefit of having listened to and observed multiple NDEers struggle to convey the depth of emotion they feel. Couple this with the advantage (in many cases) of being a writer by trade, and some of the NDE investigators do a pretty good job of describing the love of God:

"The vast majority of near-death survivors have positive, uplifting experiences. Theirs is both the opportunity and the thrill of being totally engulfed by overwhelming love, a kind of love quite beyond precedent, beyond description. There is nothing else quite like

it—a feeling, a knowing of oneness and worth, of total freedom and total acceptance. No demands. No stipulations. No conditions. No criteria. Just love—boundless, infinite, all-encompassing love—a love so forgiving, so total, so immense, nothing can contain it. Love encountered on 'The Other Side' makes any kind of earthly love dim by comparison.

"It is God's love. You just know...

"Over and over again, I hear survivors tell of the love they experienced and how they want to emulate that love, to develop and expand that love, so it will become a daily reality in their lives. They want to keep it alive and growing." (P. M. H. Atwater, Coming Back to Life, p. 66)

So far, so good.

The individuals we've quoted thus far were obviously good God-fearing folk. No one would begrudge them a pleasant reception. But what about the black sheep, the ne'er-do-well, the renegade? Those of us who, like Mary Poppins, are "practically perfect in every way," and are just itching for the day when the godless heathens finally get their comeuppance, can surely rejoice in the knowledge that death will be that day of reckoning.[12]

---

[12] Mary Poppins is the protagonist of a series of children's books of the same name, written by P. L. Travers from 1934 to 1988, centering on a magical English nanny. The expression "practically perfect in every way" comes from the

Don't break out the champagne just yet.

Consider the story this NDE researcher told about the day he ran into some motorcycle gang members (society's ultimate bad boys) and discovered that one of their fellow bikers had experienced an NDE:

> *"I stopped by my neighborhood bar while I was running some errands... I was unnerved to see two rough-looking men sitting together drinking beer... It didn't take long to realize that they were members of a motorcycle gang... I became more uneasy when a third person walked up to them and began pointing at me!*

> *"The tension mounted when the heavier of the two bikers looked over at me silently. Then he offered an almost imperceptible smile and cocked his head in the direction of the other patron.*

> *"'Do you know anything about people who die and come back?' he finally asked.*

> *"The third patron spoke at this moment. 'Yeah, he does. Go ahead and ask him.'*

> *"The biker then asked me what I knew about people resuscitated from death, so I briefly explained what psychology had learned about*

1964 musical movie of the same name by Walt Disney Productions, directed by Robert Stevenson, starring Julie Andrews, Dick Van Dyke, and others.

the near-death experience. The man then opened up completely, since he felt he really had to talk to somebody. It seemed that a few months previously, a friend and fellow gang member had been involved in a motorcycle crash. The rider had nearly been killed, but his life was saved by the emergency team at a local hospital. When he finally recovered, his left leg remained paralyzed and the doctors didn't know whether he would ever regain control of it. Despite this threat to his mobility and lifestyle (it was doubtful whether he would ever ride a motorcycle again), he seemed unusually serene when his friend visited him...

"...When the accident occurred, he found himself floating down a bright tunnel. The tunnel seemed endless and the light illuminating it became brighter and brighter until it engulfed him. While he couldn't see anyone near him, he sensed that he was in the presence of God. It was a kindly presence, a presence that loved him and accepted him completely and without judgment. Much to his surprise, the crash victim wasn't intimidated by the being, even though totally awed by it. Then the presence spoke to him and explained that everything would be all right and he would live. They also apparently discussed his life experiences and what changes he would make upon his recovery.

"'They just talked,' the biker said to me. 'Just like you and me, like friends. It was really great.'

"...He said that God was really cool.

"The reason for the crash victim's serenity became clear later, when the two bikers talked further. The patient explained that the presence warned him that some paralysis would be left in his leg, but gave the exact date when it would lift... From what my informant said, the paralysis did spontaneously heal right on schedule and his friend recovered completely."
(The Return from Silence, pp. 11–13)

"He said that God was really cool."
Not your usual description of the God of the Universe!

A few caveats:
First, this was an NDE. The man was coming back to life, which means he was being given a second chance. Would things have been different if this really had been the end for him?

Second, we can't imply from this that our reception won't be influenced by how we live our lives. Quite the contrary. The law of the harvest is very much in operation on the other side and a life devoid of compassion here won't reap accolades there. Justice must have her due. You'll notice that the man was given suggestions about some things he should do differently upon his return to life. Apparently, how we live our lives is important.

Third, we need to be careful not to stereotype (and you know the kind of people who stereotype)! Being in a motorcycle gang doesn't necessarily make you bad.

And fourth, though the biker identified the being of light as God (as do many NDEers), this wasn't necessarily the Big Boss himself. Beings of light don't wear name tags and they don't generally introduce themselves. My impression is that most arrivals are greeted by a representative of God, an angel perhaps.

In spite of these caveats, however, the biker's reception was revealing:

"He said that God was really cool!"

Bikers aren't generally held up as paragons of propriety and surely if anyone should merit a rocky reception it would be a biker. Not so, apparently. His experience was anything but distressing, and this example is *not* an aberration. Could it be that God (or whoever the being was) is just as comfortable chatting with a biker as he would be with a bona fide saint like you or me?

We'll cover this question in a later chapter, but the take-home message is that the moment of death is apparently *not* the time when the final judgment of God comes crashing down on the new arrival. Lady Justice *will* have her due, but that doesn't lessen God's love for his children in the least. Unconditional love is exactly what it says: unconditional!

What *is* abundantly clear from the near-death literature is that God loves *all* his creations more profoundly than we can possibly imagine. The tyrannical God of the Old Testament is a myth, perpetuated by pandering preachers and self-righteous zealots. God's love is unconditional, unrestrained, all encompassing, and utterly overwhelming to mere mortals—even to a biker! God really *is* love.

What we've explored so far in this chapter on love is the "passive" impact of the love of God on the NDEer (the experience is, of course, anything but passive!). As astonishing as this discovery is, the real question is whether the experience of *receiving* love translates into a desire to actively *give* more love upon returning to life? This book is, after all, about therapy. Does the knowledge gained make a difference in the life of the individual?

Absolutely!

It seems that very few can be exposed to the love of God and not be changed by it. This from author Phyllis Atwater:

> *"Over and over again, I hear survivors describe how much more loving they are, how filled to overflowing with love they are, how much more life and its living means to them, how precious everything is. They speak of loving their spouses more, their children more, their friends and co-workers more, everyone and everything—more. Said one man in southern California, whose experience was in 1964, 'I love my wife and children more than I ever thought I could. I love everyone. My experience taught me real love, unconditional love!'"*
> (Coming Back to Life, p. 66)

And these from the survivors themselves:

"My joy comes from another's smile. I also notice that I reach out and touch people more... I seem to make people feel better... I can see the pain in other people's eyes. That's why they hurt other people because they really don't understand... The most important thing that we have are our relationships with other people... It all comes down to caring and compassion and love for your fellow man... Love is the answer. It's the answer to everything." (Heading Toward Omega, p. 127)

"I think it's far easier just to want to love everybody than I ever loved before, that's for sure..." (Ibid, p. 127)

"Well, to me, a lot of things people think of as important are just not very important. I find that love, giving of love, is sufficiently important... to me the human heart is what it's all about, and the rest isn't very important." (Ibid, pp. 127–128)

"The only emotion I feel is love... I don't get caught up much anymore in anger with my kids or my husband... Jealousy and all those other things have been gone for years." (Ibid, p. 128)

The phenomenon cuts across cultures and languages. This from Hazeline from Singapore (made all the more endearing by her broken English):

"You know what I felt when I saw that light? When I saw that bright light, I felt that someone loves me very much (but no idea who it was). I was very overwhelmed with that bright light. And while I was there, I felt the love and that love I never felt before. That light welcoming me very warmly and loves me very much. My words to the light before I woke up was this: I wanted to stay here, but I love my two kids.

"Reason why I felt very overwhelmed? I felt that only that light ever love me and no one does. All people knows only to beat me, hurt me, criticized me, offended me, and many more. Nobody love me like that kind of love before.

"As a single mother/parent I have to love my children unconditionally. My mission is to raise them up in a proper manner and help poor people." (Near-Death Experiences, pp. 102–103)

Gulden from Turkey:

"I meet people with more joy. I hardly get angry. My daily life is full of love and peaceful. I feel pleasure by helping to strangers." (Ibid, p. 103)

Mohammed from Egypt:

"I feel that love is the one thing that all humans must feel towards each other, only then we would be happy." (Ibid, p. 103)

I've been very fortunate. My life has been filled with love. From parents and grandparents, to a wife, children, grandchildren, and friends, I've been surrounded by people who personify and exemplify what real love is.

In addition to earthly love, I've also felt the love of a kind, benevolent God.

But as real and as wonderful as all this is, it's been experienced through filters: the filter of the veil that separates us from God, and the hazy filter of living in a cruel world that too often seems intent on quenching love. The love of God is real, but it's tempered by the distance separating us. The love of family and friends is also real, but it's sometimes conditional. As long as we live in an imperfect world, love has to remain, to some degree, an abstract principle: a tantalizing foretaste of the real love that resides somewhere else in the universe.

In one blinding epiphany, however, all these filters evaporate when an individual emerges into the brilliant light of heaven. Love is suddenly more than just an abstract possibility. It becomes a tangible reality.

Which is why I can honestly say that I have been profoundly affected by the assurances of near-death survivors that universal love exists in the universe. I have learned as much about love from NDEers as I have from a lifetime of experience and study. Near-death survivors are not spouting an erudite thesis on the theory of love, they're expressing the exuberant joy of what it actually feels like to be engulfed by a love that is more powerful and real than anything they've ever imagined. It's a love that surpasses understanding.

Their message is consistent and unvarying: the love that exists in death is simply breathtaking (pardon the pun). It's a love that can pierce the hardest of hearts and that can lift the most lowly in spirit.

"It is God's love. You just know." (P. M. H. Atwater, Coming Back to Life, p. 66)

But let's get back to planet Earth, Bob. This book isn't about death, it's about *near*-death. Everyone who's been able to write about this divine love has had to leave it behind and come back. One can only imagine how difficult it must be to return to this cold world having had a taste of what might be—of what will be.

Difficult? Yes. But the wrenching is not without meaning. Survivors seem to have the philosophy that, as long as they have to be separated from the love of God, at least they can try to bring a taste of his love to this love-starved world. If this isn't their time to bask in the love of heaven, at least they can try to introduce the rest of us to the concept and perhaps create a little heaven here on Earth.

Where does all this leave you and me? How helpful is it for us to learn about the existence of perfect love when we probably aren't going to get close to experiencing it as long as we remain alive? Like a child growing up in a dysfunctional, love-deprived home, can we look at the happy, loving environment that is heaven and feel anything other than envy? After all, reading about a concept as experiential as love just isn't the same as being engulfed by it.

All this is true, but it fails to take into consideration one of the most fundamental verities of life: that the real test of our ability to love is whether we can do so in an environment where love is at a premium.

In this toxic environment, can we love those who are hard to love? Can we be accepting of people who are critical, judgmental, or negative? Can we resist the natural tendency to lash out at those who throw our love back in our faces? Can we respond instead with kindness and empathy? Can we love our enemies?

None of this is easy to do. It's contrary to our nature.

But if we could learn to love like that—fully and without condition or reservation—what an advantage it would give us now as well as in the next life. It's my belief that the gates of heaven are open to anyone who can learn to love as unconditionally as those who reside there. We'll know we're ready when we can accept people the way they are and love them regardless. It's the kind of love NDEers feel in the light.

Perversely, in this regard, we actually hold an advantage over the near-death survivor: if we can learn to love unconditionally, *without having experienced unconditional love*, now that's an achievement worth writing home about!

So, I'm trying to be a little kinder to those I run into day by day. I'm trying to see the good in people and to understand why they do what they do. I'm trying to view every encounter as an opportunity to lift and encourage. I'm trying to be nicer to cats (dogs are easy to love—they

don't count). I set a few insects free rather than kill them
(except mosquitoes and roaches, of course). In short,
I'm striving to learn the vernacular of love now so that
I'll be a little more fluent in that realm where love is the
native tongue.

I'm far from where I need to be, but near-death survivors have taught me to reach, and in the reaching, this
world doesn't seem quite as dark. Life is richer. Love
is returned.

The Beatles were right: *"All you need is love."*
Love—and a little therapy, Bob ...*Death Therapy!*

Chapter 3

Return from Tomorrow

*"What we have done for ourselves alone dies
with us; what we have done for others and
the world remains and is immortal."*
—Albert Pike[13]

Moneyball

IN 2002, THE TERM "MONEYBALL" ENTERED
the lexicon of professional baseball.

In that year, the Oakland Athletics had an operating
budget of $41 million, the New York Yankees: $125 million. In baseball, as in most arenas, money talks.

Grossly out-financed, the Athletics simply couldn't
compete with the likes of the Yankees unless they could
find a way to level the playing field. Their new general

---

[13] Albert Pike (1809–1891) was an attorney, soldier, writer, and Freemason. He
is the only Confederate military officer with an outdoor statue in Washington,
DC.

manager, Billy Beane, embarked on a risky experiment. It was something that had never been tried before in baseball, something that flew in the face of a century of baseball wisdom. Instead of going after the flashy players (as in *expensive!*) who had the textbook swing, blinding speed, or perfect throwing action, Beane sought out the overlooked baseball journeymen (as in *cheap!*) who weren't flashy, but who excelled in such boring statistics as on-base percentage, or low earned run average.

The theory was that results count more than appearances: it doesn't matter how good you *look* if you keep losing games. The batter with the beautiful swing may be great at getting fans in the bleachers, but he isn't going to help you win games if he gets on base less than the player with the ugly swing.

Even before the season began, things looked bad for Oakland. They lost three key players to wealthier teams and didn't have the money to attract superstar replacements. So Beane went in search of players who were cheap, but who could still get the job done.

His theory was untried and unproven, and an early losing streak caused management, coaches, and fans to question its viability. Beane stuck with the plan, however, and as the season wore on, the A's fortunes slowly improved. They were becoming a respectable team with a winning record. Not too bad in a league where they were vastly outspent.

On August 13, 2002, Oakland won the first game of a winning streak that would rewrite baseball history. They went on to string together nineteen wins in a row, and in so doing, tied an American League record held since 1947 (ironically by the Yankees). Only the Kansas City Royals stood in the way of owning the record outright.

The game with the Royals began well enough for Oakland. They amassed a seemingly insurmountable 11–0 lead in the first three innings. Surely the record was in the bag.

Inexplicably, the Royals clawed their way back, and managed to tie the game at 11–11.

With a place in history at stake, Oakland's pinch hitter, Scott Hatteberg (one of Billy Beane's bargain-basement recruits), hit a home run to secure the victory and the longest winning streak of the modern baseball era.

Now, even wealthy teams take Moneyball seriously.

No offense to baseball fans, but I'd rather watch paint dry than sit through a baseball game (and this is coming from someone who hails from the land of crown green bowling and five-day cricket matches!). Nonetheless, Billy Beane's story is inspiring.

The connection between Moneyball and near-death experiences is not obvious (although, as I think about it, having to sit through an entire baseball game is probably about as close as I could get to simulating death!), but the premise of Moneyball does emphasize a truth that NDEers quickly learn: that the flashy successes we achieve in life carry little weight on the other side. Rather, it's the little things that count. Fame, fortune, and accolades mean little if they don't translate into real results.

Which brings us to Private George Ritchie.

December 1943 found Private Ritchie in basic training at Camp Berkeley, Texas, preparing to be shipped to Europe.

He was an ambitious twenty-year-old with aspirations of becoming a medical doctor until the harsh realities of World War II threw a wrench into his plans. He did at least have a couple of days' leave before the war would become his new reality, however, and he was excited at the prospect of spending Christmas with his family. He never imagined that he would, instead, soon be spending time with his Maker.

The day before he was to catch the train home he became feverish and ill. Reluctantly, he trudged down to the infirmary where he was found to have a fever of 106 Fahrenheit and fulminant pneumonia. Leave was cancelled, and he was admitted to the base hospital.

His disappointment at not being able to go home turned to alarm as his breathing became more and more laboured. This progressed to delirium and, for several hours, George lay in bed, semiconscious and gasping for air.

Suddenly he woke up, his fever gone and his breathing back to normal. He felt great! He was cured. Maybe he could still make it home for Christmas. Feeling much better about life, he got up to walk.

Something was different, however—he was able to walk through walls!

It finally dawned on him: his spirit had left his body. It didn't occur to him that he had died, so he did what any self-respecting, newly homeless spirit would do, and went in search of his body.

The problem was: he'd forgotten where he'd left it! This out-of-body stuff was new to him and, not realizing that he'd have to return to home base (so to speak), he'd neglected to leave a trail of spiritual breadcrumbs.

After scouring the hospital for some time, he finally found his body, but he wouldn't don his physical "suit" again until he returned from perhaps the most comprehensive tour of the afterlife ever granted a human being. He wrote a book about his experience and called it Return from Tomorrow.

Everyone remembers Raymond Moody's Life After Life as the book that brought NDEs to the attention of the public, but it was actually George Ritchie's NDE that really started the near-death revolution.

Getting back to the story... (Private Ritchie has just located his body).

Oddly enough, the only way he knew that this was his body was by the ring on its finger. This is how he described it:

> *"I had never seen myself.*
>
> *"Not really. Not the way I saw other people. From my chest down I had seen myself 'in the round' of course, but from the shoulders up, I now realized, I had seen only a two-dimensional mirror-image staring at me from a piece of glass. And occasionally a snapshot, equally two-dimensional. That was all. The roundedness, the living, space-filling presence of myself, I did not know at all."* (Return from Tomorrow, p. 43)

It had never occurred to me that we might actually have trouble recognizing ourselves. It's a little strange to think about, but we have never seen ourselves from the neck upward with our natural eyes, only the two-dimensional image in a mirror. Others see our heads in three dimensions. It must be a little disconcerting to see ourselves for the first time from the vantage point of an observer. I'm not sure of the significance of this, except that it typifies the reaction common to many who look on their physical body for the first time with spiritual eyes: a curious but detached interest in the vehicle that has transported them all these years. In many respects, the beat-up and worn-out physical body seems like a totally unsuitable tabernacle for this svelte spiritual body. When it comes time to squeeze back into the physical shell, it must be like having to put your old grimy clothes back on after taking a refreshing shower. There is a certain sentimental fondness for the physical body, however: sort of like the old ragged coat you can't quite bring yourself to throw away.

The light in Private Ritchie's room began to increase until it reached an intensity that was unfathomable. Imagine a brilliance that puts our sun to shame:

> *"It was like a million welders' lamps all blazing at once. And right in the middle of my amazement came a prosaic thought probably born of some biology lecture back at the university: 'I'm glad I don't have physical eyes at this moment,' I thought. 'This light would destroy the retina in a tenth of a second.'"* (Ibid, p. 48)

But it wasn't actually the light that would destroy the retina:

"No, I corrected myself, not the light.

"He.

"He would be too bright to look at. For now I saw that it was not light but a Man who had entered the room, or rather a Man made out of light...

"The instant I perceived Him, a command formed itself in my mind. 'Stand up!' The words came from inside me, yet they had an authority my mere thoughts had never had. I got to my feet, and as I did came the stupendous certainty: 'You are in the presence of the Son of God.'...

"This was the most totally male Being I had ever met. If this was the Son of God, then his name was Jesus. But... this was not the Jesus of my Sunday School books. That Jesus was gentle, kind, understanding—and probably a little bit of a weakling. This person was power itself, older than time and yet more modern than anyone I had ever met." (Ibid, pp. 48–49)

A little note of caution here: this was one of the rare instances in which the being was actually identified by name. For the most part, beings of light do not identify themselves, although Christians often just assume that it's Jesus who's come to meet them. It could just as well be an angel, however, and when the light emanating from the being is as bright as *"a million welders' lamps all blazing at once,"* it might be difficult to tell the difference.

Anyway, as bright and appealing as the being of light was to the eyes, it paled in comparison to the love that emanated from him:

> *"Above all, with that same mysterious inner certainty, I knew that this Man loved me. Far more even than power, what emanated from this Presence was unconditional love. An astonishing love. A love beyond my wildest imagining. This love knew every unlovable thing about me—the quarrels with my stepmother, my explosive temper, the sex thoughts I could never control, every mean, selfish thought and action since the day I was born— and accepted and loved me just the same."*
> (Ibid, p. 50)

Concurrent with the being's arrival was a comprehensive review of Private Ritchie's life:

> *"When I say He knew everything about me, this was simply an observable fact. For into that room along with His radiant presence ... had also entered every single episode of my entire life. Everything that had ever happened to me was simply there, in full view, contemporary and current, all seemingly taking place at that moment."* (Ibid, p. 50)

"'What did you do with your life?'

"It seemed to be a question about values, not facts: what did you accomplish with the precious time you were allotted? And with this question shining through them, these ordinary events of a fairly typical boyhood seemed not merely unexciting but trivial. Hadn't I done anything lasting, anything important? Desperately I looked around me for something that would seem worthwhile in the light of this blazing Reality.

"It wasn't that there were spectacular sins, just the sexual hang-ups and secretiveness of most teenagers. But if there were no horrendous depths, there were no heights either. Only an endless, shortsighted, clamorous concern for myself. Hadn't I ever gone beyond my own immediate interests, done anything other people would recognize as valuable? At last I located it, the proudest moment of my life:

"'I became an Eagle Scout!'

"Again, words seemed to emanate from the Presence beside me:

"'That glorified you.'

"It was true. I could see myself standing in the center of the award circle, flushed with pride, the admiring eyes of my family and friends turned on me. Me, me, me—always in the center. Wasn't there any time in my life when I had let someone else stand there?

"I saw myself walking forward at a church service at age eleven, asking Jesus to be Lord of my life. But I saw how quickly that first excitement turned into a dull routine of church-on-Sunday. Worse, I saw the smugness and self-esteem that went with it. I was better than the kids who didn't come to church. I was even better than lots who did: there was my perfect attendance pin to prove it.

"And all at once rage at the question itself built up in me. It wasn't fair! Of course I hadn't done anything with my life! I hadn't had time. How could you judge a person who hadn't started?

"The answering thought, however, held no trace of judgment. 'Death,' the word was infinitely loving, 'can come at any age.'

"Well, sure. I knew that babies and little kids died. Somehow I had just always assumed that a full life span was in some way owed me.

"What about the insurance money coming in when I'm seventy?'... A few months ago I had taken out the standard life insurance policy offered to servicemen; in some subconscious part of me had I believed this piece of paper guaranteed life itself? If I'd suspected before that there was mirth in the Presence beside me, now I was sure of it: the brightness seemed to vibrate and shimmer with a kind of holy laughter—not at me and my silliness, not a mocking laughter, but a mirth that seemed to say that in spite of all error and tragedy, joy was more lasting still.

"And in the ecstasy of that laughter I realized that it was I who was judging the events around us so harshly. It was I who saw them as trivial, self-centered, unimportant. No such condemnation came from the Glory shining round me. He was not blaming or reproaching. He was simply ... loving me."
(Ibid, pp. 52–54)

"What did you do with your life?"

That's the question all of us will face someday. It strikes right at the heart of human existence: Why are we here? What are we to learn from our time on Earth? How should we spend our time? What is the purpose of life?

Like Private Ritchie, we will probably struggle to come up with a good answer. The achievements by which we typically measure success in life (awards, degrees, even church attendance) just don't seem to carry much weight in the life review. Checking off the bullet points of our résumé will likely elicit the same rejoinder: *"That glorified you."*

No, Private Ritchie is about to learn that what really counts in life is not what we've done to improve our own station, but rather what we've done to help others. Our grand accomplishments will likely feel rather anticlimactic to us, but we might be pleasantly surprised to learn that the little acts of kindness that seemed so inconsequential at the time will not be trivialized in the least by the being of light.

We can sympathize with Ritchie's frustration that, as a young man, he simply hadn't had time to amass much of a résumé worth talking about. However, the gentle observation that "death can come at any age" is a timely reminder that no one can take life for granted. Truth is: time is not something we are guaranteed. Maybe death *will* come at the end of a long and productive life, but there are a host of factors that can derail the plan: cancer, a heart attack, a Mack truck. The important thing is that we make good use of the time that we have.

Another revelation from George Ritchie's experience is the presence of humour in the being of light. Others have expressed similar observations, and this aspect of the NDE came as a welcome surprise to me. We don't typically associate death with joy and laughter, but more than a few survivors tell us that these are very much a part of the experience. The humour is never mocking or sarcastic. It's always uplifting and kind. Its purpose seems to be to put the person at ease.

Back to the question: "What have you done with your life to show me?"

"Already I understood that in my first frantic efforts to come up with an impressive answer, I had missed the point altogether. He wasn't asking about accomplishments and awards.

"The question, like everything else proceeding from Him, had to do with love. How much have you loved with your life? Have you loved others as I am loving you? Totally? Unconditionally?

"Hearing the question like that, I saw how foolish it was even to try to find an answer in the scenes around us. Why, I hadn't known love like this was possible. Someone should have told me, I thought indignantly! A fine time to discover what life was all about—like coming to a final exam and discovering you were going to be tested on a subject you had never studied. If this was the point of everything, why hadn't someone told me?

"But though these thoughts rose out of self-pity and self-excuse, the answering thought held no rebuke, only that hint of heavenly laughter behind the words:

"'I did tell you.'

"But how? Still wanting to justify myself: how could He have told me and I not heard?

"'I told you by the life I lived. I told you by the death I died. And if you keep your eyes on Me, you will see more...'" (Ibid, pp. 54–55)

"I did tell you."

We'll tackle the thorny issue of religion in a later chapter, but suffice it to say at this point that no book on the afterlife would be complete without examining the central role of Jesus in the history of the world. Jesus's claims were unique. He claimed to be the literal Son of God and the Saviour of all mankind.

Whatever you may think of Christ, you'd be hard-pressed to find anything in his life or teachings that demonstrated anything but a profound love for all. The depth of that love was brought home to George Ritchie when he got to experience it first-hand. Experiencing it and doing it justice are two different things, however, and all he could manage was:

"I hadn't known love like this was possible."

Which brings us to Private Ritchie's indignant exclamation: *"Someone should have told me!"*

I suspect that most of us will have that same reaction when we reach the other side: Why didn't someone tell me about this? The time for finding out what's on the exam isn't when I'm walking into the exam room! If I'd known, I would have prepared differently. I would have changed the way I lived.

I suspect we'll all get the same gentle answer from the Son of God: *"I did tell you. ... I told you by the life I lived. I told you by the death I died."*

Jesus personified God's love. In addition, in non-Christian (even non-religious) cultures, there is almost always a revered person whose life was the epitome of humility and love.[14] Now we can add to their example the passionate testimony of George Ritchie and a host of other near-death survivors. They've sneaked a peek at the test and returned to let us know what to study. The only question that remains is what we'll do with this knowledge. How will we prepare for the test?

In reality, there's only one question on the test: Did you learn to love others the way you are loved?

There's nothing wrong with pursuing the flashy plays in life, Bob. They make us feel good and they might earn a murmur of adulation from the crowd. But they won't count for much if they were all for our own benefit and did little to help others. A home run is impressive, but if it isn't part of a team effort, it may carry little weight. A series of singles can be just as effective, especially if they bring others home. It's the little acts of kindness that count in life, not the grand accomplishments that edify only ourselves.

That's what *Death Therapy* is about, Bob: learning what's important in life by studying the near-death experiences of others. People like George Ritchie have taken

---

[14] Siddhārtha Gautama (or Buddha); Muhammad, the founder of Islam; Mencius or 孟子 of China; Mahatma Gandhi; Albert Schweitzer; Oskar Schindler; Mother Teresa; among others.

the test and returned to tell the rest of us what to study. We know what's on the test!

And *Death Therapy* is the answer! Guaranteed!

Chapter 4

Light

*"I said to the man who stood at the Gate
of the Year,*
*"'Give me a light that I may tread safely into
the unknown.'*
*"And he replied, 'Go out into the darkness and
put your hand into the hand of God.*
*"'That shall be better than light and safer than
a known way.'"*
        —Minnie Louise Haskins,
"The Gate of the Year"[15]

Quoted by King George VI in his 1939
Christmas Broadcast, as Britain stood on
the brink of war.

---

[15] Excerpt from "The Gate of the Year," the popular name given to this poem, written in 1908 and published in 1912. The title given to it by the author was "God Knows."

Bumps on a Log

I'M FASCINATED BY ALLIGATORS. I'm also deathly afraid of them. So, it was with some trepidation that I accepted an invitation to spend the night camping in Brazos Bend State Park (otherwise known as "Alligator Park"), near Houston, Texas. It was rumoured that alligators roamed free in the park. The thought of spending the night in a tent, separated from the alligators by only a flimsy sheet of nylon, was not particularly appealing to me. Nevertheless, curiosity won out and a sunny Texas afternoon found us driving into Alligator Park.

We came to a fork in the road. Little wooden signs at ground level pointed to the right and to the left. The sign to the right was marked "Campers" and the one to the left, "Alligators." I was relieved that there appeared to be at least some separation between humans and reptiles.

I just hoped those alligators could read!

We got the tent set up and set out to look for gators. Posted prominently at the approach to the bayou was a big sign that explained the rules of the park. There were a lot of them, but I was here to see alligators, not to read signs. Besides, I'd seen alligators in the zoo. How complicated could it be? One rule would have sufficed:

KEEP AWAY FROM THE MAN-EATING REPTILES.

As we walked down the path, I scanned the far bank of the river for gators and was amazed to see a whole family of them basking in the afternoon sun. They were seemingly ambivalent to the presence of humans mere feet away. I looked to see what was separating them from me. The only barrier seemed to be the bayou, and that was obviously no barrier at all since other alligators were lazily swimming down and across it. No fences! No walls! No guards with guns! Nothing!

Okay, so maybe the rules were there for more than just the mentally challenged. I made an about-face and dutifully read them.

There were several, but a few stood out:

1) ALWAYS STAY ON THE PATH.

Made sense. The path was between the bayou on one side and the swamp on the other. It was raised three or four feet above both. Apparently, alligators have trouble climbing, and while they could get onto the path by crawling up the gentle inclines where the dirt path had eroded away, the raised elevation gave us bipeds a distinct advantage. The path was for humans; the bayou and swamp were for reptiles. Good so far.

2) NEVER APPROACH THE WATER'S EDGE.

A corollary to "ALWAYS STAY ON THE PATH." Obviously, the water was the alligators' playground. Evolution had adapted them well to the murky waters of the bayou and, although most of their movements were deliberate and slow, they were capable of striking with lightning speed if anyone was foolish enough to approach their domain. No arguments there.

3) KEEP PETS ON A LEASH AND CHILDREN CLOSE TO YOU. ALLIGATORS CONSIDER DOGS AND SMALL CHILDREN TO BE AN APPETIZING MEAL.

Yes, it really did say that. It made the standard "DON'T FEED THE REPTILES" warning take on a whole new meaning.

4) NEVER BE ALONE IN THE ALLIGATOR AREA AND LEAVE BEFORE DARK.

Excellent advice. I read later that alligators are uniquely adapted to hunt in the dark (although they are most active in the twilight of dusk and dawn). They are formidable predators at any time, but at night their peculiar characteristics make them fearsome killing machines. Their eyes, ears, and nose sit above the surface of the water while the rest of their large body remains submerged. Night vision, hearing, and a sense of smell are all highly developed and are attuned to the slightest hint of a potential meal. They even have special dermal pressure receptors along both the upper and lower jaws that are capable of detecting the faintest ripple in the water's surface. They can remain motionless for hours, but when a potential prey is recognised their powerful tail can propel them to speeds of up to 30 mph in the water with an acceleration that could humble a Porsche.

I made a mental note: stay with the crowds and don't be around after dark.

This next rule was intriguing:

5) IF AN ALLIGATOR IS CROSSING THE PATH, YIELD RIGHT OF WAY.

First, the whole concept of a sort-of reptile/human intersection was mind-boggling. Did we need traffic lights? A four-way stop? Roundabout?

What really got to me, however, was the fact that they felt the need to post a sign specifying who has right of way! I mean, really? When an alligator wants to cross the path in front of you are you really going to argue about who got there first? However, as I watched the antics of some of the people around me, I conceded that the sign was probably warranted.

Armed with new information on alligator lore, I spent a very pleasant couple of hours enjoying the spectacle. There were gators everywhere, peacefully going about their business. They seemed oblivious to the people walking on the path mere feet away from them. I was content to admire them in their natural habitat, unhampered by fences or moats. They were content to bask in the afternoon sun and be admired. A curious cohabitation had evolved. Reptiles and humans both seemed to understand the rules of engagement and had learned to coexist in a harmonious relationship.

I can't say that I lost my aversion to alligators, but I did gain a new appreciation for these wondrous creatures.

I slept well in the tent that night.

***

The next morning, I awoke before dawn and decided to take our dog, Brandi, for a walk before it got too hot. Brandi was a boxer, the type of family pet that only comes along once in a lifetime: faithful and obedient. The children adored her.

With my alligator phobia assuaged, I decided to return to the bayou to enjoy the spectacle again and get Brandi's take on these strange creatures. She was on a leash and I wasn't going to violate any rules. (Besides, the alligators knew the rules. What could go wrong?)

As we reached the elevated path I looked at the far bank where a whole family of alligators had been basking in the sun the previous day. Nothing. I scanned the water for the tell-tale ridgeback snaking down the bayou. Again, nothing. Same for the swamp to my left. Not an alligator to be seen. Perhaps they were off somewhere in the swamp... in a dawn assembly... planning their day.

Somewhat disappointed, I continued down the path, all the while scanning the bayou and the swamp for any signs of life. It soon became evident that we weren't going to see any alligators this morning.

The sun was beginning to rise and the temperature along with it. Brandi looked longingly at the water. I was tempted to take her down to the water's edge for a drink. After all, whatever the alligators were doing this morning, they weren't doing it here.

But the warnings were clear:

STAY ON THE PATH. NEVER APPROACH THE WATER. NEVER BE ALONE IN THE ALLIGATOR AREA (oops!).

We kept walking.

As I continued to scan the water, a nagging thought was struggling to rise to conscious level, a vague sense of danger.

Something was wrong!

There was something in the water, something that wasn't right. What was it? The anomaly clawed its way out of the fog of my subconscious.

Logs!

At a point on the trail where the bank was broken down and a gentle slope led down to the bayou, there was a little log with two bumps on it, floating in the water, four or five feet from the "beach." Nothing unusual there. The problem was that I'd seen an identical log at the last little beach—and the one before that. Same log, same two bumps.

And then it hit me:

Not bumps on a log... *alligator eyes!*

With that icy feeling that grips you when you realize you've wandered into danger, it suddenly dawned on me that scores of alligators were lurking near the water's edge just waiting for a thirsty animal to come down for a drink! Those cold, unblinking eyes were hungrily following our beloved family pet, their mouths watering at the prospect of breakfast.

The rising sun was beginning to illuminate the swamp on the other side of the path. Same logs, same bumps!

The alligators weren't off somewhere attending to their morning ablutions; they were already hunting—and Brandi was on the menu!

With a chill of self-recrimination, I realized that I'd just violated the most fundamental rules of the park: I was out in the murky light of dawn (prime hunting time for an alligator). I was alone except for our sweet, furry pet (breakfast-on-a-leash), and I'd almost let Brandi go down to the bayou for a drink.

It would have made for a pithy end to the story if I could recount an epic battle with an alligator. The problem with epic battles, however, is that they don't always have a happy ending. Imagine coming home without the dog and trying to explain to your children that their beloved pet was breakfast for a hungry alligator because their father is a moron! I still shudder to think what could have been.

Happily, the outing ended uneventfully. Brandi remained blissfully unaware of the existence of alligators. The alligators remained hungry. My kids still talk to me. I gained a new appreciation for just who the idiots are that the signs are trying to educate.

Alligators are creatures of the night. Mere objects of curiosity during the day, the tenants of Alligator Park become fearsome predators when the sun goes down. In the blackness of night, and in the murky grey of dusk and dawn, gators reign supreme. In the bright light of day, they bow to the superior firepower and intellect (in theory at least) of *Homo sapiens* and our ability to protect our young.

Humans are very much creatures of the day. We are adapted to function in the bright light of day. The human retina, for example (in contrast to cats, dogs, and alligators), contains more cones than rods. Cone cells have the ability to perceive colour and high definition, but only function well in the light. Rods see in the dark.

Many of our common expressions extol the virtues of light. We speak of being *enlightened*, of *seeing things in a new light*, or of *shedding light on a problem*. Good things happen in the light.

It isn't surprising, therefore, that NDEers devote an inordinate amount of time talking about *the Light* (some even feel the need to capitalize the word). The exposure to the Light is one of the most impactful aspects of the near-death experience. Some even describe the Light as having a personality.

It isn't simply that the Light of heaven is a brighter version of its earthly counterpart. It *is* that and more, but it also has properties that we don't normally associate with light, properties that have the power to radically change a person.

To begin with, the stunning brilliance of the Light stands in marked contrast to the darkness of the tunnel that precedes it. The tunnel isn't particularly distressing (in fact, many describe it as quite peaceful and quiet), but it *is* dark, and it clearly isn't the place where you want to hang your hat ("tunnel" being the operative word).

The tunnel is a conduit from this world to the next. The only illumination is a pinpoint of light in the distance that draws the individual irresistibly toward it. The axiom to *"go toward the Light"* is very real. The traveller doesn't need a second invitation.

The Light has many striking properties. One of them is certainly its incredible intensity but, believe it or not, this may actually be one of its more mundane features. Still, its brightness is nothing to sneeze at. Remember how George Ritchie described it?

> *"It was like a million welders' lamps all blazing at once."* (Return from Tomorrow, p. 48)

Another creative description:

> *"The light was incredibly bright, like sitting in the middle of a lightbulb."* (Consciousness Beyond Life, p. 170)

I regularly treat patients in the emergency room with flash burns to the eyes. Usually, it's a result of arc welding without proper eye protection but it can also occur from the sunlamp in a tanning salon or from skiing in bright sunlight (or any number of circumstances where an ultraviolet light source lingers too long on an unprotected cornea). The damage is usually temporary, but it can cause a lot of pain.

Now, multiply these earthly sources of light by a million and you begin to understand the intensity of the Light of heaven. This light never hurts the eyes, however:

> *"I floated ... up into this pure crystal clear light, an illuminating white light. It was beautiful and so bright, so radiant, but it didn't hurt my eyes. It's not any kind of light you*

can describe on Earth." (The Return from Silence, p. 228)

We typically don't think of light as having colour, but this Light radiates colours we've never encountered on Earth. People have difficulty describing it, but "golden yellow-white" seems to be as close to consensus as we're going to get:

> "*It was yellow-white and brilliant, but not painful to look at even directly.*" (Closer to the Light, p. 119)

> "*The whole thing was permeated with the most gorgeous light, a living, golden yellow glow, a pale colour, not like the harsh colour we know on Earth.*" (The Return from Silence, p. 74)

> "*Soft, silky, very brilliant gold.*" (Life at Death, p. 61)

The Light is very pleasant to look at, but even if you wanted to look away from it, you couldn't do it. It's everywhere. It suffuses everything and everyone:

> "*I began to discern different figures in the light—and they were all covered with light, they were light, and had light permeating all around them...*" (Consciousness Beyond Life, p. 172)

On Earth, light is perceived only through the medium of sight. While the visual spectacle is certainly a striking part of the appeal of the Light of heaven, it's only one facet of the experience. This Light has many other characteristics, all of which are powerful and evoke profound emotional reactions. The feeling most often cited by those who are exposed to the Light is that of being loved, completely and unconditionally:

> *"It was feeding my consciousness feelings of unconditional love, complete safety, and complete, total perfection... It just powed into you."* (Otherworld Journeys, pp. 124–25)

> *"The light was an overwhelming feeling of Love. It was a blinding, brilliant light that is indescribable. It was so inviting, it felt so good, and I didn't want to leave."* (Consciousness Beyond Life, p. 314)

> *"The light can perhaps best be described as personified love. Pure, unadulterated, magnificent, incredibly wonderful love."* (Glimpses Beyond Death's Door, p. 83)

Feelings of peace and tranquility come in a close second:

> *"The most gorgeous light bathed me in unimaginable tranquility. This was a world I never wanted to leave again."* (Consciousness Beyond Life, p. 78)

In short, the Light is perfection itself:

"I felt it as I experienced the Light. It's the pinnacle of everything there is. Of energy, of love especially, of warmth, of beauty." (Consciousness Beyond Life, p. 34)

"Bliss ... rapture ... joy ... ecstasy, all of the above, and in such measure that it cannot be compared or understood. As the light continued to surround me and engulf me, my consciousness expanded and admitted more and more of what the light embraces: peace and unconditional love." (The Return from Silence, p. 122)

"As I reached the source of the light, I could see in. I cannot begin to describe in human terms the feelings I had over what I saw. It was a giant infinite world of calm, and love, and energy, and beauty. It was as though human life was unimportant compared to this. And yet it urged the importance of life at the same time it solicited death as a means to a different and better life. It was all being, all beauty, all meaning for all existence. It was all the energy of the Universe forever in one place.

"As I reached my right hand into it, feelings of exhilarating anticipation overwhelmed me. I did not need my body anymore. I wanted to

leave it behind, if I hadn't already, and go to my God in this new world." (Closer to the Light, p. 120)

The one property we touched on briefly, and which is probably the Light's most unique feature, is the sense that it has a personality, that it's more of a some*one* than a some*thing*:

"In the distance I saw a light that I had never seen on Earth. So pure, so intense, so perfect. I knew it was a being I had to go to." (Consciousness Beyond Life, p. 34)

"I didn't actually see a person in this light, and yet it has a special identity, it definitely does. It is a light of perfect understanding and perfect love." (The Return from Silence, p. 228)

The Bible tells us that *God is light*, but whether the "identity" in the Light is God himself is up for debate. The whole concept of light being a "someone" is so far outside our mortal experience that definitions tend to be vague:[16]

"It wasn't God, but it wasn't not God." (Transformed by the Light, p. 189)

Whatever (or *whoever*) the Light is, it changes people. The feelings people have while bathed in its glow stay with

---

[16] 1 John 1:5

them for life. One young man had his NDE when he was five years old. He said this when he was twenty-five:

"I will never forget that Light. It is with me all the time." (Closer to the Light, p. 116)

In summary, the Light of heaven encompasses every positive aspect of the near-death experience: love, joy, peace, beauty, power, perfection. It is the embodiment of everything that is good. The Light has the power to change lives. In fact, you probably couldn't be exposed to it and *not* be changed.

Anyway, back to Earth, Bob. Back to the swamp. The harsh reality for you and me is that we're probably not going to feel the full impact of the Light of heaven until the day we actually die. In the meantime, we're just going to have to seek for light and enlightenment wherever we can find it. True it is that worldly light is a very dim substitute for its divine cousin, but we should still try to fill our lives with as much of it as we can. We should also remember that even a small light in a dark world goes a long way.

How can we ensure we are always found in the light?

By staying on the path; always taking the high road. By staying out of the swamp where predators lurk. By sharing our light with others. By protecting the innocent. By being found on the side of right, no matter what. By working in the daylight and sleeping at night.

Our task, Bob, is to generate as much light as we can in this dimly lit world, taking comfort in the knowledge that even a tiny candle in a dark place can be a beacon for others to follow. It's the contrast that makes the difference.

We can't bask in the Light of heaven just yet, but we can certainly generate a few sparks while we're waiting.

So, go toward the Light, Bob (figuratively for now) ...the *Death Therapy* way.

Oh yes, and when that alligator wants to cross the path in front of you...

...give him the right of way!

Chapter 5

Saved by the Light

"If guilt were fat, I would have weighed five hundred pounds." —Dannion Brinkley[17]

The Lifespan of an Ant

WE ARRIVED HOME FROM CHURCH ONE Sunday afternoon to find a column of ants crossing the driveway. This got our children into a discussion about how long an ant lives. One of the boys thought they lived a few days, the other a few weeks. What *is* the lifespan of an ant? I have no idea.

Our five-year-old daughter, Brittany, listened to the discussion, looked at the ants, considered the fact that we had to step over them to get to the house, and finally chimed in: *"Well it all depends on when you get stepped on!"*

---

[17] From the book *Saved by the Light: The True Story of a Man Who Died Twice and the Profound Revelations He Received*, by Dannion Brinkley and Paul Perry, published in 1994 by HarperCollins.

Ah, the wisdom of a child! We all like to think that we have a long and fulfilling life ahead of us, but the reality is that you never know when you're going to get stepped on. A life-changing event can intervene at any time—like being struck by lightning.

Saved by the Light

Dannion Brinkley was hardly a model youth. By his own admission, he was something of a nightmare. In his school years, not a day went by in which he didn't get into a fight. He was the quintessential school bully.

His proclivity for violence didn't end with graduation. By enlisting as a sniper in the Marine Corps, he was able to find further avenues to indulge his mean streak—the war in Vietnam provided fertile ground. He was seemingly locked into a life of callousness and cruelty.

All that changed dramatically on September 17, 1975, when, at the age of twenty-five, Dannion Brinkley was struck by lightning.

He was talking on the phone during a thunderstorm (always a bad idea on a landline!). A powerful bolt of lightning struck the house and was channelled through the phone cord, right into Brinkley's ear. Electricity coursed through his body, bathing every cell in what felt like battery acid. The current instantly welded the nails in his shoes to the nails in the floor of the house. He was literally blown out of his shoes.

Writhing in pain, and barely clinging to life, he was transported to the hospital. His prognosis was dismal.

It wasn't long before he went into cardiac arrest. He describes what happened next:

> "*From intense pain I found myself engulfed by peace and tranquility... It was like bathing in a glorious calmness...*
>
> "*I looked to my right and could see a silver form appearing like a silhouette through mist. As it approached I began to feel a deep sense of love that encompassed all of the meaning of the word. It was as though I were seeing a lover, a mother, and best friend, multiplied a thousandfold. As the Being of Light came closer those feelings of love intensified until they became almost too pleasurable to withstand...*
>
> "*I felt comfortable in his presence, a familiarity that made me believe he had felt every feeling I had ever had, from the time I took my first breath to the instant I was sizzled by lightning. Looking at the Being I had the feeling that no one could love me better, no one could have more empathy, sympathy, encouragement, and nonjudgmental compassion for me than this Being...*
>
> "*The Being of Light engulfed me, and as it did I began to experience my whole life, feeling and seeing everything that had ever happened to me...*

"This life review was not pleasant. From the moment it began until it ended, I was faced with the sickening reality that I had been an unpleasant person, someone who was self-centered and mean.

"The first thing I saw was my angry childhood. I saw myself torturing other children, stealing their bicycles or making them miserable at school. One of the most vivid scenes was of the time I picked on a child at grade school because he had a goiter that protruded from his neck.... At the time I thought it was funny. But now, as I relived this incident, I found myself in his body, living with the pain that I was causing...

"From fifth to twelfth grade, I estimate that I had at least six thousand fistfights. Now, as I reviewed my life in the bosom of the Being, I relived each one of those altercations, but with one major difference: I was the receiver.

"I wasn't the receiver in the sense that I felt the punches I had thrown. Rather, I felt the anguish and humiliation my opponent felt.

"I also felt the grief I had caused my parents. I had been uncontrollable and proud of it...

"I had often bragged to my friends about how I had hurt my parents. Now, in my life review, I felt their psychological pain at having such a bad child...

"The depth of emotion I experienced during this life review was astonishing. Not only could I feel the way both I and the other person had felt when an incident took place, I could also feel the feelings of the next person they reacted to. I was in a chain reaction of emotion, one that showed how deeply we affect one another. Luckily, not all of it was bad.

"One time, for instance, my great-uncle and I were driving down the road when we saw a man beating a goat that had somehow gotten its head stuck in a fence. The man had a branch, and he was hitting the goat across the back as hard as he could while the goat bleated in fear and agony. I stopped the car and jumped across a ditch. Before the man could turn around, I was pounding him as hard as I could in the back of the head. I only stopped when my great-uncle pulled me off; I freed the goat and we left in a cloud of burnt rubber.

"Now, as I relived that incident, I felt satisfaction at the humiliation that farmer had felt and joy in the relief the goat had felt. I knew

that in the animal's own way, he had said 'thank you.'

"But I wasn't always kind to animals. I saw myself whipping a dog with a belt. I had caught this dog chewing on our living room carpet and lost my temper... Reliving this incident, I felt the dog's love for me and could tell that he didn't mean to do what he was doing. I felt his sorrow and pain.

"Later, as I thought about these experiences, I realized that people who beat animals or are cruel to them are going to know how those animals felt when they have a life review.

"I also discovered that it is not so much what you do that counts, but why you do it. For example, having a fistfight with someone for no real reason hurt me far more in the life review than having one with someone who had picked a fight with me. To relive hurting someone just for fun is the greatest pain of all. To relive hurting someone for a cause you believe in is not as painful." (Saved by the Light, pp. 5–15)

If all this wasn't painful enough, the review of Dannion Brinkley's life then shifted to his years in the Marine Corps:

"*My main job was to 'plan and execute the removal of enemy politicians and military personnel.' In short, I was an assassin...*

"*...We were sent to 'terminate' a North Vietnamese colonel...*

"*...I squeezed off the round and felt the rifle kick. A moment later I saw his head explode and his body crumple before the shocked troops.*

"*That is what I saw when the incident happened.*

"*During my life review, I experienced this incident from the perspective of the North Vietnamese colonel... I felt his confusion at having his head blown off and sadness as he left his body and realized that he would never go home again. Then I felt the rest of the chain reaction—the sad feelings of his family when they realized they would be without their provider.*

"*I relived all of my kills in just this fashion. I saw myself make the kill and then I felt its horrible results...*

"*...I saw myself unloading weapons in a Central American country. My task was simply to transfer these weapons from an airplane to our military interests in the area. When this* *transfer was completed, I got back on the airplane and left.*

"But leaving wasn't so easy in my life review. I stayed with the weapons and watched as they were distributed at a military staging area. Then I went with the guns as they were used in the job of killing...

"...I remember watching children cry because they had been told that their fathers were dead, and I knew these deaths were caused by the guns I had delivered." (Ibid, pp. 16–19)

As the life review concluded, Brinkley braced for the inevitable onslaught of divine wrath. What actually followed was not expected:

"I looked at the Being of Light and felt a deep sense of sorrow and shame. I expected a rebuke, some kind of cosmic shaking of my soul. I had reviewed my life and what I had seen was a truly worthless person. What did I deserve if not a rebuke?

"As I gazed at the Being of Light I felt as though he was touching me. From that contact I felt a love and joy that could only be compared to the nonjudgmental compassion that a grandfather has for a grandchild. 'Who you are is

the difference that God makes,' said the Being. 'And that difference is love...'

"...Again I was allowed a period of reflection. How much love had I given people? How much love had I taken from them? From the review I had just had, I could see that for every good event in my life, there were twenty bad ones to weigh against it. If guilt were fat, I would have weighed five hundred pounds.

"As the Being of Light moved away, I felt the burden of this guilt being removed. I had felt the pain and anguish of reflection, but from that I had gained the knowledge that I could use to correct my life. I could hear the Being's message in my head, again as if through telepathy: 'Humans are powerful spiritual beings meant to create good on the Earth. This good usually isn't accomplished in bold actions, but in singular acts of kindness between people. It's the little things that count, because they are more spontaneous and show who you truly are.'" (Ibid, pp. 5–21)

Despite the obvious compassion coming from the being of light, one would still think that condemnation and harsh judgment were soon to follow. Justice, after all, cannot be denied. To the contrary:

"His forgiveness was remarkable. Despite the horribly flawed life we had just witnessed, deep and meaningful forgiveness came to me from this Being. Rather than issuing harsh judgment, the Being of Light was a friendly counsel, letting me feel for myself the pain and the pleasure I had caused others. Instead of feeling shame and anguish, I was bathed in the love that embraced me through the light, and had to give nothing in return." (Ibid, pp. 24–25)

A bolt of lightning harnesses up to a billion volts of electricity. The trauma to Brinkley's body was devastating. Even though he survived those first critical hours, he was by no means out of the woods. His subsequent recovery and rehabilitation would be long, slow, and tenuous. His spiritual transformation, on the other hand, was immediate and sure. A mean-spirited reprobate became a caring, considerate saint virtually overnight. The urge to hurt people vanished, replaced by an all-consuming desire to spend the rest of his life helping them. Dannion Brinkley returned to life a changed man.

His new life was not without its challenges, of course. One struggle, common to many who have been to heaven, was dealing with the harsh realities of this imperfect world after revelling in the awesome perfection of the next. Additionally, the intense pain and frustrations resulting from his injuries would be unwelcome companions for years to come.

However, the encounter with the light had given him more than just a desire to live a better life. It had also endowed him with strength to endure soul-crushing adversity:

> *"I began to realize the change that had taken place in me as a result of the near-death experience. Regardless of my [physical] condition, the experience gave me the inner strength to endure. In my worst moments, all I had to do was recall the love that I felt emanating from those heavenly lights and I could press on. I knew that it would be wrong to take my own life, but the fact is, I never even thought of doing so. When things got bad, all I had to do was think of the love in that light and they got better."* (Ibid, p. 68)

It would be a long time before Dannion's physical recovery would catch up with his spiritual transformation. He was anxious to start building a new legacy. He had a lot of lost time to make up and he wasn't about to endure another life review filled with pain and regret. He was determined that the next time his life would come up for review, things would be different. The desire to hurt others was gone, burned from his soul by a billion volts and the love of a pure being. From now on, every thought and action would be focused on how he might help people. As soon as his strength allowed, he started building a legacy of kindness that would soon outstrip the cruelty of his former life.

A Second NDE

Serious injuries have a way of coming back to haunt us. Fourteen years after the lightning strike, the enduring trauma to his body caused Brinkley to succumb to an insidious infection that slowly but surely overwhelmed him. He sensed that the end was approaching. This time, however, he wasn't at all distressed about it. He was actually excited about the prospect of "really" dying!

He had become friends with the author of Life After Life, Raymond Moody, and as his impending death approached, his friend was at his bedside.

Dr. Moody asked him: "How come you're not afraid?"

He replied: *"Because living on Earth is like being forced to go to summer camp. You hate everyone and you miss your momma. Raymond, I'm going home."* (Ibid, p. 144)

His life ebbed away, and, for the second time, Dannion Brinkley found himself in the presence of the being of light. It was a sweet reunion:

> *"He drew me towards him, and as he did he spread out, almost like an angel spreading its wings. I was engulfed by these wings of light, and as I was, I began to see my life all over again.*
>
> *"The first twenty-five years passed as they had in my first near-death experience. I saw many of the same things... Watching these early years again was painful, I won't deny that, but the agony was tempered by viewing the*

years since the first experience. I had a feeling of pride about these years. The first twenty-five years were bad, but the next fourteen were of a changed man.

"*I saw the good that I had accomplished with my life. One after the other, events both great and small were reviewed as I stood in this cocoon of light.*

"*I watched myself volunteering in nursing homes, performing even the smallest duties, like helping someone stand up or comb her hair. Several times I watched as I did jobs no one else wanted to do, like clipping toenails and changing diapers.*

"*One time for instance, I helped care for an elderly woman. She had lain in bed so long that she was stiff and could hardly move. I scooped her out of the bed like a child—she couldn't have weighed more than eighty pounds—and held her while the nurses changed the sheets. To give her a change of scenery, I walked around the building with her in my arms.*

"*I know this meant a lot to her at the time because she thanked me profusely and cried when I left. Now, as I relived the event, the perspective I had in this heavenly place let me feel her gratitude at having someone hold her again.*

"I relived a time in New York when I invited a group of bag ladies to a Chinese restaurant for dinner. I saw these women in an alley scrounging through garbage cans and felt compassion for their situation. Escorting them into a small restaurant, I treated them to a hot meal.

"When I saw this event again, I could feel their mistrust of me as a stranger. Who was this man and what did he want? They were unaccustomed to someone trying to do a good deed. Still, when the food came, they were grateful to be treated with humanity. We stayed in the restaurant for almost four hours and drank several large bottles of Chinese beer. The meal cost me more than a hundred dollars, but the price was nothing compared to the joy of reliving it." (Ibid, pp.148–149)

But this still wasn't Brinkley's "time" (which you probably guessed since he's writing about the experience!). Once again, despite overwhelming odds, he was brought back to life. He was disappointed, because he'd thought he was going home for good this time. I suspect, however, that he viewed his return to life with a certain degree of sanguinity. While he would have to wait just a little longer to enjoy his final rest, at least he had the chance to go back and continue to stack his "good works ledger" a little more on the plus side. Near-death survivors seem to gain a good appreciation that our time on Earth is not about what we can get out of it, but rather what we can give. Dannion Brinkley now spends much of his time comforting dying veterans and AIDS patients.

Dannion Brinkley's experience is unique in that he got to undergo two life reviews. The contrast in the tones of the two reviews was telling. They were as different as night and day. Like the "before" and "after" pictures of a weight-loss infomercial, the transformation of Dannion Brinkley was striking. A sinner became a saint and never looked back. Rebalancing the ledger became the priority of Dannion Brinkley's post-NDE life.

His story illustrates the remarkable transformational power of the life review. Nothing changes our priorities quite like seeing the effects of our actions on others.

Changed lives are the proof in the near-death pudding! The transformation is obviously much more noticeable in someone with a chequered past, but there is almost always a positive change in "good" people too. NDEs make bad people good and good people better.

But... back to reality, Bob: you and I are not going to have an NDE!

Near-death is not likely to intervene and change the trajectory of your life or mine. The chances are excellent that we will both arrive at that fateful life review without having had the benefit of previewing the test or even knowing how to prepare. As our entire lives are being reviewed for the first and last time, we may well feel slighted in that no one told us what to expect, and neither are we likely to have the opportunity to go back and make things right.

The question we have to ask ourselves, then, is whether it's possible for us to undergo such a mighty change now without having to be struck by a billion volts of lightning? The answer is, yes—if we want it.

The change in our lives may not be as striking or as electrifying as Dannion Brinkley's (pardon the lightning puns) but a knowledge of NDEs can spark a deep and abiding change in us nonetheless. The question for us is simply whether we're willing to learn from the experiences of others and choose to do something about it. Our motivation will have to come from within, of course, since we won't have the luxury of a miraculous intervention, but if we can change without being forced to change—well, that's the most meaningful change of all.

A lot of us are going through life not giving much thought to the effects of our actions on others. I suppose we just assume that the things we do will linger in the ether for a short while, but will soon be discarded permanently on the ash heap of history.

Not so. Actions have meaning, and the consequences of even the smallest act are eternal. One day we will confront, in vivid detail, not only the immediate impact of our actions, but also the vast ripple effects of everything we do and say. It will be an eye-opening experience, and for perhaps the first time, we will truly begin to see ourselves as others see us. Hopefully we won't be too shocked at our own appearance and will like what we see!

That introduction to our true self doesn't have to be a surprise, Bob. *Death Therapy* is about preparing for that moment now. It's like taking a selfie of our soul to see where we stand!

There are two avenues for gaining the motivation to begin preparing for the life review: we can get on the phone during a lightning storm, or we can pick up a book and read about someone who did.

Both guarantee results. But personally, I'm opting for the reading route!

Chapter 6

The Life Review

"It is our choices that show what we truly are, far more than our abilities."
—Albus Dumbledore, *Harry Potter and the Chamber of Secrets*[18]

"When you think everything is someone else's fault, you will suffer a lot. When you realize that everything springs only from yourself, you will learn both peace and joy."
—The Dalai Lama[19]

"...but then shall I know even as also I am known."
—1 Corinthians 13:12, King James Bible

---

[18] *Harry Potter and the Chamber of Secrets* is the second novel in the Harry Potter series, by J. K. Rowling, first published in 1998 by Bloomsbury.

[19] Dalai Lama is a title given to the highest spiritual leader of the Tibetan people. The fourteenth and current Dalai Lama is Tenzin Gyatso. Because of disagreements with China, he is effectively in exile.

A FEW YEARS AGO, A DISASTER OCCURRED in our home. Someone left the back door open, and by nightfall, the house was full of mosquitoes. This may not sound like a disaster to you, but I abhor mosquitoes. I grew up in the UK where there are no mosquitoes or venomous creatures of any kind (except, perhaps, for the British press), so this really was a disaster.

However, the kind hand of Providence smiled on us that day, because just a few days earlier, a friend had given me a most useful gift—an electrified mosquito zapper. It looks like a little tennis racquet, only it has metal wires instead of nylon strings. The wires are electrified by batteries in the handle. It's analogous to a cattle fence for mosquitoes, although the object isn't to scare the mosquitoes away, it's to fry their little hinies to kingdom come.

I found a couple of AA batteries, cranked up the voltage, and went to work. It was wonderful. In fighter pilot parlance, it was a *target-rich environment*.

All I had to do was waft that thing in the air, and each pass sent multiple bogies to meet their Maker. What added to the fun was that the current actually caused their little bodies to explode, producing a satisfying "pop" each time. Soon the air was filled with the sweet aroma of burning mosquito flesh. Ten minutes into the fight and they hadn't laid a glove on me, not one bite. The score was 148–0. Game over!

What began as a disaster turned out to be a most enjoyable evening.

Now, lest you get the wrong impression, let me say that I think we should be kind to all of God's creations. But, when it comes to mosquitoes, I defer to the wisdom of a five-year-old:

Susanna is the daughter of some friends of ours. We were living on Galveston Island at the time (affectionately referred to as "Galvatraz" or "The Rock" by us medical students), and if you've ever been to the island you'll know that mosquitoes can be more than just an annoyance. Some are big enough to carry you off.

One evening, Susanna was watching her dad go through the nightly ritual of ridding the house of mosquitoes. This was before the advent of the electrified zapper and he was using a good old-fashioned fly swatter (which I'm not knocking: it's simple and reliable and you have the advantage of being able to keep score by counting the blood spots on the wall).

Anyway, it was Easter, and Susanna had just had a lesson in church about the resurrection. She had learned that all creatures will be resurrected someday. With this on her mind, and as she watched her dad consign a few more of God's creatures to that great swamp in the sky, the wheels started turning. She asked her mother if mosquitoes will be resurrected. Her mother thought for a minute then replied that, yes, she supposed that even mosquitoes will be resurrected.

Just then her father slapped a particularly fat mosquito. Susanna looked at the big red spot on the wall, heaved a big sigh, and said:

"Oh well, I suppose we'll just have to smash him again!"

That's what I'm talking about!

I don't know if mosquitoes will be resurrected, and to be perfectly honest, I really don't see the point. If a mosquito's only *raison d'être* is to suck my blood, I just don't see them having much of a role in heaven. (If I'm wrong, it's going to be a long eternity!)

Anyway, while I'm hazy as to the eternal destiny of the insect world, what I *am* certain about is that death is not the end for you and me, and that one day we will be required to stand before our Maker and give an accounting of our lives.

Consciousness endures the death of the physical body and, at that fateful moment, every human being will face two very stark realities: one, that we are exactly the same person we were the moment before we died, and two, that we will have to relive, in vivid detail, every significant event of our lives, from cradle to grave.

The implications of these two realities are that neither faults nor virtues are swept under the rug at the time of death. Rather, everything we've said or done while we were alive will be on full display.

That is a rather daunting prospect, and many have been able to convince themselves that a benevolent God would never require such a thing of them. They cling to the hope that the moment we pass the portal of death, we'll be immediately fitted for angels' wings and crowned with halos (or, conversely, I suppose, that we'll grow horns and be handed a pitchfork). Some liken the process of death to a caterpillar breaking out of its cocoon and emerging a beautiful butterfly; its drab former life already a distant memory. They believe that we'll emerge on the other side with all our faults, blemishes, addictions, and character defects instantly vaporised ... like the dew before the summer sun.

Not so, at least according to near-death survivors. The first big surprise of the newly-deceased is the realization that very little has changed. Some even have trouble realizing they've died. True, their body seems to have shed some weight (all of it actually), but their intellect, aspirations, and desires haven't changed in the least, and if they remain in this new world long enough, they're going to face the reality that every thought, word, and action from birth to the present will have to be accounted for. This is the proverbial life review, and it leaves no stone unturned:

"My whole life so far appeared to be placed before me in a kind of panoramic, three-dimensional review, and each event seemed to be accompanied by an awareness of good and evil or by an insight into its cause and effect. Throughout, I not only saw everything from my own point of view, but also I knew the thoughts of everybody who'd been involved in these events, as if their thoughts were lodged inside me. It meant that I saw not only what I had done or thought but even how this had affected others, as if I was seeing with all-knowing eyes. And throughout, the review stressed the importance of love. I can't say how long this life review and insight into life lasted; it may have been quite long because it covered every single subject, but at the same time it felt like a split second because I saw everything at

once. It seemed as if time and distance didn't exist." (Consciousness Beyond Life, p. 36)

You've heard people say: "My whole life passed before my eyes." This often happens in the moments right before an anticipated disaster (such as a car accident, a serious fall, or Hillary almost becoming president). It's a real phenomenon. It's hard to imagine how someone can see his or her entire life played back in a split second. But then, we have to remember that we are highly attuned to the concept of "linear time." For us, everything happens sequentially. In a place where time and space don't exist, "split seconds" have no meaning (Einstein would approve).[20]

The miracle of our "life passing before our eyes" may progress to a full-blown life review if death (or near death) actually occurs. The difference between the two seems to be that the life review is usually conducted in the presence of a loving being of light and there is a definite purpose to the exercise: to help us carefully evaluate our life.

This review of our lives can be most impactful—hopefully more so than the experience of Babs the hen in Chicken Run:

"All me life flashed before me eyes. It was really borin.'"[21]

---

[20] Albert Einstein (1879–1955) developed the theory of relativity, a pillar of modern science.

[21] This is a line from *Chicken Run*, a 2000 animated adventure/comedy by Aardman Animations, directed by Peter Lord and Nick Park, starring Mel Gibson, Julia Sawalha, and others.

After hearing multiple accounts of the life review, Dr. Raymond Moody summarized it this way:

> *"Again and again my near-death subjects have described to me a panoramic, wrap-around, full-colour, three-dimensional vision of the events of their lives. Some people say that during this vision they saw only the major events of their lives. Others go so far as to say that in the course of this panorama every single thing that they had ever done or thought was there for them to see. All the good things and all the bad were portrayed there at once, instantaneously. It will be remembered also that this panorama was quite frequently said to have taken place in the presence of a 'being of light,' whom some Christians identified as Christ, and that this being asked them a question, in effect, 'What have you done with your life?'*

> *"In being pressed to explain as precisely as they can what the point of this question was, most people come up with something like the formulation of one man who put it to me most succinctly when he said that he was asked whether he had done the things he did because he loved others, that is, from the motivation of love. At this point, one might say, a kind of judgment took place, for in this state of heightened awareness, when people saw any selfish acts which they had done they felt extremely*

repentant. Likewise, when gazing upon those events in which they had shown love and kindness they felt satisfaction.

"It is interesting to note that the judgment in the cases I studied came not from the being of light, who seemed to love and accept these people anyway, but rather from within the individual being judged." (Reflections on Life After Life, pp. 29–30)

We all have skeletons in our closets and the thought of them being exposed for all to see is not pleasant. Indeed, much of the examination of our lives will probably make us quite uncomfortable. The intent, however, seems to be more for our growth than our condemnation. As Dr. Moody stated, whatever judgment there is, seems to come from within.

Of special importance is the requirement that we start to see ourselves as others see us, that we pay attention to how our words and actions have affected those around us.

"Then it seemed there was a display all around me, and everything in my life just went by for review, you might say. I was really very, very ashamed of a lot of the things that I experienced because it seemed that I had a different knowledge, that the light was showing me what was wrong, what I did wrong. And it was very real.

"It seemed like this flashback, or memory, or whatever was directed primarily at ascertaining the extent of my life. It was like there was a judgment being made and then, all of a sudden, the light became dimmer, and there was a conversation, not in words, but in thoughts. When I would see something, when I would experience a past event, it was like I was seeing it through eyes with (I guess you would say) omnipotent knowledge, guiding me, and helping me to see.

"That's the part that has stuck with me, because it showed me not only what I had done but even how what I had done had affected other people. And it wasn't like I was looking at a movie projector because I could feel these things; there was feeling, and particularly since I was with this knowledge... I found out that not even your thoughts are lost... Every thought was there... Your thoughts are not lost..." (Reflections on Life After Life, pp. 32–33)

Since we all will face this "test" someday, what are the things we should know about it?

First, is its comprehensive nature. Everything is fair game, *especially* the little things:

"One woman told me that the life review doesn't show just the big events of one's life, as

you might think. She said that it shows the little things, too. For instance, one of the incidents that came across very powerfully in her review was a time when she found a little girl lost in a department store. The girl was crying, and the woman sat her up on a counter and talked to her until her mother arrived.

"It was those kind of things—the little things you do while not even thinking—that come up most importantly in the review." (The Light Beyond, p. 39)

The being of light told Dannion Brinkley:

"Humans are powerful spiritual beings meant to create good on the Earth. This good usually isn't accomplished in bold actions, but in singular acts of kindness between people. It's the little things that count, because they are more spontaneous and show who you truly are." (Saved by the Light, p. 21)

The "little things" aren't limited to actions. Words, and even thoughts, come into play. We often fail to realise how much of an influence we are constantly exerting on those around us. Someone said it this way:

"Life is a state of radiation and absorption. To exist is to radiate: to exist is to be the recipient of radiation." (David O. McKay)

A near-death survivor used similar words:

> *"I had no idea, no idea at all, not even the slightest hint of an idea, that every thought, word, and deed was remembered, accounted for, and went out and had a life of its own once released; nor did I know that the energy of that life directly affected all it touched or came near. It's as if we must live in some kind of vast sea or soup of each other's energy residue and thought waves, and we are each held responsible for our contributions and the quality of 'ingredients' we add.*
>
> *"This knowledge overwhelmed me!"* (Coming Back to Life, pp. 36–37)

Life is a privilege, and with privilege comes responsibility. One of the greatest lessons we could learn in life is to begin to acknowledge the profound effect on others of everything we do and say. In order to do that, we first have to stop making excuses.

Defensiveness is rarely a good thing, because it prevents us from taking ownership of our problems:

> *"The most important thing I learned from this experience was that I am responsible for everything I do. Excuses and avoidance were impossible when I was there with him reviewing my life. And not only that, I saw that responsibility is not bad in the least, that*

I can't make excuses or try to put my failings off on somebody else. It's funny, but my failings have become very dear to me in a way, because they are my failings, and darn it, I am going to learn from them, come hell or high water.

"*I remember one particular incident in this review when, as a child, I yanked my little sister's Easter basket away from her, because there was a toy in it that I wanted. Yet in the review, I felt her disappointment and loss and rejection.*

"*What we do to other people when we act unlovingly! But it is wonderful that we are destined not to be allowed to remain unconscious of it...*

"*Everything you have done is there (in the review) for you to evaluate, and as unpleasant as some parts of it are for you to see, it feels so good to get it all out. In life, you can play around and make excuses for yourself and even cover up, and you can stay miserable, if you want to, by doing all this covering up. But when I was there in that review there was no covering up. I was the very people that I hurt, and I was the very people I helped to feel good. I wish I could find some way to convey to everyone how good it feels to know that you*

*are responsible and to go through something
like this where it is impossible not to face it.*

*"It is the most liberated feeling in the world.
It is a real challenge, every day of my life, to
know that when I die I am going to have to
witness every single action of mine again, only
this time actually feeling the effects I've had
on others. It sure makes me stop and think. I
don't dread it. I relish it."* (The Light Beyond,
pp. 37–38)

Although the entire spectrum of virtues and vices are
encompassed in the life review, a couple of virtues are constantly emphasized:

*"All of the people who go through this [the life
review] come away believing that the most
important thing in their life is love.*

*"For most of them, the second most important
thing in life is knowledge. As they see life scenes
in which they are learning things, the Being
points out that one of the things they can take
with them at death is knowledge. The other is
love."* (The Light Beyond, p. 11)

Perhaps the reason *knowledge* is so often cited as a valuable commodity is because knowledge of truth allows us
to make necessary corrections in our lives:

"I had gained the knowledge that I could use to correct my life...

"[But it still comes down to love]: *Again I was allowed a period of reflection. How much love had I given people? How much love had I taken from them?"* (Saved by the Light, p. 20)

The need to forgive others is also often brought up:

> *"After the review was over, the Being of Light gave me the opportunity to forgive everyone who had ever crossed me... I didn't want to forgive many of these people because I felt that the things they had done to me were unforgivable. They had hurt me in business and in my personal life and made me feel nothing for them but anger and disdain.*
>
> *"But the Being of Light told me that I had to forgive them. If I didn't, he let me know, I would be stuck at the spiritual level that I now occupied."* (Saved by the Light, p. 152)

One aspect of the life review that is important to realise is that it is generally conducted in the presence of a being of light. This is a crucial element because it is his (or her) unrestrained love for the individual that makes the experience tolerable. Couple this with the being's running commentary and the review of our lives becomes a most meaningful exercise:

"I looked ... at the Being of Light... I felt comfortable in his presence, a familiarity that made me believe he had felt every feeling I had ever had, from the time I took my first breath to the instant I was sizzled by lightning. Looking at the Being I had the feeling that no one could love me better, no one could have more empathy, sympathy, encouragement, and nonjudgmental compassion for me than this Being...

"His forgiveness was remarkable. Despite the horribly flawed life we had just witnessed, deep and meaningful forgiveness came to me from this Being. Rather than issuing harsh judgment, the Being of Light was a friendly counsel, letting me feel for myself the pain and the pleasure I had caused others. Instead of feeling shame and anguish, I was bathed in the love that embraced me through the light, and had to give nothing in return." (Saved by the Light, pp. 10 and 24–25)

The prospect of our many faults being laid bare for all to see is not a pleasant one...and for good reason. Only one with the clearest of consciences could look forward to that moment with eager anticipation.

For the rest of us reprobates, this day of reckoning hangs over our heads like the legendary Sword of Damocles.[22] It's

---

[22] In the fourth century BC, Damocles was a courtier to Dionysius II of Syracuse, Sicily. According to legend, Damocles was pandering to Dionysius by telling

not a pleasant thought, but it has to be this way. There is simply no room in the next life for pretense, affectation, or self-delusion. In a place where *all* knowledge is instantly available to *all*, only a pristine clarity will suffice. It's not as bad as it sounds, however: the focus seems to be on our own desire to change rather than the being's desire to punish us.

There is a lesson to be learned from the being's compassionate reaction to the ugliness of our lives: it's a powerful motivator for change. Near-death survivors teach us again and again that it isn't fear of consequences that motivates them to change, but rather the desire to try to measure up to the standard of goodness standing before them. This is a principle we can employ here and now: the best way to help someone change their behaviour is to exemplify the behaviour you wish to change.

There is no more powerful catalyst for change than modelling the outcome you wish to see in others. It will outperform criticism or threats any day of the week. It's the love coming from the being of light that is the primary catalyst for improvement in the individual:

> *"Fear of hellish punishment for earthly deeds is no longer a problem for many. When they see*

---

the king that he was truly fortunate to be a man of power and authority, surrounded by magnificence. Dionysius offered to switch places with his courtier for a day so that Damocles could experience that fortune firsthand. Damocles readily agreed, but as he sat on the king's throne he soon became aware that Dionysius had arranged to have a huge sword hung above Damocles' head, suspended by a single hair of a horse's tail. Damocles finally begged the king to be allowed to depart prematurely, having learned the lesson that with great power and privilege also comes great danger.

the review of their life, NDEers realize that the being of light loves and cares for them. They realize that he is not judgmental, but rather he wants them to develop into better people. This helps them eliminate fear and focus instead on becoming loving people.

"You have to understand that the being of light isn't telling them that they have to change. My summation, after hearing hundreds of these cases, is that people change willingly because they are in the presence of the standard of goodness, which makes them want to change their behavior radically." (The Light Beyond, p. 32)

Will It Make a Difference?

As in all aspects of *Death Therapy*, the principle is only valid if it changes the life of the student. The proof, as they say, is in the pudding. (Actually, the proverb is: "The proof of the pudding is in the eating," which makes a lot more sense, since it's rare to find any kind of proof in any kind of pudding.)

The life review does indeed change lives.

"When I got back, I had this overwhelming, burning, consuming desire to do something for other people... I was so ashamed of all the things that I had done, or hadn't done, in my

life. I felt like I had to do it, that it couldn't wait." (Reflections on Life After Life, p. 33)

"I had decided I'd better change. I was very repentant. I hadn't been satisfied with the life I had led up to then, so I wanted to start doing better." (Ibid, p. 33)

One final story of redemption:

"One of the most startling examples that I've seen of personal growth through an NDE was the case of a man I'll call Nick. He was a con artist and an outright criminal who had done everything from bilking widows to running drugs. Crime had provided a good life for Nick. He had nice cars, fine clothes, and new houses, and no problems with his conscience to annoy him.

"Then his life changed. He was golfing on a cloudy day when a thunderstorm suddenly developed. Before he could get off the greens, he was struck by lightning and 'killed.'

"He hovered above his body for a moment and then found himself speeding down a dark tunnel toward a spot of light. He emerged into a bright pastoral setting where he was greeted by relatives and other people who were 'glowing like Coleman lanterns.'

"He met a being of light that he still haltingly describes as God, who graciously led him through a life review. He relived his entire life, not only seeing his actions in three dimensions, but seeing and feeling the effects of his actions on others.

"That experience changed Nick. Later, while recovering in the hospital, he felt the full effect of his life review. With the being of light, he had been exposed to pure love. He felt that when he really died, he would have to undergo the life review again, a process that would be very uncomfortable if he failed to learn from his first life review.

"'Now,' says Nick, 'I always live my life knowing that someday I'll have to go through another life review.'" (The Light Beyond, pp. 29–30)

Well, that's the life review in a nutshell, Bob. But as always, back to real life: you and me. We're not going to experience a life review until the day we actually die. The only impetus we have for change right now are these canisters of gunpowder around our necks. Are we going to sit around waiting passively for them to explode, or are we going to take charge of our lives, begin untangling the emotional knots, and really start living? We are the producer, editor, and leading actor in our own movie and the final product is entirely up to us. We can cast ourselves as the hero in a timeless classic, or we can just sit back and wait for a rather painful review of our lives later. *Death Therapy* is the difference.

Death Therapy begins with little acts of kindness and ends when we've learned to love others as unconditionally as we are loved. It's not an easy task, Bob. But it will make for an epic movie in the end.

We may even win an Oscar.

Chapter 7

Scrooge and Marley

"Christmas? Bah! Humbug!"
—Ebenezer Scrooge (before)

"I will honour Christmas in my heart and try to keep it all the year."
—Ebenezer Scrooge (after)[23]

The Dog's Diary

8:00 a.m.—Dog food! My favourite!
9:30 a.m.—A car ride! Oh boy! My favourite!
9:40 a.m.—A walk in the park! Wow!
10:30 a.m.—Got rubbed and petted! Oh boy!
12:00 p.m.—Milk bones! Oh boy! My favourite!
1:00 p.m.—Played outside! Wow!
3:00 p.m.—Wagged my tail! Oh boy!
5:00 p.m.—Dinner! Wow!

---

[23] Ebenezer Scrooge is a fictional character from Charles Dickens's 1843 novella, *A Christmas Carol*.

7:00 p.m.—Got to play ball! Oh boy!
8:00 p.m.—Wow! Watched TV with the people!
11:00 p.m.—Sleeping on the bed! What a day!

The Cat's Diary

Day 729 of my captivity:
My captors continue to taunt me with bizarre little dangling objects. They dine lavishly on fresh meat while the other inmates and I are fed some sort of dry nuggets. The only thing that keeps me going is the hope of escape and the mild satisfaction I get from shredding the occasional piece of furniture. Tomorrow I may eat another houseplant and cough it up on the carpet.

Day 732:
Today I decapitated a mouse and dropped the headless body at their feet. I had hoped this would strike fear into their hearts since it demonstrates what I'm capable of. Instead, they condescendingly patted my head and told me "what a good little hunter" I was. Morons!

Day 738:
My attempt to assassinate my captors by weaving around their feet almost succeeded. Must try this at the top of the stairs.

Day 747:
I am finally aware of how sadistic they are. For no good reason I was chosen for the water torture. This time, however, it included a burning foamy chemical called

"shampoo." My only consolation is the piece of thumb still stuck between my teeth.

Day 750:
Today there was a gathering of their accomplices. I was placed in solitary throughout the event. Overheard them say that my confinement was due to my power of "allergies." Must learn what this is and how to use it to my advantage.

Day 755:
I am convinced the other captives are flunkies and possibly snitches. The dog is routinely released and seems more than happy to return. He is obviously a half-wit. The bird must be an informant. I see him communicate with the guards regularly. I am certain he reports my every move. My captors have arranged protective custody for him in the metal room, so he is safe—for now.[24]

Christmas

I love Christmas. I love its traditions, the music, the excitement of children, the feeling of goodwill. It really is "the most wonderful time of the year."[25]

Charles Dickens's A Christmas Carol has become a perennial favourite of mine. Every year I read the book and made our children watch the movie with me (that is,

---

[24] The author of *Dog Diary vs. Cat Diary* is anonymous. There are multiple versions.

[25] "It's the Most Wonderful Time of the Year" is a song popularized by Andy Williams, released in 1963, written by Edward Pola and George Wyle.

until they grew up and realised they had a choice in the matter—but now I have grandchildren to indoctrinate).

I don't know what it is about the story, but for me, it just wouldn't be Christmas without Dickens's timeless tale. Perhaps it's the joy of seeing a life changed, a miserly old curmudgeon become a saint. I'm not an emotional person, but even after watching the scene scores of times, I still have to fight back tears at Scrooge's joy as he wakes up on Christmas morning and realises he's been granted a chance at redemption. The reconciliation with his nephew Fred is especially heart-warming.

I know the book is fiction, but in the hands of a master, even fiction can move the soul. I find myself wanting to be like Scrooge at Christmastime (the "after" version of course).

The story behind the story is fascinating.

For many, life in Victorian London was not particularly pleasant. For some it was a grim, soulless existence and young Charles Dickens was not spared his allotment of suffering. Though he was born into a family of moderate means, he was forced to abandon his schooling at the age of twelve in order to support the family. His father, John Dickens, was something of a spendthrift and in 1824 landed himself in debtors' prison. Charles found himself working seventy-two hours a week, earning six shillings a week at a rat-infested boot-blacking factory on the bank of the Thames. Even worse for young Charles were the feelings of abandonment and betrayal he felt toward the adults who were supposed to take care of him. This was a theme that would surface again and again in his writings. The street urchin Oliver Twist is an obvious example, and even Ebenezer Scrooge himself seems to personify some of the very mixed emotions Charles felt for his profligate father.

Still, even suffering has meaning, and loss of childhood innocence, as traumatic as it was, would instil in Charles Dickens a deep compassion for the poor and the exploited working masses. He was especially sensitive to the plight of the impoverished children of London and his early writings were a constant reminder to the reader of the gross injustices of the time. This concern for the children was personified in A Christmas Carol in the form of Tiny Tim and metaphorically in the tragic twins: Ignorance and Want. In our present age of social safety nets and relative plenty, it's difficult to imagine children living constantly on the edge of starvation. The modern reader might be interested to know that almost half the funerals of the Victorian era were for children under the age of ten. Poverty could be as deadly as the plague and it didn't spare the young. Charles Dickens felt its icy grip at a very tender age.

Dickens's troubles didn't end with childhood. While he became a popular and successful author, the summer of 1843 found him once again in perilous financial straits. His popularity was on the decline and his overgenerous nature had led him to divert much of his income to worthy causes and needy family members. His fortune was gone, the mortgage was due, and creditors were circling.

It was under this crush of poverty that the inspiration for A Christmas Carol came to Dickens on a cold October evening in 1843 as he was walking along the bank of the Thames. He envisioned a tale that would not only serve as a strong condemnation of greed and social injustice, but also a story that would celebrate and elevate the joyful season that we call Christmas. Fearful that his writing career was in permanent decline, Dickens was anxious to produce a book that would ignite the public's imagination.

He succeeded on all counts, and did it just in time for Christmas. After six short weeks of writing, the book was published and released on December 19, 1843. The first six thousand copies were sold out by Christmas Eve. A Christmas Carol was an instant classic. It revolutionized Christmas, almost singlehandedly leap-frogging Christmas over Easter as the most popular holiday of the year. The Christmas we know and love today is due in large part to Dickens's transforming masterpiece.

Even though he ended up spending more on the project than he had originally budgeted, Dickens's generosity compelled him to keep the price of the book affordable. He wanted it to be accessible to the common man. As a consequence, he made very little money on the venture. He didn't mind: A Christmas Carol was his gift to the world, and besides, the rewards would come later. The book's huge popularity would create a much wider audience for his subsequent books: David Copperfield, A Tale of Two Cities, and Great Expectations. They all proved highly lucrative and cemented Dickens's place in literary history.

So, with that background in mind, let's look at A Christmas Carol and see what it can contribute to our therapy. Death Therapy is, after all, about making needed changes and learning to view the world in a more positive light.

The story begins in part:

"*...Old Marley was as dead as a doornail.*"

(How can you not love an opening like that?)

It's seven years to the day since Scrooge's old partner, Jacob Marley, passed away. It's Christmas Eve and we find the bitter, cantankerous old miser in his frigid counting house, lecturing his clerk, Bob Cratchit, on the wastefulness of using coal to keep oneself warm. It's the worst time of the year for old Ebenezer. He has to suffer the injustice of paying Cratchit a day's pay for no work, as well as endure the insufferable enthusiasm of Christmas revellers. When two kindly gentlemen come calling for donations to relieve the suffering of the poor, Scrooge sarcastically reminds them that his taxes are already supporting the poorhouses and prisons. Their argument that many would rather die than resort to the poorhouse elicits this from the old skinflint: "*If they would rather die they had better do it and reduce the surplus population.*"

When his irrepressible nephew Fred comes around to wish his uncle Merry Christmas Scrooge indignantly responds: "*If I could work my will, every idiot who goes about with 'Merry Christmas' on his lips, should be boiled with his own pudding, and buried with a stake of holly through his heart. He should!*"

Scrooge ends with the epithet: "*Christmas? Bah! Humbug!*"

That night, however, a curious series of events is set in motion. It begins with the appearance of the ghost of Scrooge's old partner, Jacob Marley. Marley noisily enters Scrooge's bedroom dragging an impressive set of chains and cashboxes. In response to Scrooge's inquiry as to why he's lugging this burden around, Marley intones: *"I wear the chains I forged in life. I made it link by link and yard by yard. I girded it on of my own free will."*

Marley's punishment for a life of greed and avarice is to wander the Earth, burdened down with chains, trying (in vain for the most part) to right the wrongs he spent a lifetime inflicting on others. He explains mournfully: *"It is required of every man that the spirit within him should walk abroad among his fellow-men, and travel far and wide; and, if that spirit goes not forth in life, it is condemned to do so after death."*

Jacob is here to try to save his old partner from the same fate and, lest Scrooge think his own penance will be any easier, Marley quickly disabuses him of the notion: *"Or would you know the weight and length of the strong coil you bear yourself? It was full as heavy and as long as this, seven Christmas Eves ago. You have laboured on it, since. It is a ponderous chain!"*

Marley informs Scrooge that he will be visited by three spirits that night, then clanks noisily off into the night, wailing pitifully as he goes.

The Ghost of Christmas Past appears as promised, a curious childlike phantom who appears to be made of light. Scrooge reluctantly accompanies him (her?) on a journey to view the Christmases of Scrooge's youth. In panoramic detail he gets to see himself as a sombre, lonely boy in boarding school, estranged from his harsh and distant father. He experiences the excitement of Christmas Eve as an apprentice to the jolly merchant Fezziwig, a brief but joyful interlude in an otherwise dismal youth and childhood. He sees his engagement to Belle, a beautiful young lady who could have provided him with love, companionship, and children to comfort him in his old age. Unfortunately, the arrangement ended when his lust for money crowded out the last vestiges of any ability he may have had to love another human being.

The vision ends with a pleasant scene on Christmas Eve, seven years ago, of a father coming home to his family: his wife, Belle, and a happy brood of children. The man tells Belle that he has just seen Ebenezer Scrooge sitting alone in his counting house. His business partner, Marley, is on the brink of death. Scrooge seems to be quite alone in the world.

The implication of the vision is that this wonderful family could have been Scrooge's. This cruel reminder of what might have been is too much for Scrooge. Angrily, he seizes the candle extinguisher cap the ghost was carrying and uses it to snuff out the light emanating from the being.

Sometimes the truth hurts!

With the spirit vanquished, Scrooge lies down to get some sleep, but sleep isn't going to come easily tonight.

Next to appear is a majestic, gregarious spectre in a sumptuous green fur robe: the Ghost of Christmas Present. His review of Scrooge's life will cover the Christmas happening now.

The tour begins in Bob Cratchit's humble home. In a few brief moments, Scrooge is going to learn more about his employee and his family than he's cared to know in all the years Bob has been clerking for him. Scrooge is taken aback by the tiny abode, the scrawny Christmas turkey, and the meagre meal the family is able to put on the table. It probably had never occurred to him that this was all Bob Cratchit could afford with the miserly salary he was so begrudgingly paid. It must also have been a revelation to Scrooge to see the love and joy the family was able to manufacture in such mean and lowly circumstances.

It's in the Cratchit home that Scrooge is introduced to Tiny Tim, a little boy in a crippled body who has every reason to feel sorry for himself, but whose every expression is filled with hope. His only concern is for others. He is the epitome of everything that is good about childhood: love, purity, innocence, humility—all the virtues Scrooge discarded long ago. Scrooge's heart is pricked by the little fellow, however, and when the spirit tells Scrooge that it's unlikely Tiny Tim will live much longer, we begin to see the first crack in Scrooge's armour.

One more lesson before they leave: Bob Cratchit proposes a toast to Ebenezer Scrooge, the founder of their "feast." Finally, a ray of light in an otherwise dismal outing: Scrooge is about to get a little recognition for his role in the family's well-being. His self-congratulation is short-lived, however, when he learns in no uncertain terms what each member of the family really thinks about him—none of it is good.

(Oh, what it would be like to be a fly on the wall and learn what people really think of us! It's one of those things we'll only find out in full in death, and I don't mean at the funeral—people have to say nice things about you at your funeral. No, the real truth about what people really think about us comes in the life review. There's no more hiding behind the shield of self-delusion.)

Scrooge gets another earful in the home of his nephew Fred. He is then abandoned by the spirit in a part of London where he least wants to be: amongst the homeless and destitute he so flippantly condemned just hours before. So much for Christmas Present.

If Scrooge thought he had endured the worst the spirits could dish out, he was mistaken. The Ghost of Christmas Yet to Come—by far the most fearful of the spirits—had no words of comfort for the old miser. Actually, he spoke no words at all.

This vision was marked only by death: cold, unfeeling, unmourned death. A man has died and his business associates at the Exchange are only willing to attend his funeral if there is food provided. Conniving lowlifes have already taken the curtains from the bed where the corpse lies and are pawning them off for a few measly pennies.

Outraged, Scrooge asks the spirit if there is anyone who feels any depth of emotion at the death of this man. Obligingly, the spirit shows him a young couple who were in debt to the man and who are overwhelmed with relief that they are no longer under the thumb of this harsh and heartless creditor. Not exactly the emotion Scrooge was looking for, but reality isn't always kind.

There is one family that is feeling tremendous depth of emotion at a death, but it's an unrelated event. Scrooge gets to witness the Cratchits mourn the untimely death of Tiny Tim. Even Scrooge has begun to warm to the plucky little lad by this point and, for the first time in decades, starts to feel an inkling of compassion for another.

But Scrooge still remains in serious denial about his own failings and refuses the spirit's invitation to discover the identity of the deceased man whom no one seems to care about (the man, of course, is Scrooge himself). The spirit will not be denied, however, and with the icy hand of impending doom tightening its grip around his stony heart, Scrooge finally comes to the realization that his time on Earth is going to end this very night.

But he's a changed man!

He just can't believe that he's been shown all these things if it's all for naught! He pleads with the spirit:

"Are these the shadows of the things that Will be, or are they shadows of things that May be, only? Men's courses will foreshadow certain ends, to which, if persevered in, they must lead, but if the courses be departed from, the ends will change. Say it is thus with what you show me!

"Am I that man who lay upon the bed? No, Spirit! Oh no, no! Spirit! hear me! I am not the man I was. I will not be the man I must have been but for this intercourse. Why show me this, if I am past all hope?

"Assure me that I yet may change these shadows you have shown me, by an altered life! I will honour Christmas in my heart, and try to keep it all the year. I will live in the Past, the Present, and the Future. The Spirits of all

*Three shall strive within me. I will not shut
out the lessons that they teach."*

You know the rest. Scrooge wakes up in his bed and realises he's not dead. Better yet, it's still Christmas morning. He jumps up, filled with joy and with resolve to spend the day doing as much good as possible. He pays the butcher to take the prize turkey to the Cratchits (anonymously of course), makes a more-than-generous donation to the poor and the needy, wishes a joyful "Merry Christmas" to all he meets, and spends the evening making up for lost time and lost relationships with his nephew Fred, his family, and friends. On Boxing Day, he tells a startled Bob Cratchit he's doubling his salary and assures him that he's going to do all he can to make sure Tiny Tim gets well.

Dickens concludes: *"Scrooge was better than his word. He did it all, and infinitely more; and to Tiny Tim, who did not die, he was a second father. He became as good a friend, as good a master, and as good a man, as the good old city knew..."*

What a wonderful story!

Although A Christmas Carol was written in 1843 (over a century before the near-death revolution), Dickens's celebration of Christmas would not be out of place alongside any modern NDE. Yes, it's fiction, and, no, none of us are going to be haunted by three Yuletide wraiths and a chain-dragging ex-partner. Nevertheless, A Christmas Carol is legitimate fodder for the serious near-death student.

It contains all the elements of a good NDE: meeting people we knew in life, encounters with otherworldly guides, a panoramic life review (complete with a vivid awareness of how our actions have affected others), education about what's important in life, and finally (and most importantly), a changed life.

It's the Death Therapist's dream! Reading the story every year makes me want to be more Scrooge-like at Christmas (now there's an oxymoron!). Would that we could all be visited by those pesky phantoms.

But that's where *Death Therapy* comes in. We don't have to have an epiphany like this to benefit from Scrooge's eventful evening. If reading about Ebenezer Scrooge can make us a little kinder at Christmas and throughout the year, then we've achieved the premise of *Death Therapy*: changing our lives by reading about the experiences of others.

Marley

But A Christmas Carol has a fatal flaw! It raises a question that has bothered me for years:

What about Marley?

What about Jacob Marley? While Scrooge's story is one of hope and redemption, our last and lasting impression of Jacob Marley is of a hapless spirit lugging his chains all over creation, wailing mournfully as he goes. Scrooge gets the break of a lifetime; Marley suffers for eternity. It's not right!

Okay, I know I'm obsessing way too much over the salvation of an imaginary person. It reminds me of an

Internet debate that arose over the question of whether J. K. Rowling intended Albus Dumbledore (Harry Potter's headmaster at Hogwarts) to be gay. The possibility ignited a firestorm of controversy in the blogosphere. In the middle of a heated online argument over the matter, one droll individual commented: *"You know, I just don't have the time to worry about the sexual orientation of fictional characters!"*

That's advice that I should probably take to heart, but I've been concerned about Marley for years. I'm genuinely worried about his welfare! Perhaps it's because it gets right to the heart of the question of the fairness of the whole near-death phenomenon: Why should a few "lucky" individuals get to discover the secrets of death and adjust their lives accordingly, while the rest of us patsies are left to fumble in the dark and find out the answers only when it's everlastingly too late? What did those fortunate NDEers do to deserve such a leg up in the death business?

With this in mind, it was with great excitement that I came across a book recently, titled Jacob T. Marley by R. William Bennett. The story is spun around A Christmas Carol but written from the point of view of Scrooge's erstwhile business partner, Jacob Marley.

Again, I know it's just fiction, but it did give me some much-needed closure in regards to Marley.

To be brief (something I've failed miserably to do thus far), I'll summarize the story:

Jacob Marley was blessed with a gift for mathematics. While a blessing, it was also, more tellingly, a curse. The young man developed a deep aversion to anything that didn't make mathematical or financial sense (in other words, anything that didn't contribute to his net worth). This included marriage, children, family, friends, pity, compassion, etc., etc. Jacob became an expert at extracting the maximum return possible from every contract he made, oblivious to the misery it inflicted on the other party.

It followed, then, that when Ebenezer Scrooge showed up on Marley's doorstep, Jacob instantly recognised a kindred spirit. Scrooge still retained a few vestiges of humanity at this point in his life (and was actually contemplating marriage to Belle), but all internal debate ended for Scrooge when his new mentor showed him the path to real wealth—a path which left no room for Belle or anyone else. They became partners and Marley completed Scrooge's journey to the dark side.

Fast-forward several years: it's Christmas Eve and Jacob Marley is dying. His passing is unheralded and unmourned. Not even Scrooge can squeeze out a tear.

Jacob finds himself in a quiet, peaceful environment and is met by a being of light. He senses a long-forgotten, vaguely familiar feeling that he can't quite put his finger on. He finally realises that what he's feeling is love—not within himself, because he successfully eradicated any vestiges of love from his own life many years ago. No, the love is emanating from the being, and it's pure and unbridled.

He starts to realise that his financial prowess counts for very little in this place and that a life of greed and avarice has real consequences. He braces for the inevitable condemnation from the being of light—but it never comes. Instead, he is taught that the condemnation will come only from himself as he begins to comprehend the full extent of the misery he has caused others. His greatest regret will come from having to witness the suffering caused by his avarice and knowing that it's too late to do anything about it. That regret will never be more acute than in the case of his protégé, Ebenezer Scrooge.

While the future looks bleak, however, Jacob senses that he may not be doomed forever. Although a life devoid of compassion can't just be swept under the rug, perhaps there is a glimmer of hope, even for a miserable old miser like him. He even sees a way to turn his avaricious nature to good use: Scrooge's heart is so hardened that no earthly or otherworldly spirit has been able to dent it in any way. But Marley understands Scrooge better than anyone. He should, he practically made him who he is and no one recognises a crook better than another crook. Perhaps Marley might just be able to reach Scrooge where no one else could. He pleads for the chance to try to reach out to his former partner. His request is granted.

Seven years pass: it's Christmas Eve again. Marley has been walking the Earth, vainly trying to make amends to those he wronged in life. Mostly though, he's just been suffering from insatiable regret. Tonight, however, it's time to take a crack at the toughest nut of all, Ebenezer Scrooge. Not a moment too soon: Scrooge will die tonight if nothing changes.

Marley appears to Scrooge and announces the agenda for the evening. He's then permitted to follow the three spirits around as they try to find an opening in Scrooge's hardened shell. It will only happen if they can get Scrooge to see himself as others see him.

The first two spirits have only limited success in getting Scrooge to face the reality of his predicament and his own impending death. Scrooge's reluctance to acknowledge just how wrong he has been in life causes the Ghost of Christmas Future to lean toward removing him from the land of the living, and consigning him to the same path of penance blazed by Marley. This is too much for Marley. With ever-deepening love for his old partner and increasing anxiety for his welfare, Marley won't tolerate this punishment for Scrooge:

> "With a sureness he had not known his entire life, he turned to the spirit. 'If you need to settle a balance, if Scrooge is found wanting in his accounts with you, then balance your scale with me. I know he must learn, you have taught me so this night, but I believe he will change if you give him time. If you must, if you demand this justice, give me his chains. I will wear them with my own. I will carry them to all the places we both would have visited in our penance...

> "'Take me—give this man even if it is but one more day to honour the commitments he makes to you...

> "'I beseech thee, Spirit, give me his punishment, and give him my chance,' Jacob implored."

The spirit acquiesced.

> *"Around Jacob's shoulders the chains wound,*
> *adhering themselves to Jacob's chains and to*
> *himself. All the malice, all the hate, all the*
> *deceit of the years of Scrooge and Marley*
> *piled upon Jacob. With the weight of each link,*
> *Jacob felt he could bear no more."*

The rest (at least as it applies to Scrooge), is history. *But what of Jacob?*

Waking up in the dark mist that has been his home for seven years, Jacob discovers that Scrooge's chains, as well as his own, are gone! For the first time, in life or in death, he is free. Why? He was willing to give his life for another, to take another's punishment. There is no greater love. A sufficient price has been paid and Jacob is finally free.

The book ends with a wonderful account of Scrooge's life after that fateful night, his reputation for generosity becoming even more legendary than his former reputation for miserliness. (Now, when my family calls me *Scrooge* I no longer take it as an insult.)

And finally: the poignant reunion of Scrooge and Marley when Scrooge finally dies. Two former sinners now become saints, their affection for one another cemented by Jacob's sacrifice. The perfect ending.

Okay, so it remains that R. William Bennett's book Jacob T. Marley is still just fiction based on fiction (and he's taken a lot of liberties with Dickens's classic). We have to ask ourselves whether two works of fiction have any place in fact-based *Death Therapy* (and death is very much a fact!). Can Dickens's classic and Bennett's delightful sequel contribute anything to our understanding of death and the application of that understanding to life?

I like to believe that pearls of truth can be found even in fiction.

There are two lessons we can take away from Scrooge and Marley:

First, that the application of justice in life and in death is much fairer than we typically give it credit for. God does *not* play dice with the universe. Everyone gets a fair shake.

Second, it's always better to learn from the mistakes of others than to have to suffer the consequences of our own failings. This would hopefully forestall the need to be haunted by ghosts (or to have to engage in some haunting of our own).

At the very least, the serious *Death Therapy* devotee can learn something from Scrooge and Marley. All of us could use a Scrooge-like transformation at Christmastime (or at any other time of the year for that matter). Try immersing yourself in their story each year as Christmas approaches. It will make a difference. And as you think about Jacob Marley, realize that learning to love now (before it's "too late"), will result in a life that is so much more fulfilling than the alternative.

Even fictional *Death Therapy* can be therapeutic, Bob— and it still carries a guarantee!

Chapter 8

Reunions

"Home is the place where, when you have to go there, they have to take you in."
—Robert Frost[26]

"In every conceivable manner, the family is link to our past, bridge to our future."
—Alex Haley[27]

A "Tail" of Two Brandies

I LOVE BOXERS. THEY'RE THE COMEDIANS of the canine world. I've owned six of them in my

---

[26] This line is from the Robert Frost poem "The Death of the Hired Man," first published in 1914 in the *North of Boston* collection.

[27] Alexander Murray Palmer, or "Alex" Haley (1921–1992) was an American writer, and the author of the 1976 book *Roots: The Saga of an American Family*, which was adapted as a television miniseries of the same name in 1977. The book and miniseries raised the public awareness of African American history and inspired a broad interest in genealogy and family history.

lifetime and loved them all, but two were special. Both were Brandies: Brandy (with a "y") and Brandi (with an "i").

Brandy came to our family when I was a teenager. We lived in a tiny village, far from friends, so Brandy became my constant after-school companion. We were inseparable.

When I left the UK to spend two years abroad it was a gut-wrenching moment for both of us. Brandy moped for weeks, heartbroken, and probably wondering what he'd done to cause me to leave.

Still, time heals wounds, even in dogs, and Brandy eventually forgot about me and moved on.

When I came home two years later I wondered what kind of reception I would get. It was nothing special at first: Brandy greeted me with the same enthusiasm he reserved for all visitors, just a good-natured welcome from a gentle dog who loved people.

Gradually though, the pennies started to drop. He sniffed around me with a little more curiosity, his level of excitement beginning to rise. Then the light came on: *I know him!* He started bounding around the room like a spring lamb. His memory had failed him briefly, but not his sense of smell. *My friend is back!*

It was a joyful reunion. The months of separation melted instantly. It was as though I'd never left.

Fast-forward several years...

Tired of boisterous male boxers, we decided to get a female. We picked the most docile-looking one of the litter. The kids named her Brandi (with an "i") and right from the start we knew we'd made the right choice: Brandi was calm, loving, obedient, and anxious to please.

We were living in the Panhandle of Texas and when I went running in the fields around our home I took Brandi with me whenever I could. She loved to run. She would roam over the prairie until she flushed out a jackrabbit and would chase it to a fence or until she just got tired. She was fast. She never quite caught one, but she came awfully close.

It was cold one day, so I wore gloves for the run. As I got warmed up, I took the gloves off and put them in my pockets. When I got home I realised one of them had fallen out. They weren't expensive gloves, but I thought I'd retrace my route the following day and see if I could find it.

It quickly became evident that I wasn't going to find the glove. The wind had blown all night (as only it can in the Panhandle), scattering debris far and wide. In addition, an inch or two of snow had fallen, burying everything under a white blanket. Nonetheless, I kept a hopeful eye on the path for the glove.

Halfway around the route, I looked up and saw Brandi sitting out in the snow, a good twenty feet from the beaten path, wagging her tail and looking very pleased with herself. I called her to come but she just sat there. This was very out of character as she was always so obedient. I ran over to her, and sure enough, at her feet was the glove, buried under the snow. With that incredible sense of smell, she had been able to find something amidst the debris of the prairie that was familiar to her. (Smell is the most deep-seated of the senses, and has the ability to evoke some powerful emotions, in dogs *and* people.) Brandi didn't know I was looking for the glove. She just knew that she'd found something that reminded her of home and of people she loved.

So it is with death. One of the most poignant aspects of the near-death experience is the reunion with loved ones. For the most part, the arrival in the world of spirits is a jubilant affair and although the near-death traveller doesn't instantly recognise everyone in the welcoming committee, there is often a powerful sense of familiarity, both for the people as well as the place. The traveller feels very much that he or she is home. In short, death is both a reunion and a homecoming.

As always, the NDEers themselves tell it best:

> *"I had this experience when I was giving birth to a child. The delivery was difficult, and I lost a lot of blood. The doctor gave me up, and told my relatives that I was dying... I realized that all these people were there, almost in multitudes it seems, hovering around the ceiling of the room. They were all people I had known in my past life, but who had passed on before. I recognized my grandmother and a girl I had known when I was in school, and many other relatives and friends... They all seemed pleased. It was a very happy occasion, and I felt that they had come to protect or to guide me. It was almost as if I were coming home, and they were there to greet me or to welcome me. All this time, I had the feeling of*

*everything light and beautiful. It was a beau-
tiful and glorious moment.*" (Life After Life,
pp. 55–56)

"*Suddenly I recognized all these relatives.
They were all around thirty-five years old,
including the little brother I'd never known,
because he had died during the war when
he was two years old, before I was born. He
had grown a lot. My parents were there too,
and they smiled at me, just like the others.*"
(Consciousness Beyond Life, p. 33)

Thirty-something seems to be the ideal age in the spirit world. Survivors are consistent on this point. It's an unusual combination of youthful vigour and emotional maturity. Someone described it this way:

"*They did have a physical shape; it's hard to
describe, but it somehow combined the youth
and vigor of twenty-one-year-olds, with a
sense of perfect maturity.*" (Return from
Death, p. 53)

I find this very encouraging. It's a given that advancing age brings greater wisdom (unless, of course, you're a teenager and already know everything), but the problem is that the older we get, the more our bodies start to betray us. Zombie folklore has conditioned us to believe that death will be even less kind to our bodies. Happily, near-death survivors assure us that death actually improves our appearance:

> *"My mother was sixty when she died and way overweight, and she looked trim and a good general-health look, happy and healthy [during the NDE]. Everybody looked healthy, real, real healthy."* (Recollections of Death, pp. 48–49)

It's long been lamented that youth is wasted on the young.[28] Apparently, death grants us the best of both worlds. Even physical imperfections are corrected:

> *"They were my mother and father, both had died years ago. My mother was an amputee and yet that leg was now restored! She was walking on two legs!*
>
> *"I said to my mother, 'You and father are beautiful.'*
>
> *"And they said to me, 'You have the same radiance and you are also beautiful.'"* (Beyond Death's Door, pp. 97–99)

Imagine the shock of seeing your parents as they appeared in their prime (especially if you'd witnessed the long, slow decline of advancing age). Whatever the

---

[28] "Youth is wasted on the young" is alternately attributed to Oscar Wilde and to George Bernard Shaw.

circumstances, this reunion with parents must be a strange reversal of generational dynamics. We're simply not conditioned to picturing our parents as being younger than ourselves:

> *"A brown cloaked figure drifted out of the light toward me. As my euphoria rose still more, I, much to my delight, recognized it to be that of my mother. My mother had died at age thirty-seven when I was seven years old. I am now in my fifties and the first thought that came to my mind was how young my mother appeared."* (Near-Death Experiences, p. 220)

Family and friends are easily recognisable of course, but there is often a feeling of familiarity with people we may not have known well in life. There's either a sense that the same blood runs through our veins, or that we just knew someone well at some point in our existence. Family, friend, or mystery guest—there's a powerful and poignant sense of attraction:

> *"I felt as if I was going back somewhere I belonged. There were people all around who I sensed were loving friends."* (Return from Death, pp. 46–47)

> *"In February 1989, Stuart* [a man with spastic quadriplegia] *had his sixth out-of-body experience* [or OBE]. *He indicated he went to 'Paradise' while asleep and saw a glowing*

woman with a Scandinavian accent who had died a century ago. Stuart believed she was an ancestor of his, and he was thrilled at how loving she was. He also saw two deceased grandfathers who touched him, two deceased grandmothers, and two deceased stepbrothers. (His adopted mother confirmed that she had lost two sons prior to Stuart's OBE.) He also saw others there whose genders he could not determine, and indicated it was like a 'big reunion.'" (Journal of Near Death Studies, vol. 9, no. 2, winter 1990, p. 94)

Just as a welcoming committee goes to the airport to greet a family member who's coming home after a long absence, so, it seems, do those who have passed on before us. Their purpose in being there seems to be to make the transition to death a little easier or (if this is not their time), to gently coax the traveller to return to his (or her) body. Whatever the reason, the new arrival is greeted with joy: the wanderer coming home at last:

"I saw a group of people between me and the light. I knew them; my brother, who had died a few years before, was gesticulating delight-edly as I approached. Their faces were so happy and welcoming." (Science and the Near-Death Experience, p. 118)

"I recognized a lot of people. And one of them was my grandmother. And I saw my uncle

*Gene, who passed away when he was only
thirty-nine years old. He taught me a lot; he
taught me to play my first guitar. So was my
great-great-aunt Maggie. On Papa's side of
the family, my grandfather was there... They
were specifically taking care of me, looking
after me."* (Glimpses of Eternity, p. 153)

The moment of greeting is often marked by a sudden
rush of understanding; a return of clarity:

*"I was immersed in a feeling of total love. It was
crystal clear to me why I'd had cancer. Why I
had come into this world in the first place. What
role each of my family members played in my
life, where we all were within the grand scheme
of things, and in general what life is all about.
The clarity and insight I had in that state are
simply indescribable. Words seem to diminish
the experience—I was in a place where I understood that there's so much more than we can
fathom in our three-dimensional world. I realized that this was a great gift and that I was
surrounded by loving spiritual beings of light."*
(Consciousness Beyond Life, p. 34)

Not only is the traveller familiar with the *people* who
are there, but he often senses that he is not a stranger to
the *place*, either. There's a strong feeling that this "new"
world is not new at all. Rather, it's the place where our
journey began:

"He showed me a gate behind which I saw the same landscape. But now, with this gate in front, it suddenly looked extremely familiar. I came to the startling conclusion: I've been here before. It felt like a homecoming after an arduous journey." (Consciousness Beyond Life, p. 39)

When families get together, you sometimes learn things you didn't know before. Death is no exception. Death is the ultimate family reunion and it shouldn't surprise us that sometimes there are surprises:

"During my NDE following a cardiac arrest, I saw both my dead grandmother and a man who looked at me lovingly but whom I didn't know. Over ten years later my mother confided on her deathbed that I'd been born from an extramarital affair; my biological father was a Jewish man who'd been deported and killed in World War II. My mother showed me a photograph. The unfamiliar man I'd seen more than ten years earlier during my NDE turned out to be my biological father." (Consciousness Beyond Life, pp. 32–33)

Members of the welcoming committee are not generally strangers to us. Those bonds are powerful and enduring, and the only desire of those who come seems to be to help us:

"I encountered a group of fifteen to twenty souls (human spirits sent by God), who greeted me with the most overwhelming joy I have ever experienced and could ever imagine. It was joy at an unadulterated core level. They were sort of like a large welcoming committee...

"While I could not identify each spiritual being as someone by name (for instance, as Paul, my dead grandfather; Mrs. Sivits, my old babysitter; Steven, my neighbor; or other such individuals), I knew each of them well, knew they were from God, and knew that I had known them for an eternity. I was a part of them, and I knew they were sent to guide me across the divide of time and dimension that separates our world from God's. I also had the unspoken understanding that they were sent not only to greet me and guide me, but also to protect me during my journey." (To Heaven and Back, pp. 68–69)

What can we learn from this that will help us in life?

First, the assurance that we are returning both to people and to a place that are familiar to us should provide great comfort. That knowledge alone should greatly reduce our fear of death. In reality, the world we now live in is only a temporary residence. Death is but the doorway to our real home.

Second, this reunion with loved ones will likely be a moment of unbridled celebration and should be anticipated with joy. True, we may arrive there with some trepidation, having amassed a host of offences against a great many people (including some of those who've come to greet us). I suspect, however, that we'll find this welcoming committee to be very forgiving. They've been tested in the same crucible of life that we have and made many of the same mistakes. They'll understand. They will also have learned (from their time in this new world) the nature of unconditional love. I believe that this new perspective will lead to a greatly enlarged capacity for compassion.

That being said, we probably shouldn't rely too much on the magnanimity of those who precede us in death. We can start preparing for that reunion now—by minimizing offences and being more willing to forgive.

Third, a great many people will be there, both familiar or half-remembered, and they will have come to this meeting as anxious to see us as we have been to see them. We will have greatly missed their association in life, and I suspect that the years of separation will have been just as painful for them. They will have yearned for this reunion with equal fervour. It will truly be a bittersweet moment: while loved ones on Earth are shedding tears of grief at our passing, loved ones on the other side will be shedding tears of joy at our return. From a sombre funeral to a joyful reunion—all within moments of each other! Funerals are certainly a time for mourning, but perhaps only for those left behind.

So, cherish family and friends, Bob. Cultivate those precious bonds. Be forgiving of faults and mistakes. We're rubbing shoulders in an imperfect world and it's inevitable that we'll rub one another the wrong way on occasion. That's inevitable, but it would be a big mistake to permanently give someone close to us the cold shoulder.[29] Life is too short for that.

It isn't easy to extend patience and compassion to those who seem determined to push us away, but we would do well to try to keep those lines of communication open. Who knows what the future may hold? Deep down, those who resist closeness are often lonely souls who just need someone to recognise the pain behind their tough exterior.

Realise that we are all a mixture of both good and bad, but that the good almost always outweighs the bad. I think we'll find in death that grudges are a luxury we simply can't afford. Recognise that the highest measure of success in life may be our ability to love those who are hardest to love.

We can grumble and complain about the injustices we suffer at each others' hands or we can just get on with the business of loving one another. The former is unproductive and will consume a lot of energy. The latter will bring joy, both in life and in death. Besides, forgiving others can be quite satisfying. As Oscar Wilde said: "Always forgive your enemies; nothing annoys them so much."

Finally, be kind to your pets. There's plenty of evidence to suggest that they'll be at that reunion, too. And why not? Dogs love unconditionally. They'll be right at home in a place of unconditional love. We can learn a lot from dogs.

---

[29] It is believed by some that the phrase "give someone the cold shoulder" originated in medieval times. A guest who had outstayed his or her welcome could be served a cold shoulder of mutton by the host, as a subtle hint that it was time to leave, thus avoiding the unpleasantness of direct confrontation.

(As for cats, who knows? They're good for keeping the mice away, but beyond that, we'll have to wait and see.)

Fact is, I learned a lot from our boxers and can't wait for the time when I can see them again. I hope they'll have the ability to talk to me (even though speech was never necessary to communicate their love).

It's been decades now since I've seen Brandy, but I doubt it will take him long to recognise me this time.

As for Brandi: we mourned her passing with a bag-pipe send-off to the strains of "Amazing Grace."[30] It was a painful moment, but I suspect she was already up there, looking for gloves and frolicking with jackrabbits. When my time comes, she'll know how to find me.

Death is still a great mystery, but it's nothing to be feared. It's really just a big reunion. One of the first things we'll see as we emerge into the light is the most compre-hensive gathering ever assembled in our honour. All will be there to welcome us home. They will have come with the desire to make the transition to our new life as pleasant as possible. Each person (and pet!) will share precious memories with us and will be overjoyed to see us.

There's no point getting stressed out over this reunion, Bob: no need to get Botox, lose twenty pounds, or lament

---

[30] "Amazing Grace" is a Christian hymn published in 1779, with words written by the English poet and Anglican clergyman John Newton (1725–1807). It debuted in print in 1779 in Newton and William Cowper's "Olney Hymns" but settled into relative obscurity in England. In the United States, however, "Amazing Grace" was used extensively during the Second Great Awakening in the early nineteenth century. It has been associated with more than twenty melodies, but in 1835 it was joined to a tune named "New Britain" to which it is most frequently sung today.

that we have nothing to wear. All we need to worry about is how we're doing at the business of loving and forgiving.

See you at the party!

Chapter 9

Heaven Is for Real

"What a wonderful world."
—Louis Armstrong[31]

Hurricane Harvey

AROUND HERE, EVERYONE HAS A HARVEY story.

Harvey stormed ashore near Rockport, Texas, as a Category 4 hurricane. Then, like a drunken sailor, he staggered along the Gulf Coast, leaving devastation in his wake. He then wandered back out to sea to suck up what was left of the Gulf of Mexico and dumped it unceremoniously on an already-waterlogged Southeast Texas. One gauge measured sixty-four inches of rainfall in three days... more than our average rainfall for a full year. It's been suggested that this was a six-hundred-year weather event. I don't know where that statistic came from, but I like to

---

[31] "What a Wonderful World" is a song first recorded by Louis Armstrong, released in October 1967, and written by Bob Thiele and George David Weiss.

think that on the list of epic floods, there was Noah...and then there was Harvey.

Our daughter and son-in-law lived behind us with their four children in a beautiful little home they had mostly built themselves. It was a sad moment when we realised it was going to flood (sad for everyone except four-year-old Scarlett, who was thrilled at the prospect of the entire house becoming an elaborate swimming pool).

We got as much furniture on buckets as we could and then trudged wearily to our house, secure in the knowledge that at least *it* would remain high and dry. Elevated a good two and a half feet above the road, we had often bragged that the whole region would have to be underwater for our home to flood...

...which was exactly what Harvey had in mind.

Hour after miserable hour the rain fell in torrents. Water crept up the steps and onto the porch. We'd always loved going to sleep to the sound of the rain...not tonight.

It was surreal to witness that first rivulet of water breach the walls of our home. It had been a bastion of safety through Hurricanes Rita and Ike, and had held on through Harvey as long as it could. But there was an air of inevitability to Harvey.

We were more fortunate than most: we had an upstairs. Many were not so lucky. There were urgent phone calls in the night warning people to get out quickly as water from swollen reservoirs engulfed everything in its path. There were dramatic rooftop rescues by helicopter; daring extrications by pickup truck. An elderly neighbour was found in his kitchen, chest-deep in water, unsure what to do. He was rescued just before the floods swamped the house.

Tragic tales emerged: flash floods submerged a car and swept a mother and child half a mile from the vehicle. Rescuers finally got to them: the child barely clinging to life...and to her mother's dead body. Two heroic volunteers were on their third rescue mission when their boat drifted into live power lines. A young man was electrocuted in ankle-deep water as he was on his way to check on his sister's cat.

Selflessness and heroism also abounded:

The "Cajun Navy" volunteers were out in force at first light, navigating their shallow-bottomed boats down streets-turned-rivers until all refugees were accounted for.

"Dry" neighbours opened up their homes to the displaced, donated necessities to those who had lost everything, brought hot meals to hungry victims. Churches mobilised to provide food, water, and clothing to anyone who needed it. Thousands of selfless souls came from far and near to muck out houses...a truly thankless job.

Twenty volunteers in yellow "Mormon Helping Hands" shirts came to our home and stripped out soggy carpet, insulation, and sheetrock (I refuse to call it "drywall" anymore!), accomplishing in one day what would have taken us a month to do alone.

There were some lighter moments:

A picture of a golden retriever named Otis went viral. He was seen walking home after the waters receded—with a bag of dog food between his teeth. (You have to love a self-reliant canine!)

One of the volunteers cleaning out our home asked where the toilet was. I pointed to it, only to realise that all the walls were gone...leaving the throne clearly visible from anywhere in the house. There were new realities to get used to.

Harvey decimated lives, homes, and businesses. Some are still living with family or neighbours. Many homes remain "stripped down to the studs." Some were simply abandoned altogether. It will be months, perhaps years, before life gets back to normal.

Some good has come of the devastation, however, chief of which is the outpouring of love and goodwill that still abounds in Southeast Texas. People are taking care of people. Problems were brought to light that no one would have known about unless houses had been stripped down: termites and leaky plumbing, for instance. Houses are being rebuilt better than they were before.

My wife is getting to redecorate the house the way she's always wanted to. One thing is driving her crazy, however: she's an interior decorator and has been wanting to modernise her elderly aunt's home for years. She saw her opportunity when their house flooded, but sadly it's not going to happen. Her aunt wants the house completely restored to its 1970s Brady Bunch glory and isn't willing to compromise. It's one post-Harvey trauma from which my wife may never fully recover!

Harvey may turn out to be the most expensive natural disaster in US history. Countless lives were affected for both good and ill.

Life-changing events typically don't announce themselves. Such was the case with Todd and Sonja Burpo of Imperial, Nebraska. When they set off on a family vacation to Colorado, they had no idea how much the trip would change the course of their lives. It began innocently enough with their three-year-old son, Colton, complaining of a stomach ache, but as it became apparent that his appendix had ruptured, a simple ailment became a life-threatening emergency.

Colton's father is a pastor, and while his little boy's life hung in the balance, this man of faith found himself experiencing a crisis of faith. He prayed fervently for his son, alternating between pleading for his son's life and berating God for allowing such a thing to happen. His prayers were heard, and the boy's life was spared.

The parents were so thrilled to have their son back that they didn't dwell too much on what may have happened while he was in extremis. Why would they? They had no reason to think anything untoward had occurred.

Little by little, however, Colton began to reveal tidbits of a remarkable experience: of traveling to a world of indescribable beauty, of singing with angels, and of seeing the throne of God. The details were completely beyond the imagination of even this imaginative little boy and his parents slowly came to the realisation that, while his body was teetering between life and death, his spirit had visited another world. For Colton, there was no longer any doubt: *Heaven is for real!*

It's frightening to think of a little boy going anywhere on his own, let alone to *another world*. There was no need to worry, however: angels make the best babysitters. They made Colton feel right at home by singing his favourite songs. Yet they weren't totally accommodating:

"'Well, they sang 'Jesus Loves Me' and 'Joshua Fought the Battle of Jericho.' ... I asked them to sing 'We Will, We Will Rock You,' but they wouldn't sing that.'" (Heaven Is for Real, p. xiv)

Angels are solicitous to make the transition to death as easy as possible, and even though they apparently do requests, it appears that there are some things even an angel won't do! (Or perhaps they just didn't know the words to Queen's classic hit!)

Being the son of a pastor, Colton had been taught about Jesus. Still, the details he volunteered astonished even his pastor father: *"Did you know that Jesus has a cousin? Jesus told me his cousin baptized him... I don't remember his name, but he was really nice.'"* (Ibid, p. 63)

How many adults know that Jesus was baptized by his cousin (John the Baptist), let alone a three-year-old? And then this:

"'Jesus has markers.'

"'What?'

"'Markers, Daddy ... Jesus has markers. And he has brown hair on his face. And his eyes ... Oh, Dad, his eyes are so pretty!'

... "What are markers to a little kid?

"Suddenly I had it. 'Colton, you said Jesus had markers. You mean like markers that you color with?... Well, what color are Jesus's markers?'

"'Red, Daddy. Jesus has red markers on him.'

"Quietly, carefully, I said, 'Colton, where are Jesus's markers?'

"Without hesitation, he stood to his feet. He held out his right hand, palm up and pointed to the center of it with his left. Then he held out his left palm and pointed with his right hand. Finally, Colton bent over and pointed to the tops of both his feet.

"'That's where Jesus's markers are, Daddy,' he said.

"I drew in a sharp breath. He saw this. He had to have ...

"I was also struck by how quickly Colton answered my questions. He spoke with the simple conviction of an eyewitness." (Ibid, pp. 65–68)

The reality of Colton's experience really hit home when he announced to his mother that he'd discovered in heaven that he had another sister (in addition to his living sister, Cassie):

"I have two sisters. You had a baby die in your tummy, didn't you?"

His startled mother asked, *"Who told you I had a baby die in my tummy?"*

"She did, Mommy. She said she died in your tummy."

Sonja Burpo's miscarriage had been the most painful event of her life. They had explained it to Colton's older sister, Cassie, but didn't feel the little boy was ready for this kind of revelation. Colton had unknowingly opened a very painful wound and could see it in his mother's face.

"It's okay, Mommy," he said. *"She's okay. God adopted her."*

"Don't you mean Jesus adopted her?" she asked.

"No, Mommy. His dad did."

Tender emotions rushing to the surface, Sonja struggled to steady her voice:

"So, what did she look like?"

"She looked a lot like Cassie. She is just a little bit smaller, and she has dark hair."

Sonja's dark hair! Both Colton and Cassie have blond hair like their father. Sonja had jokingly complained that she was the one who carried the children for nine months, and both had come out with their father's blond hair. Now there was a baby girl who had her dark hair. Tears began to form.

Colton went on:

> *"In heaven, this little girl ran up to me, and she wouldn't stop hugging me,"* [clearly a distasteful display of affection to the little tyke].

> *"Maybe she was just happy that someone from her family was there,"* Sonja said. *"Girls hug. When we're happy, we hug."*

> *"What was her name? What was the little girl's name?"*

> *"She doesn't have a name. You guys didn't name her."*

> *"You're right, Colton,"* Sonja said. *"We didn't even know she was a she."*

Then, the little boy delivered the news that really started the tears flowing: *"Yeah, she said she just can't wait for you and Daddy to get to heaven."* (Ibid, pp. 94–96)

Little by little, more details of Colton's experience came out. One day he said to his father:

"'Daddy, remember when I yelled for you in the hospital when I waked up?'

"How could I forget? It was the most beautiful sound I'd ever heard. 'Of course I do,' I said.

"'Well, the reason I was yelling was that Jesus came to get me. He said I had to go back because he was answering your prayer. That's how come I was yelling for you.'" (Ibid, p. 81)

Could a simple prayer actually be the difference between life and death? It appears so in Colton's case.

Colton's father, Todd, spent several months slowly teasing more details of the NDE from the little boy. Colton volunteered information at his own pace, innocently and without guile. There was, however, one message he wanted to be sure his parents understood:

"No matter what new tidbits he revealed, though, Colton had one consistent theme: he talked constantly about how much Jesus loves the children. I mean that: constantly.

He would wake up in the morning and tell me: 'Hey Dad, Jesus told me to tell you, He really loves the children.'

"Over dinner at night: 'Remember, Jesus really loves the children.'

*"Before bed, as I helped him brush his teeth,
'Hey, Daddy don't forget ... Jesus said he really,
really loves the children!'"*
(Ibid, pp. 105–106)

While his parents grew tired of Colton's constant reminders about how much Jesus loves the children, still, it changed the way they conducted their ministry for the children in the church. It was a powerful example of the change that can occur in someone who learns second-hand what death is all about. *Death Therapy* in action! How can you ignore the earnest testimony of a little boy: *"Hey, Daddy don't forget...Jesus said he really, really loves the children!"*

One final anecdote from Heaven Is for Real:
One day, Colton darted out into a parking area. Trying to teach him a lesson, his father pointed to a dead rabbit in the road and told his son that he could end up that way if he kept running out without looking.

Colton simply grinned at his dad and said, *"Oh, good. That means I get to go back to heaven."* (Ibid, p. 113)

It's hard to scare a child who's looking forward to death! It's like threatening: "Do that one more time and I'm taking you to Disneyland!"

Three-year-old Colton Burpo brought knowledge from the next world that is astonishing in its insight and detail. It had a profound effect on everyone involved: Sonja learned about the unborn daughter she never knew. Pastor Todd changed the way he conducted his church ministry. Colton completely lost his fear of death.

And we can learn from childhood NDEs too, Bob. Children bring a purity and innocence to the near-death phenomenon that is uniquely refreshing. They lack the ulterior motives and biases that sometimes afflict grown-ups. They just report what happened and don't worry in the least how their story will be received. They saw what they saw, and nothing can change it.

If we will listen to the children and suspend our disbelief for just a minute, we may find that they have the answers to some of the most important questions in life.

Hurricane Harvey didn't discriminate between rich or poor, insured or uninsured, old or young, and neither, unfortunately, does death. Death is always an unwelcome intruder, but never more so than when a child is involved. The Burpos were narrowly spared that heartache, but Colton's experience taught them that death is really nothing to be feared. For Colton himself, death is merely the next stage of life, and even something to anticipate with joy.

That's the promise of *Death Therapy*, Bob...and it's for real.

Chapter 10

Knowledge

"Have you ever heard of Plato? Aristotle? Socrates? ... ...Morons!"[32]
(Vizzini to the Man in Black)

MY WIFE AND I JUST FINISHED A FIVE-DAY babysitting stint with our grandchildren while our son and daughter-in-law left for a little getaway. They have three kids: a four-year-old and two-year-old twins. Truthfully, I was only there part of the time, since I'd mistakenly scheduled a shift in the ER in the middle of it. It really was an honest mistake and I felt bad about abandoning my wife to the wolves. Three kids against two grandparents is unfair. Three against *one* is a massacre!

We knew we were in for a beating even before the starting bell. The gig was supposed to begin at exactly 7:05 on Thursday morning—the moment the alarm clock in

---

[32] From the Battle of Wits in *The Princess Bride*, a 1987 adventure/fantasy by Act III Communications, directed by Rob Reiner, starring Cary Elwes, Mandy Patinkin, Robin Wright, and others.

the twins' room turned green. Our daughter-in-law had given us (and them) strict instructions the night before: *"Don't let them get up before the clock turns green."*

It was an important rule. It would set the tone for the rest of the event.

Savannah (four years old) woke up long before dawn. I very patiently reiterated her mother's instructions that nothing happens until the clock turns green. Feeling pleased with my firmness at the first test of our resolve, I lay back down to savour the calm before the storm.

Savannah was already several moves ahead: she went straight into the twins' room and turned on the light to see if the clock had turned green. It hadn't of course, but the twins were now wide awake and ready for action. (This is the first rule of an insurrection: recruit the agitators.)

I spent the next hour feebly protesting: *"The clock isn't green! The clock isn't green!"* I might as well have thrown gasoline on a fire. They had a short window of opportunity and they weren't wasting a minute of it. We knew we were in for a beating. The only question was: how bad?

Our experience prompted me to come up with a list of rules for grandparents who are contemplating the unthinkable: agreeing to babysit for anything longer than an evening.

Babysitting Rules for Grandparents

Rule #1: JUST SAY NO

Take a page out of the war on drugs and *just say no!* Head it off before it gets started. You're too old for this.

The elderly are too often the victims of scams, and unfortunately, some of the most effective shakedowns are perpetrated by our own children. When your kids nonchalantly approach you with a request to watch the grandkids, alarm bells should ring. Your kids love you, but they're also desperate. All manner of pressure and manipulation are going to be brought to bear, and if you haven't made the commitment beforehand to just say no, you'll waver, rationalize, and eventually cave. They'll tighten the noose mercilessly. They'll use platitudes like: *"The kids are so excited to spend quality time with you!"* or *"You'll have so much fun bonding with the little ones!"*

Recognise this for what it is: blatant manipulation. It's a sweet, but cynical, attempt to flatter you into believing that you still have useful parenting skills to offer. What they are *not* telling you is that they are enlisting you in the fight of the century. Your kids aren't "getting away for a few days"; they're dragging their battered and bruised bodies to the ropes to hand you over to three crazed behemoths who are salivating at the prospect of fresh meat. This is bigger than the Rumble in the Jungle and the Thrilla in Manila combined, but you're not getting paid millions to do it. You're not even getting paid![33] [34]

---

[33] The Rumble in the Jungle was a historic boxing event in Kinshasa, Zaire (now Democratic Republic of the Congo), on October 30, 1974 (at 4:00 a.m.). Held at the Twentieth of May Stadium (now the Stade Tata Raphaël), it pitted the undefeated world heavyweight champion George Foreman against challenger Muhammad Ali, a former heavyweight champion. The attendance was sixty thousand. Ali won by knockout, putting Foreman down just before the end of the eighth round.

[34] The Thrilla in Manila was the third and final boxing match between Muhammad Ali and Joe Frazier. It was contested in 1975 for the heavyweight championship of the world at the Philippine Coliseum in Cubao, Quezon City, Philip-

Your health and sanity are on the line.
Just say no!

Rule #2: THIS IS A STATE OF WAR

Okay, so you failed at Rule #1. Don't feel bad...your
kids are good at this. It's a survival instinct, and let's face
it, you're an easy mark.

But now that you're committed, it's important to
acknowledge that you are now in a de facto state of war.
Remember your history: this is 1939, the grandkids are
Hitler, Rommel, and Mussolini. You are Europe and you're
about to be overrun. This is no time to cower and capitu-
late. This is the moment to channel your inner Churchill.
Stiffen your upper lip and repeat with Sir Winston: *We
shall fight on the beaches; we shall fight on the landing
grounds...we shall never surrender!*[35]

You're in the fight of your life, Bob! Grow a spine and
get through this.

Rule #3: YOU HAVE NO AUTHORITY

Don't for one minute entertain the myth that any of
the parents' credibility is going to carry over to you. You

---

pines, on Wednesday, October 1. Ali won by technical knockout (TKO) after
Frazier's chief second, Eddie Futch, conceded the fight prior to the fifteenth
round. The contest's name is derived from the frequent rhyming boast made
by Ali that the fight would be a "killa and a thrilla and a chilla, when I get that
gorilla in Manila."

[35] From a speech delivered by Prime Minister Winston Churchill to the House
of Commons of the Parliament of the United Kingdom on June 4, 1940, as
England faced the threat of invasion by Nazi Germany.

have no authority here. You know it. The grandkids know it. You've spent their formative years carefully cultivating your image as the fun and easy alternative to their mean and harsh parents, and now you're suddenly going to become a feared and respected authority figure? I don't think so.

You are the substitute teacher, the interim boss, the babysitter. You're not a corrections officer, you're just a prison guard. It's not your job to rehabilitate, instil values, or pass on valuable life experience.

Yes, you feel bad because you see all your failings as a parent showing up in your progeny, but the reality is that you're not going to correct it all in the next five days. Don't waste whatever functioning brain cells you have remaining on subtle psychological manipulations. They didn't work on your kids. What makes you think they would work on the grandkids?

No, your task is simple: sit on the grandkids (figuratively!) until the parents return. That's why it's called baby*sitting*.

You have a weight advantage. Use it!

Rule #4: KEEP THEM ALIVE

This follows from Rule #3. You have one objective and one only: to keep the grandkids alive. If you can return them to the parents free of poison ivy, beads up the nose, or self-administered haircuts, that's all wonderful, but don't overthink this.

When things get confusing (and they will), simply revert to the prime objective: *keep them alive.* You'll overload your brain if you try to make things any more complicated than that.

Rule #5: EVERYTHING IS A CON

"Mommy always takes us to Dunkin' Donuts for breakfast."
"Daddy lets us pour shampoo on the bathroom floor and skate on it."

Any sentence that begins: *"Mommy always..."* is a con. Don't give it the time of day. If you must insist on entertaining the possibility that something is legit, follow the maxim: "trust, but verify" (only ignore the part about trust).

If you feel you have to verify something with the parents, be selective in what you run by them. Asking: *"Is it true that you let Savannah stay up on a school night to watch* The Godfather?*"* isn't going to reassure your kids that you're up to the task at hand.[36]

Age has clouded your judgment and grandkids can smell weakness like a dog smells fear. They'll exploit any equivocation with all the compassion of a trial lawyer. Wise up! Dredge up whatever feeble parenting skills remain and recognise this verity:

Everything is a con.

Rule #6: AVOID NON-ESSENTIAL EXCURSIONS

So, it's Saturday morning and I have the bright idea of giving my wife a break by taking the grandkids to the supermarket for doughnuts. It's a cheap and easy way to

---

[36] *The Godfather* is a 1972 crime/drama by Paramount Pictures, directed by Francis Ford Coppola, starring Marlon Brando, Al Pacino, and others.

enhance your reputation as the kind, indulgent grand-parent. Right?

Wrong!

A remarkable transformation occurs as you cross the supermarket threshold: each grandchild grows six new arms and their brains instantly flip to "seek and destroy" mode.

You also quickly realize that whoever designed the layout of the store harboured some sort of vendetta against babysitting grandparents: they put the doughnuts, stuffed cuddly animals, and festive helium balloons all within spitting distance of each other in a sort of land-based Bermuda Triangle, the sole intention being (apparently), to ensnare the naïve, unsuspecting grandparent.

You open the doughnut cabinet to let them choose their own and all twenty-four tentacles simultaneously reach out to sample the icing on every doughnut. This means that you have to either buy the whole display or try to repair the damaged items. While you're re-icing the doughnuts, the child with chocolate icing on her fingers glides over to the stuffed animal display to check out the pink cuddly bears. You break off redecorating the dough-nuts to rescue the pink bears but as you're returning to the doughnut cabinet, the child with pink icing on his fingers is making his way to the cuddly animals (using the fresh fruit stand as cover) to finish defacing whatever animals the first child missed.

Ah, but the observant reader will recall that you entered the store with *three* kids! While you're scraping the pink icing off the brown cuddly bears, the third grandchild is joyfully liberating the helium balloons to the safety of the thirty-foot ceiling.

We received a round of applause as we left the supermarket. A first for me.

This rule is sacrosanct: *if an excursion isn't essential to sustain life or limb, don't do it!*

Rule #7: NEVER NEGOTIATE

Everyone knows that you don't negotiate with terrorists: all it does is embolden them. That being said, terrorists are ideologically driven and will sometimes listen to reason.

The same can't be said of a two-year-old!

You need to realise that the minute the parents drive off, all the normal rules of civilized society leave with them and it's officially open season on the grandparents. The grandkids have complete latitude to do whatever they want, secure in the knowledge that there'll be no real consequences. Sure, you can go through the motions of imposing discipline, but they know you're bluffing and lack the will to follow through. Their cuteness is your Achilles' heel. Again, ever since the grandkids were born, you've sold them on the idea that you are the nice ones and that their parents are the mean ones. You can't change that overnight and they'll exploit this vulnerability without mercy.

Get used to the reality that your feeble negotiating skills are no match for a two-year-old. This is Day One of a five-day fiesta...with you as the piñata! Resistance is useless, and pleas for leniency will only be seen as a sign of weakness. Your only hope is to try to absorb the blows without coming apart at the seams.

Remember: grandchildren are the quintessential terrorists.

Never negotiate.

RULE #8: LIFE IS NOT FAIR

How many times did you tell your kids that? Newsflash: life doesn't get any fairer as you get older, and babysitting is no exception.

Don't kid yourself that you're playing on a level field. You're trying to follow the rules of engagement; the grandkids have no rules. True, you're bigger and stronger, but you're also very slow. They're small and mobile. They'll hit you where they can inflict maximum damage and be gone before you even know what happened.

To illustrate: Queensberry Boxing Rule number 5 states that:[37]

"A man hanging on the ropes in a helpless state, with his toes off the ground, shall be considered down."

The grandkids have another name for this situation... *opportunity!*

The harsh reality is that there are no rules (and no referees to enforce them anyway). The best you can hope for is to live to fight another day.

---

[37] The "Marquess of Queensberry Rules" is a code of generally accepted rules in the sport of boxing. Drafted in London in 1865 and published in 1867, they were named so as John Douglas, Ninth Marquess of Queensberry, publicly endorsed the code, although they were written by a Welsh sportsman named John Graham Chambers. It is the code of rules on which modern boxing is based.

Life is not fair. If you haven't learned that by now, you're about to be taken to school.

Rule #9: BRIBERY IS AN ACCEPTABLE TOOL

Every parent knows that bribing children creates monsters. The good news for the babysitting grandparent is that they will only be *your* monsters temporarily. This grants you license to indulge any form of bribery you see fit: television, video games, jumping on the bed, sledding down the stairs, bathroom skating parties, gummy bears, doughnuts, sugary cereal, dessert with no "after you eat your vegetables" requirement. In short, everything the parenting manuals tell you *not* to do.

(Note that there are no *grandparenting* manuals! Take this as evidence that society has imposed no responsibility on you whatsoever. You are free to simply pad your resume as the fun and indulgent grownup.)

Worried about the fallout when the parents return? Don't be. By the time they figure out all that's gone on in their absence, you'll have already skipped off happily down the road. Besides, they didn't think twice about leaving you in this mess. This is your chance for payback.

And finally,

Rule #10: DECLARE VICTORY—NO MATTER WHAT.

The house may resemble a postapocalyptic wasteland; the grandkids are swinging from the chandeliers; you look like Rocky after the first fight with Apollo Creed.[38] None of that matters. Declare victory and go home.

Practice some stock phrases for the parents' return: *"Oh, they were simply angels!"* or *"What a joy to spend quality time with the little ones!"*

It's all a big fat lie. You know it and they know it, but that's the way the game is played. You need to keep up the façade that you still retain some semblance of usefulness and your kids need to believe that they didn't just take the gamble of their lives by trusting their offspring to the most inept babysitters on the planet. If you have to, remind them that you did this for free, and that (as in all things in life) you get what you pay for.

Walk out with your head held high. You met the prime objectives: they're alive and you're alive. Win-win. You went toe-to-toe with the champ for fifteen rounds. Cry out with all the emotion you can muster:

"Yo, Adrian! We did it!"

And just like that, it was over.

The ordeal taxed our physical and mental stamina to their limits. But that was nothing compared to the emotional wrenching tiny Charlotte put on us after the fact. She kept asking where Grammie and Grandad had gone and when we were coming back. The little monsters are relentless: if they don't destroy you physically when you're with them, they'll rip your heart out emotionally when you leave.

---

[38] From the movie *Rocky*, a 1976 drama/sport movie by Chartoff-Winkler Productions, directed by John G. Avildsen, starring Sylvester Stallone, Talia Shire, Burt Young, and others.

As I've reflected on the experience, I've been able to convince myself that while we clearly weren't up to the task physically, our mental reserves had seen us through. Grandparents do still have something to offer and it's largely due to the knowledge we've accumulated over a lifetime of experience. Our lives can still have meaning.

(And, in case you were wondering, we love our grandchildren more than life itself. It's why we had kids in the first place.)

Near-death experiences teach us that there are two things that count the most on the other side: love and knowledge. We've already learned about the importance of love, but what of knowledge?

"You can't take it with you."

We've all heard that expression, and while this is certainly true of our earthly possessions, we don't disembark life totally naked. NDEers report that in death they were still in possession of all the attributes that made them who they are in life: love, virtue, hate, passions, interests, anger, impatience, hope, prejudices, compassion, stubbornness, humility, pride...

...and *knowledge*.

In fact, for some new arrivals there is so little "difference" between being alive and being dead that they struggle to comprehend the fact that they've actually died. As one survivor succinctly put it:

"I was still me!" (Waking Up in Heaven, p. 12)

And whatever knowledge we take with us is apparently a priceless commodity in the next life. The importance of knowledge is a recurring theme:

"As they witness the display [life review], *the being seems to stress the importance of two things in life: Learning to love other people and acquiring knowledge."* (Life After Life, p. 65)

"If there is any consistent message that is brought back by those who have a classic NDE, it is this: after death there is more, and the purpose of life is to grow in love and knowledge." (Science and the Near-Death Experience, p. 123)

"I read and search out everything I can. I don't know why I seem to feel as if I'm preparing myself in some way for something greater. Knowledge seems to be very, very important but I don't know why I feel so compelled to learn." (Heading Toward Omega, p. 222)

Learning doesn't end with death:

"The being of light told them that learning doesn't stop when you die; that knowledge is something you can take with you. Others describe an entire realm of the afterlife that is set aside for the passionate pursuit of knowledge." (The Light Beyond, p. 35)

There is more information available in this world than we could possibly absorb in a hundred lifetimes. So what kind of knowledge is most important? The answer is that just about anything is worthy of our effort, but some subject matter carries more weight than others:

> *"The knowledge that I had gained: that was mentioned, too... What kind of knowledge? Well, it's hard to say, you know. But it was knowledge of basic things, the basic universal principles...of things that hold the universe together...I was told that that would be important over there too..."* (Reflections on Life After Life, p. 89)

> *"God wants us to search for truth in every area of life until we find it. This is not only true on the spiritual level, but also in the mental and physical levels. Any time we learn a new truth in any field we are drawing closer to God."* (My Life After Dying, p. 32)

> *"I don't scorn professors anymore. Knowledge is important. I read everything I can get my hands on now... It's not that I regret taking the path I did in life, but I'm glad that I have time now for learning. History, science, literature. I'm interested in it all. My wife fusses at me about my books in our room. Some of it helps me understand my experience better... All of it does, in one way or another, because, as I say, when you have one of these experiences,*

you see that everything is connected." (The
Light Beyond, p. 45)

Ironically, the purpose of acquiring knowledge seems
to be not so much to comprehend the complexities of life,
but rather that we gain a better understanding of the basics:
Ben (a forty-seven-year-old policeman who had an
NDE at age fourteen) said it wasn't as if he suddenly *"...
knew everything. It was more like I suddenly realized that
life is a lot more simple than most of us think."* (Closer to
the Light, pp. 112–113)

The attainment of knowledge is not an end in itself. All
the knowledge in the world means nothing if it doesn't
make a difference in our lives. In other words, if we don't
act on what we learn, and if the changes aren't for the
better, then the knowledge really hasn't benefited us much:

> *"None that I know of...have pursued knowl-
> edge for the sake of knowledge. Rather, they
> all feel that knowledge is important only if it
> contributes to the wholeness of the person..."*
> (The Light Beyond, p. 44)

A housewife in her late thirties had an NDE following
surgery. She learned this from the being of light:

> *"He showed me all that I had done, and then
> he asked me if I was satisfied with my life... He
> was interested in love. Love was it. And he
> meant the kind of love that makes me want*

to know if my neighbor is fed and clothed and makes me want to help him, if he is not.

"The kind of knowledge meant was deeper knowledge, sort of as it related to the soul... wisdom I would say." (Reflections on Life After Life, p. 89)

It always comes back to love and how we treat people.

Knowledge and Fashion

Knowledge needs to lead to wisdom and love, but on a bit of a tangent, apparently knowledge can also lead to a better wardrobe:

"All the people in heaven are seen dressed in accord with their intelligence; and since one person surpasses another in intelligence...one will have more outstanding clothes than another. The most intelligence [sic] have clothes that gleam as if aflame, some radiant as if alight. The less intelligent have shining white clothes without radiance, and those still less intelligent have clothes of various colours." (Heaven and Hell, p. 137)

If Emanuel Swedenborg is right, clothing in heaven is purchased with the currency of knowledge (or more specifically, intelligence). Just imagine the implications: supermodels in hand-me-downs; nerds on the cover of Vogue!

Take-home message for the fashion-conscious: if you want to look good, hit the books.

(My apologies to supermodels for the obvious stereotyping. I don't mean to infer that intelligence and good looks are incompatible. Not that a supermodel is likely to be reading this book anyway. Oops! I just stereotyped again!)

There are no mysteries on the other side. NDEers indicate that knowledge is instantly available to anyone who wants it. In fact, you just have to think of a question and immediately the answer is there. It's a disconcerting yet exhilarating phenomenon. No question is off limits, apparently. Many NDEers have stated that they were able to comprehend all the mysteries of the universe. Nothing was withheld.

> *"Because this is a place where the* place *is knowledge... Knowledge and information are readily available—all knowledge... You absorb knowledge... You all of a sudden know the answers."* (Reflections on Life After Life, p. 13)

> *"That very same moment, in a split second, I gained access to a wealth of knowledge, a complete knowing and understanding. All knowledge. Universal knowledge. I understood the origins of the cosmos, how the universe works, and why people do what they do. Their positive actions, but also why they hurt one another,*

deliberately or not. Wars and natural disasters, everything has a purpose, a reason. It all makes sense. I understood the past, the present, and the future. I saw evolution. Everything and everyone evolves and develops together. I saw and understood—without any judgment—the connection, the coherence, the logical and sometimes major consequences of every single act. I mean at every level and down to the smallest detail... The way all kinds of mechanical, electrical, and electronic equipment, gadgets, and engines work. Everything. I knew and understood all about mathematics, electronics, physics, DNA, atoms, quantum mechanics, and quantum physics... I also saw where evolution is headed, what its ultimate goal is. I realized that this grand scheme not only includes me, but everything and everybody, every human being, every soul, every animal, every cell, the Earth and every other planet, the universe, the cosmos, the Light. Everything is connected and everything is one. 'I see!' I thought happily. 'I get it. It's all so simple. So obvious. It all makes sense...'"
(Consciousness Beyond Life, pp. 34–35)

There's a caveat to this, however, and it's a big one. Although the secrets of life are often given to those who request them, it seems to be an incontrovertible rule that the full gamut of this knowledge cannot accompany the individual back to life. Continuing the narrative from the above account:

> "...No, I wasn't allowed to bring back the knowledge itself. Why, I don't know... Perhaps we're not supposed to have such universal knowledge in the here and now, in our physical form? Perhaps we're here to learn? Perhaps there's another reason?" (Ibid, p. 35)

> "[Dr. Moody:] 'You mentioned earlier that you seemed to have 'a vision of knowledge,' if I could call it that. Could you tell me about it?'

> "'It seemed that all of a sudden, all knowledge—of all that had started from the very beginning, that would go on without end—that for a second I knew the secrets of all ages, all the meaning of the universe, the stars, the moon—of everything. But after I chose to return, this knowledge escaped, and I can't remember any of it. It seems that when I made the decision [to return] I was told that I would not retain the knowledge...

> "'This all-powerful knowledge opened up before me. It seemed that I was being told that I was going to remain sick for quite a while and that I would have other close calls. And I did have several close calls after that. They said some of it would be to erase this all-knowing

*knowledge that I had picked up...that I had
been granted the universal secrets and that
I would have to undergo time to forget that
knowledge. But I do have the memory of
once knowing everything, that it did happen,
but that it was not a gift that I would keep if
I returned...*

*"'The memory of all these things that happened
has remained clear, all except for that fleeting
moment of knowledge. And that feeling of all
knowledge disappeared when I returned to
my body...'"* (Reflections on Life After Life,
pp. 10–11)

This ability to suddenly and instantaneously acquire
all knowledge begs the question: why make the effort to
tax our puny, overloaded mortal brains now with tidbits
of suspect information when we can just wait until death
and download torrents of truth onto a massive spiritual
hard drive at a trillion gigabytes a second?

Good question, indeed. Dr. Moody had the same
thought and asked it of the person just quoted:

*"'One thing I wonder. I've spent a lot of my life
seeking knowledge, learning. If this happens,
isn't that sort of thing rather pointless?'*

*"'No! You still want to seek knowledge even
after you come back here. I'm still seeking
knowledge... It's not silly to try to get the*

answers here. I sort of felt that it was part of our purpose... but that it wasn't just for one person, but that it was to be used for all mankind. We're always reaching out to help others with what we know.'" (Reflections on Life After Life, pp. 10–11)

"We're always reaching out to help others with what we know."

There, I believe, is the key. The acquisition of knowledge is a good thing when it causes us to be more useful to our fellow men. We're not learning just for our own benefit. We're learning so that we can help others.

But here's the rub: if knowledge is such a good thing, and near-death survivors are privy to the greatest knowledge of all, why take it away from them upon their return? Why allow a peek into Pandora's box only to slam it shut?[39] Wouldn't a floundering world benefit greatly from understanding the secrets of the universe and of death?

One answer to this paradox is that near-death survivors *are* bringing back all the answers this troubled world needs. Their message is really very simple: live in the light, be tolerant and kind, seek useful knowledge, learn to love. That's all the knowledge we really need. These are

---

[39] According to Greek mythology, in an effort to punish a happy mankind, the gods gave to beautiful but also curious Pandora a box or jar with all the evils. Her curiosity got the better of her and she opened the box to peek, thereby releasing them all on the world that previously had no such evils. Once these evils escaped the box, there was no way to get them back into the box.

the things that matter in death. They are the things we should be pursuing in life.

This is the very essence of what *Death Therapy* is about, Bob: making the best use of our time on Earth by vicariously learning from the near-death experiences of others. It's about realizing that we don't have to wait for our own death to find out what life is all about. A knowledge of death is the most practical knowledge available to mankind because it unlocks the secrets of life and has the power to change lives.

And if you're contemplating the unthinkable (babysitting), this knowledge might even *save* your life!

Chapter 11

Children

"Grief fills the room up of my absent child,
"Lies in his bed, walks up and down with me,
"Puts on his pretty looks, repeats his words,
"Remembers me of all his gracious parts,
"Stuffs out his vacant garments with his form"
Constance lamenting the death of her son,
Arthur, in *The Life and Death of King John*,
Act III, Scene IV, by William Shakespeare

"A person's a person, no matter how small."
Horton Hears a Who! by Dr. Seuss[40]

I N 2014, TWO UNRELATED BUT DISTURBING stories appeared in the news. One concerned the dis-

---

[40] *Horton Hears a Who!* is a children's book written and illustrated by Theodor Seuss Geisel under the pen name Dr. Seuss and was published in 1954 by Random House.

covery of a mass unmarked grave in Tuam, Ireland.[41] It contained the remains of 796 children between the ages of two days and nine years. They were the "Home Babies:" children of unwed mothers who had been housed in an "orphanage" to "protect their family's good name."

There were several of these "Mother and Baby Homes" scattered throughout Ireland in the first half of the twentieth century. Embarrassed parents sent their unwed, pregnant daughters to the homes to distance the family from the stigma of an out-of-wedlock birth. There, the mothers worked for little or no pay to atone for their sins (even though the pregnancy was often the result of rape or unwanted advances from men in positions of power). The children were also considered to be tainted by sin and were punished by separating them from their mothers soon after arrival at the home. They weren't treated well either— the child mortality rate in the Homes was four times the national average. Malnutrition and neglect made the children easy prey to measles, tuberculosis, and other diseases.

The Home Babies were allowed to attend the local school, but it was made clear that they were not to mingle with the "normal" kids. Catherine Corless was one such "normal" child who came from a two-parent home, but attended school with the Home Babies. She had this to say:

"They were always segregated to the side of regular classrooms. By doing this the nuns

---

[41] A representative article from that time: "Galway Historian Reveals Truth Behind 800 Orphans in Mass Grave," https://www.irishcentral.com/opinion/cahirodoherty/galway-historian-reveals-truth-behind-800-orphans-in-mass-grave

telegraphed the message that they were different and that we should keep away from them.

"They didn't suggest we be nice to them. In fact, if you acted up in class some nuns would threaten to seat you next to the Home Babies."

There was no point wasting a coffin or burial plot on these pariahs. When they died, they were simply wrapped in a shroud and thrown into what appears to have been a septic tank along with the rest.

It's difficult to wrap our twenty-first-century brains around such indifference.

The other story that came to light in 2014 reflects the attitude of some toward children in this enlightened new millennium. Actually, this scandal concerned our treatment of the *unborn*.

An investigation of the National Health Service in the United Kingdom found that the bodies of thousands of aborted and miscarried babies were being incinerated along with other "clinical waste." In an example of ruthless efficiency, some foetal remains were even being burned in "Waste to Energy" plants: the power generated from the aborted "waste products" was being used to heat the very hospitals where the abortions were performed.[42]

(Kudos to the "green energy" initiative for saving the planet—one foetus at a time!)

---

[42] A representative article from that time: "Aborted Babies Incinerated to Heat UK Hospitals," http://www.telegraph.co.uk/science/2016/03/15/aborted-babies-incinerated-to-heat-uk-hospitals/

One of the most heart-breaking aspects of my job is having to tell an expectant mother that she's suffered a miscarriage. Even if it occurs very early in the pregnancy, the sense of loss isn't lessened much. It was still a human life in the making. In many of the "Waste to Energy" cases, the NHS failed to consult the parents about what they wanted to do with the remains. If questioned after the fact, the authorities would generally tell the parents that the "products of conception" (as an aborted baby is euphemistically referred to in the medical field) had been "cremated."

The investigation embarrassed the NHS and the practice was immediately stopped.

These two scandals appeared in the news within months of each other. Both illustrated the ambivalence with which children's lives are sometimes viewed, and demonstrated an appalling lack of compassion for the feelings of the parents. The irony was stunning: the Home Babies in Ireland were taken from the mothers who would have loved them, to be "taken care of" by those who saw them as merely the inconvenient by-products of sin. In our own day, the aborted babies of the NHS were likewise treated with disdain, more thought being paid (apparently) to the demand for cheap energy than the grief of the parents.

No parent should have to endure the death of a child, but it happens. And, while funerals are rarely happy occasions under the best of circumstances, when a child is involved, hope, meaning, or peace can be very elusive.

Death is no stranger to the Emergency Room. As an ER physician, I've seen my share of it. It's never easy for the family and friends of the deceased, but the pain is at least mitigated when death comes at the end of a long and productive life. When a child dies, however, there's little comfort to be found. There's always the feeling that a life was cut short prematurely.

I've participated in hundreds of resuscitations; some successful, some not. Fortunately, the vast majority were elderly patients, and like anything that you do on a regular basis, even cardiac arrests become routine after a while. Most are quickly forgotten.

When a child is involved, however, the memories never fade. There are some things that will never be "routine."

I remember the morning a frantic mother rushed in with her lifeless new-born in her arms. The baby was cold, blue, and pulseless. We worked on her for the better part of an hour, but it was too late. The mother had fallen into an exhausted sleep with her baby lying in the bed beside her. Sometime during the night she'd rolled over and smothered her precious infant.

Another day the paramedics called, en route with a young boy with serious head trauma. The moment we laid eyes on him we knew he wasn't going to make it. He had a misshapen head and an open skull fracture with brain tissue showing. We went through the motions, but it was without hope. His mother had backed her heavy SUV out of the driveway, unaware that the little boy was playing under the vehicle.

There are no words of comfort in such moments. Attempts to find meaning seem trite. One can only hope that time will ease the pain.

What do near-death survivors have to say on the matter? Can NDEs offer any comfort? What exactly *does* happen to children when they die? Is there someone on the other side to take care of them?

What about the unborn who don't even make it to birth? Do they qualify as a "person"? Did they forfeit their chance for fulfilment, life, and happiness?

This chapter is based on the NDE of a seventy-one-year-old man. You may wonder what the near-death of an elderly grandfather has to do with children. Surprisingly, it was this man who learned more about the fate of children who die young than perhaps any other near-death survivor. Logic would suggest that a bereaved mother would have been a more likely candidate. Nevertheless, Marvin Besteman's vision of the children has provided tremendous comfort to the many parents who have endured the anguish of the loss of a child. Whenever Marvin spoke about his near-death encounter, people always honed-in on one aspect of the story: his vision of the children.

Marvin Besteman was a veteran of the US Army, a retired banker, and an avid golfer. He whiled away his days on the links and drinking coffee with his buddies at Arnie's Bakery. Life was good.

At age seventy-one, Marvin's peaceful retirement was threatened when he was diagnosed with a rare tumour of the pancreas. He was taken to surgery and the mass was successfully removed. In the hours following the operation, Marvin was in agony. He was given progressively higher doses of painkillers and sedatives to try to control the pain,

and at some point in the process, his breathing stopped.
His spirit embarked on a dramatic otherworldly journey.
He introduces his experience with a brief summary:

> *"In that short round trip, I was reunited with*
> *loved ones; saw babies, children, and angels;*
> *peeked at the throne of God and Book of Life;*
> *and had a conversation with the apostle Peter,*
> *who I must say was a little bit shaggy looking."*
> (My Journey to Heaven, p. 11)

I'm not sure that describing the keeper of the gate of
heaven as *"a little bit shaggy looking"* is wise, since tradition
has it that Peter is the one who will be deciding our fate.
Then again, I'm sure Peter values honesty. Besides, anyone
who spent his days fishing in a boat on the Sea of Galilee
isn't likely to be gracing the cover of GQ anyway. I doubt
he would be offended.

Marvin's first awareness that his situation had changed
was when two men walked into his room and began to
disconnect him from the many tubes and wires coming
out of his body. They clearly weren't hospital personnel:

> *"Don't ask me how I knew the two strangers*
> *who had just walked into my hospital room*
> *were angels; I just knew they were. Beyond*
> *any doubt, these were angelic visitors, come*
> *to take me home.*
>
> *"I wasn't one bit worried about it, either. A*
> *feeling of deep calm washed over me as these*

two men approached my bed, one on either side of me. They were smiling and quiet. My angels looked like regular guys, except regular guys usually don't wear white robes. Both looked in their mid-forties and stood about 5'8" to 5'10". One had longish brown hair, and the other one had shorter hair...

"And no, actually none of them had wings."
(Ibid, p. 31)

That's the question everyone wants to ask: Do angels have wings? For the most part, the near-death literature indicates they don't. This is how these men were dressed:

"My angels looked like men I might see on the golf course or at a hockey game, except of course they were wearing long-sleeved robes. Their clothes were white and gauzy, almost filmy, but not quite see-through, and they hung about two or three inches from the floor. Both angels wore ropes or long rags belted around their waists." (Ibid, p. 38)

Marvin was taken up by the angels through a sky *"soaked in color and light:"* verdant greens that reminded him of the fairways during the Masters and vibrant turquoise blues that far outstripped the luxurious hues of the Caribbean. He eventually alighted on solid ground at the end of a queue of people standing in front of a monumental gate.

"Standing in a short line of people, I observed the other thirty-five or so heavenly travelers, people of all nationalities. Some were dressed in what I thought were probably the native costumes of their lands. One man carried a baby in his arms...

"My geezer body felt young and strong and fantastic. The aches and pains and limitations of age were just gone. I felt like a teenager again, only better.

"The music I heard was incomparable to anything I had ever heard before. There was a choir of a million people, thousands of organs, thousands of pianos. It was the most lush and beautiful music I had ever heard..." (Ibid, p. 14)

"There were three children in line, each of them around four or five years of age. These little ones were not standing still, but moving around, wiggling in their spots in line, like children do. They all had big smiles on their faces.

"It's terribly sad, I know, to think about children dying, and of course these precious kids had died or they wouldn't have been in that line. Their loved ones were experiencing the heartrending loss of a child—perhaps the

*worst and deepest loss anyone can ever expe-
rience. I wish I didn't know how awful that
is, but I do. So what I'm about to tell you is
said from a heart that has felt the wretched
loss of a child. I don't share this piece lightly.
But I promise you, dear one, those children
were delighted to be in that place. Their eyes
were shining with life and pleasure, just like
everyone else."* (Ibid, p. 76)

Marvin patiently waited in line, drinking-in the sights
and sounds of this new world. He wasn't the least bit worried about the interview he was about to have. The peace
he felt was overwhelming. Finally, he reached the front of
the queue:

*"'Hello, Marv. Welcome to heaven. My name
is Peter.'"* (Ibid, p. 14)

Marvin had a delightful interaction with Peter. This
wasn't an interrogation, it was a welcome. No one was
being turned away, including Marvin Besteman.

Beyond the outer gate was another gate, as beautiful
as the first. But unlike the rest of the new arrivals, Marvin
wasn't granted admission through this inner gate. It wasn't
that he was less worthy than the others, just that this
wasn't his time.

While Marvin stood in the courtyard between the
inner and outer gates, waiting for Peter to sort things
out, he made good use of his time by trying to see what
was beyond the inner gate. There was an invisible barrier

preventing him from entering through the second gate, but he was able to see clearly through it nonetheless. What he saw would become the defining moment of his near-death journey and set his experience apart from the rest. He got to see heaven's babies:

> *"The first thing I saw when I looked out into the huge kingdom before my eyes were all the babies...*
>
> *"There were millions of babies, from the tiniest unborn baby, about the size of my pinkie finger, to babies who were preterm to babies who were born full term, and every age on up from there.*
>
> *"I felt a physical jolt of shock at the sheer numbers of babies, babies upon babies upon babies, each one cherished and loved...*
>
> *"On Earth, there would be no way for the unborn babies to live outside their mothers' bodies, but yet here they were, alive and thriving. I knew these babes would grow and bloom here, perfectly safe, entirely happy, and wholly loved. The second their lives ended, by whatever sad circumstance, on this side, the babies arrived in a world more wonderful than any dreams their parents might have had for them. And if they were unwanted*

on Earth, for any reason, those babies were wanted in heaven, highly valued and beloved.

"Somehow, I knew all these things to be true without being told...

"I knew beyond a shadow of a doubt that they were as happy and contented as could be...

"No matter how those lives ended, I knew without being told there was breath, hope, and life abundant there, even in the tiniest foetus." (Ibid, pp. 123–125)

"When I speak to groups about my heaven experience, pretty much every single time the dominant questions are about the babies:

"What did the babies look like?
"Who was holding them?
"Who was taking care of them?
"Were the babies happy?

"And on and on, people want to know every little detail of what I saw in regard to those babies. So many people I've met after my talks are thinking about their own little ones, babies who were miscarried or maybe even aborted." (Ibid, p. 126)

"One of the top questions folks ask me about the babies is, who was holding them? The answer is, nobody was holding them, because babies in heaven simply don't need to be held...

"And they really were as comfortable, happy, and fulfilled as any baby I have ever seen on this Earth...

"That's not to say that babies in heaven are never held. I bet they are held and often, because all things are wonderful and pleasing in that place, and what's more wonderful and pleasing than holding a baby?

"There was a layer of space between the babies and that green grass. You could almost say they were resting on air pillows... They were also cradled in the perfect love of God, wholly joyful and basking in the warmth of his light and presence." (Ibid, p. 129)

Well, there you have it.

It's anybody's guess as to why a seventy-one-year-old male, ex-army, ex-banker, golf-playing retiree would be the one to see the vision of what happens to babies when they die. Why not a distraught, recently bereaved mother? Why not a woman who had suffered a miscarriage? Marvin Besteman had experienced the loss of a child, but surely there are countless others who have felt such a loss more keenly and proximately. In addition, I doubt there are many men who can come close to comprehending the agony a mother goes through when she loses a child.

One thing's for certain: Marvin Besteman didn't visit the afterlife yearning to know what happens to children when they die. I doubt the question even crossed his mind until he saw the babies. But see them he did, and when Peter returned with confirmation that he needed to go back, he knew that part of his mission in the years that remained would be to share with grieving parents what he had seen. Peter told him as much:

> *"Marv... I've talked to God, and God told me to tell you that you had to go back, that he still had work for you to do on Earth. He still has work for you to finish there."* (Ibid, p. 171)

The news didn't sit well with Marvin. He was already feeling quite at home in this place and not even the prospect of abandoning his family could trump the desire to stay. In truth, he'd already forgotten about them!

> *"After my trip to heaven, Ruth asked me if I had ever thought about her during my time there. Had I ever once thought of our children, our grandchildren? ...*
>
> *"And the answer is, no, I didn't think of my beloveds, as much as I adore them. In fact, had...God given me the choice to go back to Ruth, Julie, Amy, and Mark, on Earth, or*

stay in heaven, there's no doubt I would have chosen to stay in heaven...

"Oh yes. Those kids and grandkids are my heartbeat, and I'd move mountains for them if need be. But had they seen and heard what I did in that glorious world, they would understand that no one who sets foot in heaven would ever want to come back." (Ibid, pp. 68 and 167)

What Marvin Besteman saw and heard should offer comfort to every grieving parent who has endured the heartache of the loss of a child. We will get to see heaven's babies for ourselves someday, and when we do, I suspect we will never grieve again. Until that day, we have the testimonies of near-death survivors like Marvin Besteman to confirm what we really already knew: that our deceased children are gloriously happy and that they are growing up in the most loving environment imaginable.

Losing a child will always be painful, Bob, but glimpses of the next life assure us that the sense of loss is only present on this side of the veil. The children are in a place where they are infinitely valued and cherished. We shouldn't underestimate the pain a bereaved parent must feel, but near-death stories like Marvin Besteman's assure us that our grief won't last forever.

Chapter 12

Suicide

*Lady Nancy Astor to Winston Churchill:
"Winston, if you were my husband, I'd poison
your tea!"
Churchill: "Nancy, if I were your husband,
I'd drink it!"*

"May you live in interesting times."
—English translation of a Chinese curse[43]

Zip-lining in Honduras

A FEW YEARS AGO, WE TOOK OUR FOUR
children and their spouses on a cruise to Central
America. The highlight of the trip was zip-lining in Roatán,
Honduras. Eschewing the relatively tame zip-line at the
cruise terminal, we ventured deep into the Honduran
jungle for a more authentic experience.

---

[43] This is common in English to be known as a Chinese curse, but no actual
Chinese source has been produced.

We had three Spanish speakers in our group and they were able to negotiate a bargain-basement price for the adventure. I wasn't sure this was such a good idea: we were about to be dangling high above the jungle, trusting our lives to the very people we had just swindled!

It turned out that the actual zip-lining was the least dangerous part of the experience. Getting to the top of the hill was the hard part. Thirty of us (okay, maybe only twenty-eight) piled into the bed of a tiny beat-up pickup truck which had apparently already reached "antique" status in the '70s. It creaked and backfired its way up a steep muddy "road" with precipices on both sides. Our guides seemed pleasantly surprised that we reached the top with no losses. On the plus side, it made the zip-line descent seem tame by comparison.

The safety lecture was brief and incomprehensible. I think we were instructed in the finer points of turning somersaults on the line, coupled with a plea to right one-self in time to avoid smashing into the tree below, all the while fending off monkeys, iguanas, and dengue fever. The guide then leaped out into the void yelling the Honduran equivalent of *Bonzai!!!* apparently intent on demon-strating to the sceptical Americans just how much abuse the rusty zip-lines were capable of absorbing.

The braking mechanism consisted of one of the guides throwing his body into the path of the speeding zip-liner, moments before we connected with the tree. Their timing was excellent.

It was comforting to know that there was a hospital nearby (well, it was either a hospital or slaughterhouse. Possibly, both).

The adventure ended without incident and all agreed that zip-lining in Honduras was the high point of the cruise (literally).

I can't help looking back, however, and wondering if our life insurance provider might have designated this activity a suicide gesture. Fortunately, we didn't have to find out and a good time was had by all.

Monique Hennequin was given a unique opportunity to learn first-hand the implications of suicide. She was thirty-one years old when she gave birth to a healthy baby by caesarean section. Hours later, she experienced severe abdominal cramps and was taken back to surgery where she went into shock and multi-organ failure. The cause of shock was later found to be a perforation of the colon, which allowed intestinal contents to leak into the abdominal cavity.

She survived the surgery, but later had a cardiac arrest. During the arrest, she experienced a beautiful and uplifting near-death encounter. She was resuscitated, but remained in critical condition and on a respirator.

Upon awakening, Monique was so annoyed at being resuscitated, and so desperate to return to the loving environment she had visited that she managed to bite her breathing tube in half. This precipitated another respiratory arrest and a second near-death experience. This one wasn't nearly as pleasant.

These are Monique's descriptions of her two experiences, beginning with the first. They were markedly different and the contrasts are instructive. It's a long read, but worth the effort:

"After a final, desperate attempt at moving my body, I gave up. My heart was beating like mad, and even my rapid breathing gave me no air; I felt as though I was suffocating.

"...[H]ow on Earth could my life end here in the intensive care unit? What was to happen to my children, my job, and the assignments that wouldn't be finished, my house? There was so much left unsaid and undone...

"The last thing I heard was a long beep from the monitor and an alarm that apparently sounds when you flatline...

"Everything went black, and somehow I was relieved because I felt no pain or fear whatever. I felt safer than ever, and I had a sense of nostalgia. A childlike innocence and naïveté came over me, as if I was going to the movies with Daddy, and at the same time I felt more mature than everything I was leaving behind (including my own life)... I continued to feel protected, by somebody rather than something. It became lighter, and I saw myself enveloped as it were by a situation from my past...

"I proceeded to other situations that had raised question marks in my life. The how and why of my actions became clear to me because I saw, sensed, and knew how people had felt

during (and frequently also after) contact with me. I viewed several episodes from my life. I recognized and felt everything as though I had gone back in time and completely in the actual moment...

"*I lingered at those incidents where I had trouble recognizing my responsibility until I was ready to accept it. To everybody I had ever hurt, either intentionally or unintentionally, I wanted to explain why and express my sincerest apologies. Nobody condemned me, and at all times I felt this warm support. How could this support love me? Could it not see how naïve I had been in life? And that I had been motivated by ambition, selfishness, fear— and, yes—even by joy or euphoria?*

"*Fortunately, I also saw and felt all the wonderful, happy, rewarding, and joyful moments that my thoughts, words, and actions had given others (and thereby myself). Everything was shown simultaneously—my entire life! Some things even made me laugh. I didn't spare a thought for my surroundings and was completely engrossed in my life...*

"*Everything around me went black, a warm black, and I realized that pure, warm, soft black is also light, a kind of energy, palpable even without a body...*

"I rose higher and higher, further away from life and closer to what feels like real existence...

"As I approached my 'level,' I became lighter and happier and felt almost elated about what lay ahead...

"A sense of happiness and grace washed over me and glowed deep inside me. I felt privileged to be a part of this. Why me? What good had I done to deserve this? ...

"Here and now I had the opportunity to instantly know everything...

"Time did not exist here, and a loving tranquility suffused the field.... This moment of eternal omniscience is still indescribable to me. The surge of love and the explosion of information were overwhelming...

"My smile felt bigger than ever, and I was complete as well as perfectly happy and in the place where I belonged...

"Even if I could reach only one single person on Earth and let him or her feel this tranquility, my return would be worthwhile. I realized that I couldn't stand around here much longer, or I wouldn't be able to return to achieve my goal...

"*I made a well-considered choice, and this determined what happened next. A preview, showing me all the opportunities of the life ahead of me, as if it had already been lived, flashed before me. My smile was palpable again, and I was pleased with the life ahead...*

"*And I was ready now; I really wanted to be on this logical and coherent Earth, to be aware and live accordingly. Nature is perfect...*

"*With a violent and painful jolt, I returned to an immobile body. ... The loving smile and the tranquility of where I came from were obviously gone too. Nor was I grateful; what a sluggish, harsh reality this was.*

"*I didn't know how many hours or days I had been lying there, feeling frustrated in the body that I couldn't get going again, when I decided that it was pointless. ... I became angry and felt betrayed. I thought that I had been abandoned by the source I came from...*

"*I wanted to return to this heaven. ... I thought that the only way back was via death, and I began to wonder how I could rid myself of the machinery that kept my body alive. I felt imprisoned in this life and wanted to free myself at all costs. ... With my jaws and teeth, I bit down as hard as I could until the intubation tube was severed. I tried to swallow it as quickly as possible. The alarm, the oxygen, the nurses—they were gone in a flash. 'Good,' it went through me; 'that will teach them not to keep me here. I'm off!' But it wasn't good; it was neither a good thought nor a good deed...*

"*This time I saw nothing: no colors, no warmth. ... I was confused; where was I supposed to go, what was happening? ... A sense of panic came over me. I didn't understand what was happening and what had to be done except that this was damn serious and that I was now at a different 'layer' in the atmosphere than last time.*

"*In the distance, very far away, I saw a pinprick of light. The end of the darkness? Was I supposed to go there? Did I want to go there? I looked around me; everything was black— black, quiet, cold, and lonely. I was completely alone. Alone with my thoughts and feelings. The expression 'godforsaken' made sense to me now. ... I had built a wall between myself and my heart, between myself and trust, between myself and gratitude. And above all between myself and love. The love of the heart that enables a clear conscience, peace, health—in one word, everything. My wall cast a shadow over me so I couldn't see the light. Love and the higher consciousness are in the light; they are the light. And in order to see this, I had to break down this wall. Fear—I was full of fear. I think there's no bigger wall than fear except perhaps anger, which was still there too. How could I escape this misery? Why did nobody help me? I got more anxious and felt nothing but pain, anguish, grief, and loneliness.*

"The regret intensified, and I understood that I had made a huge mistake. Why had I not had any faith and patience? I felt deeply ashamed. ... I recognized my weakness and felt that love, trust, and faith were the greatest strengths I needed...

"I was of no use to anything or anyone by isolating myself like this, and I encountered immediate pain. The pain of having chosen the life that might have been and having given up so easily ... I wouldn't reach the 'heaven' where I belonged via this road, not via 'death,' but would reach it instead via a life filled with faith, trust, love, and gratitude. 'Help!' went through me, and I felt like I was breaking.

"All of a sudden my father [who had previously died] drifted around the corner, like a huge shadow. He didn't look up at all. He moved solemnly. ... Whatever I tried, he kept moving and never once looked at me. I was so desperate to see, touch, question, almost beg him what to

do. Should I join him, go after him, or head in another direction? Somehow I sensed that if we made contact, there would be no going back. Not to my 'heaven,' my level, not to my body and the life I had chosen. There was a reason he didn't look at me, a reason he didn't grab hold of me. He had only come to clarify everything for me. It felt like his final duty as a parent before he could proceed to the light. I had to understand everything now. And again, the decision would be mine. If I wanted to, he would accompany me to that pinprick of light, but I knew that this light didn't have the same intensity as before. To get to the source, I would have to move through yet another 'level.' So again (or still) the choice was mine: I could choose life or choose this other light without pain, cold, or lovelessness. It remained to be seen if I would suffer again in a physical body, and deep down I knew the answer.

"I could tell from my father's body language that he didn't want me to accompany him. I loved him, even here and now, behaving like this. Suddenly I felt what he felt, I knew what he knew. He clarified things instantly, including what I had to do. This wasn't my 'final destination,' this was his world, this was his (and temporarily my) domain, and it was his level and his light over there in the distance. I had to go back of my own free will.

*Surely I knew that next time I would end up
at my own level and at the source? But I was
anxious and kept following him. ... I couldn't
for the life of me catch up with him. I tried to
scream, cry, beg, but nothing got through to
him. I felt the pain in him: the pain of not
being able to hug me and help me decide. I
tried to stop and scream like a small child in
a supermarket, in the hope that he would stop
and help me. He continued to the light, which
grew closer and closer. I had to make my decision now; the end ... was approaching. I could
almost touch him. Almost ... Right before my
eyes he entered the overwhelming light. Such
power! Such love! One more step and I'd be
with him. With him and with many others.
He had arrived; he had finally found peace...*

*"What next for me? If I wanted to return, I
had to go 'backward' immediately or I would
be received into the light. As an example of
how I felt at that moment: imagine you're on
one of those moving walkways that take you
to the gate at the airport. You reach the end
without doing anything, but you do have to
'get off' to avoid taking a tumble. If you don't
want to get off, you have to walk backward at
what feels like a very brisk pace...*

*"I had no time to weigh up the two options. I
felt like I was suffocating; I had to decide. ...*

The decision this time to return to my body on Earth was actually the only time that felt like I was 'dying.' The decision to walk backward and return as quickly as possible seemed inexplicable to me. It was the more painful of the two options, and I knew I would be suffering a lot of pain. Ahead of me everything was good, full of love, warmth, honesty, knowledge, everything I had always wanted here on Earth. Then why return to that hell when I knew for sure that what I saw in front of me I would never have on Earth?

"...But I knew that it would have been pointless to stay. What is the point of enlightenment if I can't reach out to others? Sharing knowledge, love, honesty, and awareness—that's it! I had to reach out to myself ... and others...

"The intention behind my earlier choice ... came back to me very clearly: 'Even if I can only reach one person to feel this, it will be worth all the pain.' As soon as I became aware of this, I felt the connection, the warmth, and the support of where I belonged, and I no longer felt isolated and alone. I had reconnected to the source and knew that I needed my body.

"Suddenly I was back in my body...

"*I knew that my first experience was a natural one and that my so-called negative experience was an unnatural one that sprang from lovelessness. However, the latter NDE taught me most about love and conscious choices because I had to feel right down to my toes what free will, faith, and love can achieve and that I'm always only one thought removed from the source, irrespective of the horrible state I'm in.*

"*At no point during my NDE did I feel that somebody other than myself forced me to do anything. I made all the decisions...*

"*The greatest reality for me was there! ... Everything that is visible here on Earth feels like a feeble reflection of reality...*

"*The feelings are even harder to explain. I can't give any examples of the love, the acceptance, and the source except perhaps something as simple as new-born lambs or ducklings in spring, bright reflections in the water, or the smile of a child with an even brighter sparkle in its eyes...*

"*Every day I'm happy that I chose the difficult route and that I've been through this heaven and hell...*" (Consciousness Beyond Life, pp. 203–221)

What a remarkable journey! Shortly after bringing a new life into the world, Monique Hennequin went from fighting *for* her life, to fighting to *end* her life, to understanding just how precious life really is. She is living proof of T. S. Eliot's statement: "...the end of all our exploring will be to arrive where we started and know the place for the first time."

In his awe-inspiring book, Man's Search for Meaning, Viktor Frankl describes the unspeakable atrocities he and his fellow prisoners endured in Hitler's concentration camps. The sheer brutality of the camps quickly extinguished any "delusion of reprieve" the inmates may have harboured, and as hope gave way to despair, almost everyone eventually entertained thoughts of suicide.

It is remarkable then, to read of the lengths to which some prisoners would go to cling to life, even hiding *in* the latrines to evade the death squads. Why is it that humans can hold on to life with such tenacity while at the same time longing for the release of death? And does it matter whether we end our lives by our own hand, or are we expected to endure any adversity life throws our way and allow nature to take its course? These are the terrible questions millions grapple with.

Suicide presents an awful dilemma.

I've treated hundreds of suicidal patients in the ER. An overdose of pills is the most popular method chosen. Usually, it's little more than a cry for help. Some attempts are more serious and require more extreme resuscitative measures. Then, of course, there are a few who successfully end their lives by their own hand.

In all instances, there is tremendous internal conflict about the rightness of the decision. I'm certain the choice to end one's life never comes lightly. You can see the doubt in the methods chosen: most are *gestures* rather than *attempts*. For every case where the final result is left to little doubt (such as a gunshot to the head), there are a hundred patients who choose a method with a high likelihood of failure: swallowing pills, cutting a wrist, etc. Even the most determined often leave themselves a small avenue of escape.

The most bizarre case I encountered was a man who dissected a hole through his own chest wall (under local anaesthesia!), stuck a scalpel into his heart, then sat back to watch his heart pump the blood out of his body. Pretty final, right?

After watching the blood pump for a minute or two he experienced a change of heart, stuck his finger in the hole to plug the leak, and called for help. He survived.

No matter how dismal life may be or how hopeless the circumstances, we seem to intuitively know that suicide is not the answer. There is something in us that tells us that life is precious, that it is to be protected at all costs, and that meaning can be found in even the most distressing of trials. Viktor Frankl noticed that the prisoners who were able to survive the concentration camps were often the ones who could find some sort of meaning amidst the horror. He attributed his own survival to the hope (in vain as it turned out) that his wife might still be alive. He reasoned that if we can find a *why*, we can bear almost any *what*.[44] That's why he titled his book, Man's Search for Meaning.

---

[44] Similar to the quote by philosopher Friedrich Nietzsche: "He who has a why to live can bear almost any how."

It's not as simple as that, of course, and I would never presume to judge someone who's desperate enough to consider suicide. I haven't walked in their shoes.

The issue of suicide has posed ethical and legal questions for centuries. In ancient Rome and medieval Japan, suicide was viewed as an extreme act of defiance against an oppressor or was done to absolve the shame of defeat. It was considered the honourable path under certain circumstances. Those cultures were aberrations, however, and for the most part, suicide was denounced as a crime against God and nature. In the early church, people who succeeded in committing suicide were denied a Christian burial, while those who were unsuccessful were excommunicated from the church (in other words: damned if you succeed, damned if you don't). Suicide continues to be a crime in some parts of the world (punishable how, exactly?), and while it has largely been decriminalized in Western society, it's still generally stigmatized and discouraged.

But we now live an era when the choice to do whatever we want with our bodies is viewed by some as an unassailable right. A woman's "right" to terminate the life of her unborn baby is now the law of the land in many countries. Increasingly, the "right" to prematurely end one's own life is also becoming the norm. The "right-to-die" movement has become progressively more vocal, with some countries and organizations really pushing the envelope of assisted suicide. Switzerland is an interesting case in point:

Patients with severe or terminal illness now have the option of going to Switzerland for assistance in ending their lives. In fact, the phrase: "going to Switzerland" has even become a euphemism for assisted suicide. It's given birth to a whole new cottage industry and a term that baffles the imagination: "suicide tourism!"

(Parenthetically, Switzerland is by far the most beautiful country I've ever visited. It seems a little ironic to travel to such a beautiful place only to end your life in the cold sterility of a suicide clinic.

Also, a confession: I've been promising my wife for years that someday: "I'm going to take you to Switzerland." I promise I have no nefarious intent. My only desire is for her to see the beauty of the Alps... not to jump off them!)

From excommunication to suicide tourism. What an interesting world we live in!

As with so many of the controversial issues of life, near-death survivors are not conflicted on the question of suicide. The take-home message from the vast majority of suicide-induced NDEs is loud and clear:

Suicide is *not* the answer.

I'm sure there are some die-hard right-to-die folks who would take issue with such a blanket statement, but they aren't likely to get much sympathy from NDEers. The simple truth is that very few suicide attempters who've seen how suicide is viewed in the next life, would ever attempt it again:

> *"Since then, suicide has never crossed my mind as a way out. It's a copout to me and not the way to heaven. I wish you luck in your research and hope my experience will help someone*

from taking his own life. It is a terrible waste."
(Coming Back to Life, p. 18)

"I didn't go where [my wife] was. I went to an awful place. ... I immediately saw the mistake I had made. ... I thought, 'I wish I hadn't done it.'" (Life After Life, p. 143)

"When I was a teenager, I tried to kill myself because my uncle was molesting me. I took a handful of pills and then went outside. I was very upset and fell to my knees and began to cry.

"I felt groggy and then fell over on my side. It was then that I heard a voice. ... There standing over me was my grandmother. She had killed herself years ago because of chronic heart disease.

"She looked down at me and got right to the point. 'What you are doing is wrong,' she said. 'You aren't supposed to kill yourself.'" (Saved by the Light, pp. 102–103)

"A young girl who was abused by both parents attempted suicide at age seven. She nearly succeeded. She experienced the love and comfort of the Light and also heard a voice which said, 'You have made a mistake. Your life is not yours to take. You must go back.' She retorted, 'No one cares about me.' The answer

was not what she expected: 'You're right. No one on this planet cares about you, including your parents. It is your job to care for yourself.'" (Closer to the Light, p. 159)

An eleven-year-old tried to kill himself. This was his experience with the being of light:

> *"He was kind but not very sympathetic. He said, 'Well, you'll just have to stick around and see what you can do with your life.'"* (Closer to the Light, p. 61)

> *"A girl who attempted suicide as a teenager got this response: I was shown the beauty of my body and of every body. I was told that my body was a gift and I was supposed to take care of it, not kill it."* (Transformed by the Light, p. 152)

Tough love!

One thing is certain about encounters with beings on the other side: they aren't very sympathetic (at least as it relates to suicide). There isn't a lot of enabling going on.

Dr. Raymond Moody's conclusions:

> *"All mentioned that after their experiences, they would never consider trying suicide again. Their common attitude is that they had made a mistake, and that they were very*

glad they had not succeeded in their attempts."
(Reflections on Life After Life, p. 41)

Research shows that plenty of suicide attempters who *didn't* have a near-death experience will try it again, sometimes many times over. As for those who *did* have an experience, very few repeat the attempt. That's a telling statistic considering that most (non-suicidal) NDE survivors can't wait to get back to that beautiful world.

So, why does the near-death literature speak so adamantly against suicide? The reasons are many:

The first, and perhaps most compelling reason, is that it just doesn't work. It doesn't solve the problem:

> *"If you leave here a tormented soul, you will be a tormented soul over there, too."* (Life After Life, p. 143)

> *"All of these people agree on one point: They felt their suicide attempts solved nothing. They found that they were involved in exactly the same problems from which they had been trying to extricate themselves by suicide. Whatever difficulty they had been trying to get away from was still there on the other side, unresolved."* (Reflections on Life After Life, p. 45)

> *"If the NDE was experienced during a (failed) suicide attempt, people usually refrain from*

> *making a second attempt because the experi-*
> *ence taught them that they remain burdened*
> *with the problems they tried to escape. They*
> *come to realize that it is better to solve problems*
> *in this life because the other dimension offers*
> *scant opportunity for solving their earthly prob-*
> *lems."* (Consciousness Beyond Life, p. 65)

The second problem is that, not only does suicide fail to relieve the burdens on the individual, but if successful, it also inflicts enormous burdens on those left behind. While this must surely be a consideration to the one contemplating suicide, I suspect that most are so consumed with their own problems that their ability to rationally assess the fallout on others is greatly diminished. This isn't a criticism of the individual, but it *is* the stark reality for those who loved and cared about them.

As we've already discussed, the remarkable life review allows us to instantly and fully comprehend the effects of our actions on others and to feel the pain from *their* perspective. Death doesn't permit the luxury of ignorance. One can only imagine the agony of regret that must immediately assail the suicide attempter:

> *"I felt the pain of those who had resuscitated me,*
> *of those who had devoted their efforts to me*
> *and thought that I was going to pull through.*
> *I became angry with myself."* (Consciousness
> Beyond Life, p. 215)

"In their disembodied state they were unable to do anything about their problems, and they also had to view the unfortunate consequences which resulted from their acts." (Life After Life, p. 143)

"Another man who survived an apparent clinical death of some duration said that while he was 'over there' he had the impression that there was a 'penalty' to pay for some acts of suicide, and that part of this would be to witness the suffering on the part of others that this act would cause." (Reflections on Life After Life, p. 40)

A third reason which is very often touted by returnees is the feeling that they still have a mission to perform if they are to reach their full potential:

"Like any other survivor, the suicide victim often returns with a sense of mission, a sense of a job yet to be accomplished, and often that job turns out to be a desire to inform other potential victims that suicide is not the answer." (Coming Back to Life, pp. 17–18)

"Others who experienced this unpleasant 'limbo' state have remarked that they had the feeling they would be there for a long time. This was their penalty for 'breaking the rules' by trying to release themselves prematurely from what was, in effect, an 'assignment'—to

fulfil a certain purpose in life." (Life After Life, pp. 143–144)

"No, I would not do that again. I will die naturally next time, because one thing I realized at that time is that our life here is just such a small period of time and there is so much which needs to be done while you're here. And, when you die it's eternity." (Reflections on Life After Life, p. 46)

Before we end this chapter on suicide, a word of comfort to those who may have suffered the agony of seeing a loved one take his or her own life. While suicide appears to rarely be an acceptable way out, there is strong evidence to suggest that heaven's love is not denied those who succeed in their suicide attempt. One could argue, of course, that all these are the testimonies of those who survived. With what we've learned, however, why would we expect it to be any different for those who aren't fortunate enough to be granted a second chance at life? Given the level of understanding on the other side, certainly those not in their "right mind" who committed suicide would have to be given some leeway.

"Some near-death episodes emerge from the trauma of suicide. On the average, these suicide scenarios are positive and uplifting but lack much of the complexity and involvement of those resulting from other forms of death. Still, these near-death scenarios are important,

perhaps doubly so, because each tends to confirm the importance of life and illustrate for the confused victim how truly loved and special he or she really is." (Coming Back to Life, pp. 17–18)

"*Most people experience the NDE precipitated by a failed suicide attempt as largely positive, given that it is accompanied by a sense of acceptance, love, and understanding.*" (Consciousness Beyond Life, p. 352)

And finally, this from Annie, a depressed teenager who indulged all the vices: drugs, alcohol, and boys. She swallowed a handful of barbiturates and a lot of vodka at a party right after her boyfriend announced he was dumping her:

"*I remember feeling love and peace and also feeling as though I had escaped from all the tension and frustration in my life. I felt kind of enveloped by light. It was a wonderful feeling...*

"*I was shown the beauty of my body and of every body. I was told that my body was a gift and I was supposed to take care of it, not kill it. After hearing this, I felt very, very ashamed of what I had done and hoped that I would live. I began to beg the light for life. The feeling that came back was the strongest feeling of love I have ever experienced, even more than the feeling of love I have for my own children.*

"My friends had taken me to a hospital, because the next thing I remember was waking up in the emergency room...

"Immediately after the experience I felt as though I had been given a mission in life, like I was born to accomplish something. The experience gave me an inner energy that has never left me." (Transformed by the Light, pp. 151–153)

Annie got her life back together. She immediately gave up the drugs and alcohol and found new friends. Twenty years later she is happily married with four children.

The world is confused about suicide. Suicide survivors who had an NDE aren't. They will tell you that life is precious, a gift of inestimable worth. They would advise you to hold on to life with every faculty you possess, that no matter how desperate things may seem, suicide is rarely the answer. Even suffering has meaning, and if we could just catch a glimpse of what lies ahead for those who endure it well, we would never think of short-circuiting the process before its time. If we could take a step back and look at the big picture, we would understand that the rewards for holding on are well worth it. The sun *will* rise tomorrow ... but only if we stay around to see it.

It's *Death Therapy* at its finest, Bob, and it very much applies to those who no longer think life is worth living.

And even for those who are left behind, who still feel the sting of the loss of a loved one to suicide, *Death Therapy* offers hope. It teaches us that in the arithmetic of eternity, even the tragic consequences of suicide are accounted for. Somehow, things will be made right in the end. *Your loved one is finally getting some real help, and it's the best therapy available!*

As for you and me, Bob, it would behove us to heed the counsel of those who know, and no one knows more about the implications of suicide than those who've been there and lived to tell the tale. Their stories and insights are compelling, if we'll read with an open mind.

Hold on to life, Bob. Take that trip to Switzerland you've been planning...

...just make sure you buy a return ticket.

Chapter 13

Hope and Redemption

"*In 2007, only 17 percent of people aged thirty or younger said they had some doubt that God was real. In 2012, that number went up to 32 percent. That's roughly a third of young Americans surveyed who aren't sure if they believe God is real.*

"*Then there is a recent comment from Professor Stephen Hawking, the famous Cambridge scientist. 'There is no heaven or afterlife,' he said in a 2012 interview. 'That is a fairy story for people afraid of the dark.'*" (*Waking Up in Heaven*, p. 5)

"*I was five years old when my stepfather took me by the hand, led me into a dark room, and introduced me to Satan.*"

(Crystal McVea, Ibid, p. 15)

The Seventh Continent

IN THE NORTH PACIFIC OCEAN LIES AN enormous, amorphous mass, misleadingly dubbed the "Seventh Continent." Its more official name is the "Great Pacific Garbage Patch." Massive quantities of plastic waste from the coasts of North America, China, and Japan get caught in the circulating currents of the North Pacific Gyre and are relentlessly sucked into this colossal vortex. The garbage patch has been estimated to be somewhere between the size of Texas and twice the area of the United States.

That sounds dramatic, but contrary to popular belief, the garbage patch is not a floating refuse pile like you'd expect to see in a landfill, and no, it isn't visible from space. It's not even visible from a boat. The garbage patch is merely an increase in suspended (often microscopic) plastic particles in the upper water column of the Pacific. It's more of a plastic "soup" suspended below the surface of the ocean than a floating "island" of plastic milk jugs. Size estimates of the mass depend on how high a concentration of plastic particulate matter one considers to be abnormal.

This is not to suggest that the Pacific garbage patch isn't a problem. It is ... at least if you're a black-footed albatross. About one-third of the indigenous albatross chicks die, often as a result of being fed plastic polymers by their parents.

Does anyone really care about the mortality rate of black-footed albatross chicks? Probably not, but the toxin-containing plastic particles in the garbage patch are also ingested by jellyfish ... which are eaten by fish ... which are eaten by you and me!

Why not just clean it up? The enormity of the mass makes that difficult, although viable solutions have been proposed. Some have even suggested innovative ways of making use of the recycled plastic. Belgian architect Vincent Callebaut has designed blueprints for a massive aquatic structure that he calls an "oceanscraper."

Shaped like a giant jellyfish, a plastic mangrove–covered marina would float on the surface of the ocean, with "tentacles" spiralling down to the ocean floor. Within the tentacles would be a series of underwater "eco-villages." Callebaut claims his oceanscrapers could each house over twenty thousand people and realize the dream of subaquatic living.

Artists such as Marina DeBris have used plastic from the Pacific vortex to create "trashion": clothes made out of garbage. While her goal is to educate people about the existence of the garbage patch, my wife would tell you that in my case, trashion would actually be a significant upgrade in style.[45]

An Abusive Childhood

Sometimes, it can seem like our personal life becomes the designated dumping ground for all the "garbage" this world has to offer. Like a voracious whirlpool, we accumulate failure upon failure until our problems become so overwhelming that any hope of resolution can seem impossible. Such was the case with Crystal McVea.

---

[45] Marina DeBris is not her real name ... that would be too serendipitous!

Crystal had every right to believe that there was no God, or that, if he did exist then he certainly didn't care about her. Her problems began at birth. Her father abandoned the family soon after she was born, and her first episode of abuse occurred when she was three, at the hands of a babysitter. The abuse defined her childhood:

> *"The reality of being sexually abused at a young age is that it identifies you—it becomes a part of who you are."* (Ibid, p. 32)

Through it all, she begged God for forgiveness for not being strong enough to stop the abuse and pleaded with him to deliver her from the misery. Her prayers fell on deaf ears:

> *"Night after night, week after week, I prayed. But, to my dismay, nothing changed. I concluded that if God was real, He wasn't interested in my problems."* (Ibid, p. 55)

The abuse cycle followed its predictable course into the teenage years: loser boyfriends, a child out of wedlock, failed suicide attempt, abortion, another child...

> *"And where was God in all of this? ... The concept of God as a loving father had no meaning for me."* (Ibid, p. 34)

But God *was* listening—more intently than Crystal would ever have suspected. There were little mercies along the way, too. Bright spots in an otherwise dismal child-hood. Then she met the man who would become the love of her life—Virgil. Little by little, she began to find a measure of peace.

At the age of thirty-two, Crystal developed a severe case of pancreatitis. It landed her in hospital on a Dilaudid pump to control the pain. Dilaudid is a potent analgesic. If it isn't administered carefully, it can lead to respiratory arrest:

> *"The very moment I closed my eyes on Earth was the same moment I opened them in heaven."* (Ibid, p. 11)

Her spirit separated from her physical body, but the essence of who she was had not changed:

> *"And even without a physical body I knew that I was still 'me.' The same me that had existed on Earth, the same me that had just told my mother I loved her before I died. At the same time, though, I had the stunning realization that I was the 'me' that had existed for all of eternity, long before my time on Earth.*
>
> *"Unlike on Earth, where I was plagued by doubts and fears, in heaven there was nothing but absolute certainty about who I was ... I was flooded with self-knowledge, and all the junk that cluttered my identity on Earth instantly fell away, revealing, for the first time*

ever, the real me. 'Before I formed you in the womb, I knew you,' God says in Jeremiah 1:5. And now I knew myself.

"Imagine that—the first person we meet in heaven is ourselves." (Ibid, p. 12)

Again, that sense of timelessness and the discovery of our true self.

Like most NDEers, Crystal struggled to find the words to describe her new surroundings. She also expressed the sentiment that many others have noted—that the next world somehow feels more "real" than this one:

> *"I grasp at words like 'beautiful' and 'brilliant' and 'amazing,' but they are wildly inadequate. What I experienced in heaven was so real and so lucid and so utterly intense, it made my experiences on Earth seem hazy and out of focus—as if heaven is the reality and life as we know it is just a dream."* (Ibid, pp. 12–13)

Her efforts to describe "the light" mirror those of other NDEers:

> *"It was closest to the color we call white, but a trillion times whiter than the whitest white you've ever seen or could imagine, it was brilliant and beaming and beautifully illuminating...*

"There was also the sensation of cleanliness. It was a feeling of absolute purity and perfection, of something completely unblemished and unbroken. ... It was like being bathed in love. ... And it felt familiar, like something I remembered, or even recognized.

"The best way to put it is this: I was home."
(Ibid, p. 13)

Brilliant, clean, pure, perfect, unblemished ... and familiar! These descriptions of the light are recurring themes, along with the difficulty of distinguishing the light itself from the Beings of Light who were present:

"I was instantly aware of two beings in front of me and to my left, and I knew right away who they were—they were angels.

"But they weren't just any angels—they were my angels.

"I recognized them immediately. There was so much brightness coming off them that I couldn't make out any features. But they weren't shapeless blobs; they definitely had a form, which was roughly that of a human body: long and slender...

"And what I instantly felt for them was love...

"I felt like they had been a part of my existence and my journey forever. ... I felt so unbelievably safe and free in their presence, so happy and fulfilled...

"What's more, I realized there was instant and complete communication between us. ... There was no room whatsoever for secrets or shame or misunderstanding or anything negative." (Ibid, pp. 37–38)

Hope and Redemption

Crystal didn't "see" God as such, but all her senses told her she was "in his presence." She had longed for this time when she could unload all the pent-up questions and frustrations she had harboured for years. It wasn't necessary:

"Back on Earth, I had so many questions for God. 'If I ever meet Him,' I'd say, 'I'm going to ask Him how he could let someone molest me when I was a child. How could he abide brutality against children or the suffering of starving people or cruelty toward the weak? How could He allow such evil to exist in the world?'

"Why, I would ask Him, was he such a punishing God?

"But in heaven, all those questions immediately evaporated. In His presence I absolutely understood that in every way God's plan is perfect. Sheer, utter perfection. Does that mean I can now explain how a child being murdered fits into God's plan? No, I understood it in heaven, but we aren't meant to have that kind of understanding here on Earth. All I can tell you is that I know God's plan is perfect. In His radiance, it all makes perfect, perfect sense." (Ibid, p. 91)

Crystal would probably have been more than satisfied if this had been the extent of her NDE. But there was one more surprise in store for her, and this one would remove any doubt that God had been listening to her pleadings all along. It would also leave her in no doubt that his love for her was absolute and always had been:

"I moved with God and my angels through the tunnel toward the glowing entranceway. I knew exactly where we were headed and I believed I couldn't possibly feel any more joy than I did. But then I became aware of yet another presence in the tunnel just ahead. This was the person God had brought me to meet.

"The girl was skipping and prancing and laughing just like little kids do on Earth. She was bending and dipping her basket into the brightness at her feet and filling it up like she

was filling it with water. She would dip the basket and scoop up the brightness and pour it out and do it again. And every time she dipped the basket and came up with it dripping this magical brightness, she laughed.

"*Every time she laughed, my spirit absolutely swelled with love and pride for her. I wanted to watch this little girl play for the rest of eternity. I wanted to run up to her and take her in my arms and tell her how much I loved her. The love just kept building, endless and radiating waves of love so deep and so intense and so unstopping I truly, truly believed my soul was going to explode and I was going to cease to exist. And all the while the little girl just kept dipping her basket and scooping up light and laughing like little girls do. It touched me so deeply, it was more than I could bear. I prepared myself to burst, to shatter into a million pieces, because I knew I couldn't possibly contain all the love I felt for this child.*

"*And then God lifted this feeling from me.*

"*It was almost as if I had been wearing some kind of magic glasses that suddenly He took off of me. And I knew it was God who lifted this feeling, because as soon as it was lifted, I looked back at the child and immediately understood who the child was.*

"The little girl with the golden basket was me.

"And then another understanding passed between God and me, and I knew this is what He'd been trying to show me all my life. He'd been trying to show me how very much He loved me.

"I knew God was allowing me to see myself as He saw me...

"I was imbued with this penetrating under-standing that God had always loved me, like He loves all His children. And so, for the first time ever, I was filled with love for myself. How could I not love myself? I was God's per-fect creation!

"What's more, God chose to show me myself at the age of three. This was not a random age. I was three years old when the abuse began."
(Ibid, pp. 163–165)

With all her questions answered and her faith in God restored, one would think that Crystal would be ready to return to the land of the living. After all, she had a loving husband and four children who needed her and would be devastated if they were to lose her. It wasn't that simple:

"What I do remember clearly—and what lin-gered for a long time—was how I felt about

being back in my human form. To put it mildly, I was pretty ticked off. I simply loved being with God so much and wanted to go back so badly that I came to resent all the people who saved my life. ... Why did you make me come back? I asked them over and over in those first few hours. 'This was not my choice.'

"*Now, some of you may say, 'Hold on a minute, weren't you thrilled to come back with your husband and your children?' Some of you may even wonder, 'How could you choose to stay in heaven when you knew your family would be so crushed to lose you?' Those are good questions, and I've thought about them a lot in the last three years. And the answer I come up with is always the same: more than anything, I wanted to be with God.*

"*Believe me, before this happened I could not understand how it was possible to love anyone or anything more than your own children. But that was before I found myself in the presence of God. Like I said, that changed everything. I understood instantly that the love of God is greater and more powerful than any other kind of love. And I didn't only understand it; I felt it and heard it and saw it and tasted it with every fiber of my being. When I was in my spirit form, there was simply no other conceivable option for me but to be with*

God. I know it sounds funny to say, but not even my babies made me want to return to my human form...

"I just really, really missed God. I longed to be with Him again, and I felt like I was still bathed in the glow of His greatness. ... I mean it wasn't like I had met the president or a celebrity or something. This was the Creator of the Universe! The Lord God of Israel!

"That is not something you can just shake off."
(Ibid, pp. 176–177)

Still, hard as it was to return to the fray, this was not the same Crystal McVea who had departed this Earth just nine minutes earlier. She was a changed person and could never go back to her old life. Just as the years of abuse had (in her own words) become the defining aspect of her identity, so her near-death experience would now define the new Crystal. She lost no time getting to work:

"The big stuff—the resentments I'd lived with for so many years—just melted away. I'd been angry with someone who owed Virgil money— and I'm talking a lot of money, not just a few hundred bucks, but a life-changing amount. But afterward I told him, 'I know we're never getting that money back, and it's okay. We have to pray for them.' ...

"I just felt liberated from all the baggage I'd carried my whole life. I asked Virgil's mother to forgive me for pushing her away. I asked Virgil to forgive me for making him choose between his family and me. I asked my brother to forgive me for not paying enough attention to him when we were young, and I asked my mother to forgive me for always making her the target of my anger. I even called my father in Illinois, and I asked him to forgive me too...

"I also stopped being so attached to my possessions. ... Honestly, I wouldn't have cared if we did give everything away and moved into a one-room shack. After I died I came to realize that my fortune was my family and friends and the love of God, and the rest didn't matter all that much.

"I found I loved and cared about everyone. ... I was filled with sorrow and pity for anyone who had ever wronged or hurt me, and I prayed for them because they were God's perfect creations. ... Knowing what I knew, I didn't want a single person in the world, not even my worst enemy, to stand outside God's radiance—I wanted everyone to be there with me in the glory of His greatness...

"Nothing bothered me or made me angry anymore, and I overflowed with compassion and

love. I had been powerfully transformed by those nine minutes, and in every way that mattered I was a new creation.

"After a lifetime of doubt I was a loving child of God, and nothing would ever be the same again." (Ibid, pp. 179–181)

Crystal McVea's experience is an amazing affirmation of the love of God. It's a story of hope, redemption, and the wonders of eternity. She stopped breathing, woke up in heaven, and a vision of herself as a child resolved the struggles of a lifetime.

I know what you're thinking, Bob. You're thinking: well, that's great! I could turn my life around too if I got to go to heaven, cavort with angels, bask in the love of God, and learn the secrets of the universe.

True enough, but we both know we aren't going to get that "lucky." Just like that Pacific Garbage Patch, we're going to accumulate an ocean of toxic waste over time, but you and I are not going to enjoy the benefit of a detoxifying NDE. The question is, can we draw sufficient inspiration from people like Crystal McVea to put our past in perspective and allow us to move on? *Death Therapy* affirms that we can.

Near-death experiencers speak of a loving God in heaven who hears and answers prayers. They teach that life has purpose and meaning, and that even tragic childhoods can have a happy ending. If God can turn a life around as he did for Crystal McVea, he can do it for you and me. And the best part is: we don't have to die to experience the miracle!

Chapter 14

Religion

"How thoughtful of God to arrange matters so that, wherever you happen to be born, the local religion always turns out to be the true one." —Richard Dawkins, avowed atheist[46]

"Christians say that God came amongst us as a man, do they not? Yet the Muselmen [Muslims] say he was only a prophet, and that God has no name. ... We fight and kill each other so readily, yet if I had been born in the East, would I not believe the stories they believe, and if they had been born here, would they not be Christians?"
—David Clement-Davies, Fell[47]

---

[46] Clinton Richard Dawkins (born 1941) is an English ethologist, evolutionary biologist and, author. He is an emeritus fellow of New College, Oxford, and was the University of Oxford's Professor for Public Understanding of Science from 1995 until 2008.

[47] David Clement-Davies is a British fantasy fiction writer.

RECRUITING SUICIDE BOMBERS HAS TO BE one of the more challenging careers, and the task just got much harder.

Tradition has it that would-be jihadists can expect to enjoy the companionship of seventy-two virgins upon their arrival in the afterlife. The actual quantity of women anxiously awaiting the arrival of the dashing young warrior isn't entirely clear; some say seventy-two, others seventy. Some estimates are as low as forty-eight.

What is not in question is the quality of the virgins: dark-eyed maidens of stunning beauty, whose only desire is to guarantee the new martyr an eternity of bliss. Worth blowing yourself up for? Perhaps.

One wonders, of course, what's in it for the virgins and what qualifies them for this singular honour. Tradition seems silent on the matter.

While there may be some minor disagreement in regard to the quantity and quality of the whole jihadi/concubine scenario, what is really causing consternation is the recent revelation that scholars may have had the whole thing wrong from the start. Researchers are now suggesting that martyrs to the cause may not be rewarded with seventy-two virgins after all—but rather with seventy-two *raisins*![48] Yes, *raisins*.

Somewhere along the way, something got lost in translation.

And before you blow the whole thing off as a simple doctrinal faux pas, you need to consider what's at stake here: you can't ask a virile young man in the prime of

---

[48] This was aired on a May 21, 2016, CNN special titled, "Why They Hate Us," in an interview of Irshad Manji by Fareed Zakaria.

life to blow himself to kingdom come for a bowlful of dried grapes!

Or maybe you can.

It may not actually be as bad as it sounds. Calling them "dried grapes" is a bit of poetic license on my part. A better translation by those in the know is: "white raisins of crystal clarity." These aren't just any old raisins. Who knows, maybe our young hero will be quite content with his bowl of Sunkist Jihadi Bran ("two scoops are all you need"). A regular, balanced eternity is nothing to scoff at.

The one thing you can't do, however, is to just brush this under the rug, and in light of recent research, what exactly does the recruiter now tell the fresh-faced freedom fighter? Should he level with him? My guess is that they'll just keep quiet about the whole thing. I mean, it's not like he's coming back to spill the beans! And if, on the off chance he has an NDE and *does* come back to reveal the truth about the whole virgin/raisin controversy, his indignation could easily be dismissed as merely sour grapes (sorry!).[49]

Perhaps the recruiter can present it as a choice between the virgins or the raisins. While that may sound like a no-brainer, one should remember one very inconvenient truth: that close on the heels of *every* virgin ... comes a mother-in-law!

Seventy-two mothers-in-law! ... forever!

Those raisins are looking better all the time.

---

[49] This refers to an Æsop fable about a fox who justifies his inability to get to some grapes overhead by concluding that they are probably sour and therefore he wouldn't want them anyway. (This explanation still doesn't excuse the awful pun.)

All frivolity aside, everyone must worry at some point about the reception we can expect when we die. Even those who have convinced themselves that consciousness ends with the death of the physical body have to wonder a little. In the case of our suicide bomber, what sort of reception can he really expect to encounter (tradition notwithstanding)?

Death Therapy provides some clues. In Chapter 5, we learned about the near-death experience of Dannion Brinkley. You'll recall that young Dannion was the quintessential school bully, and that he continued to find an avenue for violence as a sniper in the Marine Corps. In his life review of the Vietnam years, Brinkley relived one of his missions: the assassination of a government official. He had been unable to complete the job because the man was always surrounded by an entourage of bodyguards and secretaries. His team finally decided to simply blow up the hotel where the man was staying:

> *"We surrounded the hotel with plastic explosives and levelled it at sunrise, killing the official along with about fifty people who were staying there. At the time I laughed about it...*

> *"I saw this incident again during my near-death experience, but this time I was hit by a rush of emotions and information. I felt the stark horror that all of those people felt as they realized their lives were being snuffed out. I experienced the pain their families felt when they discovered that they had lost loved ones*

*in such a tragic way. In many cases I even felt
the loss their absence would make to future
generations...*

*"In the life review I was forced to see the death
and destruction that had taken place in the
world as a result of my actions. 'We are all a
link in the great chain of humanity,' said the
Being. 'What you do has an effect on the other
links in that chain.'"* (Saved by the Light,
pp. 18–19)

That was a life review of a "legitimate" killing in a "legitimate" war, many years after the fact. Imagine the reception our suicide bomber would get on suddenly finding himself on the wrong side of the veil along with scores of innocent men, women, and children whose lives he's just snuffed out with a C4 waistcoat! Violence is rarely justified even under the best of circumstances. Violence meted out under the guise of religious mandate surely leaves one on thin ice.

In this chapter, we're going to look at the role of religion in the near-death experience. It's been said that you should never discuss religion or politics in polite company.[50] In no way am I inferring that you, the reader, aren't polite company, but since I've already abandoned any pretence of politeness, let's plunge headfirst into both religion *and* politics.

The fate of the religious fanatic is probably fairly easy to predict, but what about the billions of moderate believers,

---

[50] How ironic that *polite* and *politics* come from the same root!

of any persuasion, who are simply trying to live the basic tenets of their faith? Take Islam, for instance: the very name means submission and peace. Can a devout Muslim expect a warm welcome on the other side ("warm" as in pleasant, not as in fire and brimstone!)? It depends on whom you ask but, historically, Christianity hasn't had a lot of tolerance for anyone with non-Christian beliefs. The Spanish Inquisition and Crusades were prime illustrations.

What of today? My wife and I got a glimpse into how *some* modern Christians view Muslims when we were in Jerusalem on a beautiful spring day in 2012. We were in the Mahane Yehuda Market at lunchtime and entered a tiny restaurant in the Muslim quarter. We were the only customers. While we were eating, a small Christian tour group stopped at the entrance and peered in. Their leader, a middle-aged American woman, asked the owner if he had room for them. He assured her that he did. She then asked him if he believed in the one true God and that Jesus died for his sins. He replied honestly that he worshipped Allah and that he revered Jesus as a prophet. (What he should have said was: "What does any of that have to do with the quality of my food?")

The woman briefly consulted the group, then said loudly: "We won't give our business to someone who doesn't believe in the one true God!"

She stalked off, with her hungry little protégés meekly in tow.

We felt sorry for the owner and asked him if this was a regular occurrence. It was clear that it was, but he merely shrugged his shoulders submissively and said: "If it is God's will..."

It was also clear which one of them exemplified the teachings of Jesus that day.

(The meal was fabulous, by the way.)

This penchant for condemning anyone who doesn't believe as we believe has been the way of the world for centuries and is part of what's driving people away from organised religion today. Many are just tired of the conceit. The claim to salvational exclusivity is not exclusive to Christianity (many faiths believe they've found the one true path to eternal bliss). But Christians are often the worst offenders, especially when you consider that Jesus taught incessantly about tolerance and forgiveness. The problem lies in the way his teachings are interpreted. The typical line of reasoning goes something like this:

Jesus is the Way. No one gets to heaven except through him. Whether or not we accept him in this life is the single determining factor for where we end up in eternity. There is one heaven and one hell, and at death we go one way or the other. There are no other options and no second chances. There is no provision made for someone born into a non-Christian family even if he or she has no real opportunity to hear about Jesus. You either accept Jesus in this life, or prepare for Inferno.

Very little thought is given to the capriciousness of this argument. It paints God as an erratic deity: anxious to heap lavish rewards on those who revere him in the approved way, quick to condemn those who don't.

The Protestant Reformers of the sixteenth century wrestled with the timeless question of who was worthy to be "saved." The oppressive dogmas of the Dark Ages hadn't offered much cause for optimism. The Reformers were good and well-intentioned individuals who bravely challenged the prevailing views of the day, often at great personal cost. But, while they made considerable strides in the advancement of freedom from religious tyranny, they still struggled to reconcile the role of God in the salvation of men. How do you harmonize the concept of an impartial God with the obvious disparities in opportunities to learn about him? Why were some privileged to grow up in a Christian home in a Christian nation, while others were never granted such advantages, simply because of the circumstances of their birth?

Though he deserves credit for tackling the issue, John Calvin's solution to the paradox was, in some ways, a cop-out. In the end, he simply ascribed it all to God's will. He called it predestination: God, in his infinite wisdom, has chosen a lucky few for salvation, while the rest of mankind are damned for eternity. Not the most equitable of solutions, but who are we to question God? On the bright side, it did at least remove the annoying requirement of taking responsibility for one's own salvation, since it was all placed squarely on God's shoulders. And if it was obvious you weren't part of the happy elite, at least you were free to simply enjoy a life of decadence and plan on just taking your lumps at the end. No amount of good works could cause God to change his mind, so you may as well yuck it up while you could. Why agonize about something over which you have no control?

Lost in this argument was any allowance for free will: you can't circumvent the predestined will of God.

The God of the Middle Ages seems so provincial in our eminently enlightened modern era. Yet, despite our sophistication, we have to ask ourselves whether things have really changed that much. Isn't Christianity still claiming the same "chosen" high ground Calvin staked out almost half a millennium ago? To illustrate:

One child is privileged to be born in a Christian nation. He accepts Christ and is "born again." His salvation is assured.

Another child is born to a devout Muslim family. She isn't taught about Christ, and yet she practices all the good tenets of Islam (faith, prayer, charity, etc.). She's living the essential teachings of her religion, but has no incentive to learn about Jesus or to follow him.

In the view of many Christians, it doesn't matter how well (or poorly) either of them live their respective faiths. By decreeing the circumstances of their births, God chose one for salvation and the other for damnation.

Predestination at its best!

Not content with simply being numbered among the elect, some Christians are even choosy about which of their fellow Christians they'll allow to join them in the rarefied realms above. They seem to view salvation as a sort of game of ecclesiastical King of the Mountain ... with limited seating at the summit. In their view, it's not enough just to worship Jesus, you have to worship the *correct* Jesus. Four years ago, I discovered I'd been following the wrong one!

A pastor of a megachurch in Texas was firmly committed to his pick for the Republican nomination, Rick

Perry. He saw an avenue to promote his man by declaring him a "competent Christian" while simultaneously labelling the front-runner, Mitt Romney (a Latter-day Saint like me) a non-Christian. This begs the question why Romney shouldn't be allowed to self-declare his allegiance (or, for that matter, why any of us shouldn't).

It didn't seem to matter that the name of our church is The Church of *JESUS CHRIST* of Latter-day Saints (*EMPHASIS* added), or that its almost sixteen million members place Jesus firmly at the centre of our faith. No, to remain in the pastor's good graces (as well as the three out of four ministers who apparently sided with him), you have to worship the "right" Jesus in the "right" way. Evidently, we Latter-day Saints are barking up the wrong tree. Our salvation appears to depend on an opinion poll, and right now the odds aren't looking too good!

The pastor also labelled Mormonism a cult. He did soften the blow a little, by opining that while he considered it to be a "theological" cult, he didn't think it was a "sociological" cult. The nuance was probably lost on most people, but he went on to explain that what he meant by "sociological" cults were such tragedies as the mass suicides in Jonestown and the Branch Davidian massacre in Waco. I think he was trying to throw Latter-day Saints a bone by suggesting that, although we are theologically misguided, at least he wasn't expecting to wake up one morning and read about a bloodbath in an obscure Mormon community (clearly, he's never attended a BYU/University of Utah football game in Provo!).

Anyway, bottom line for the pastor: sixteen million Latter-day Saints are bound for hell (along with some other undesirables) mainly because we backed the wrong Jesus.

(Just for the record, the pastor seems to be a good man and his love for Jesus and his fellow evangelicals is commendable. I have tremendous respect for anyone who is willing to devote his or her life to service to others. I'm just saddened that some are not willing to allow that we're all travellers on the same journey and that we're all just trying to navigate our way through life as best we can.

Jesus was very tolerant of honest truth-seekers and very inclusive: I can't find one instance where anyone who came to him in sincerity and humility was ever turned away. He reserved criticism only for the proud Pharisees and Sadducees who believed they had an exclusive claim to salvation and used their perceived superiority to lord it over lesser mortals [i.e., everyone else].)

So, here we are in the twenty-first century, still quick to condemn those who don't conform to our particular version of the truth. In many respects, we're still fighting the same struggle that started with Cain and Abel arguing over whose offering was more acceptable to God.[51] That little dispute ended in bloodshed, and sadly we don't appear to have come very far in six millennia. So many modern-day conflicts continue to have their genesis in religious ideology and bigotry. With a few notable exceptions, people seem convinced that they've found the one and only path to heaven whilst all around them remain deluded and lost, and instead of reaching down to offer a helping hand, many would rather extend a stiff arm to keep the opposition down

---

[51] This is generally outlined in chapter 4 of Genesis, in the Bible.

in the mud. Sadly, that's the current state of our society and the root cause of so many of our problems.

What of death? Will the religious wars continue beyond the grave? Will zealous recruiters line our path to the pearly gates, anxious to sign us up before some other faction gets their talons in?

Clearly not.

There is absolutely no place for religious conflict in the next world (or at least in that part of it where light and knowledge prevail). To the contrary: it all appears to be monotonously serene, almost boring. There is no room for religious one-upmanship and anyone who enters the light believing that their particular brand of religion grants them special dispensation, will quickly be disabused of the notion. They will soon learn that the one thing that truly isn't tolerated on the other side ... is intolerance!

Religious affiliation just doesn't seem to matter over there. It's all about what we've done with our lives:

> *"...[W]hen I met the Risen Christ He wasn't impressed by what church I had joined, but asked me what I had done with my life to show Him. He was asking me if I had been kind and loving to those around me."* (My Life After Dying, p. 116)

> *"I was fairly religious, but in a superficial way. I was more or less caught up in the ritual and the trappings of religion. And afterwards, for the short period after, I realized that the ritual*

and all that really meant nothing. It was the faith and the deep-down meaning that was of importance...

"It is the smug sectarian quality of some religious groups to which core experiencers tend to object, not to the basics of religious worship itself." (Life at Death, p. 164)

"My doctor told me I 'died' during the surgery. But I told him that I came to life. I saw in that vision what a stuck-up ass I was with all that theology, looking down on everyone who wasn't a member of my denomination or didn't subscribe to the theological beliefs that I did.

"A lot of people are going to be surprised when they find out that the Lord isn't interested in theology. He seems to find some of it amusing, as a matter of fact, because he wasn't interested at all in anything about my denomination. He wanted to know what was in my heart, not my head." (The Light Beyond, pp. 39–40)

Even the most ardent of devotees don't get much credit for their zeal if it doesn't translate into a genuine love for people:

"I am known as one of the most enthusiastic of Christians. Enthusiastic was the word used before my experience. The enthusiasm was outward and since has drawn inward into a yearning to be real and to be the me I was created to be in yielding my own life up to preferring others before myself. Before, I wanted the world to see and help me and admire the beautiful walk with God I had. Now I want to love people with the love God loved me as the Light of His love ebbed through me as I dissolved in it for a moment of life-changing revelation. That love does not exploit nor call attention to itself." (After the Beyond, p. 81)

This awakening to the existence of divine love is a game changer for many. Their experience introduced them to the existence of overwhelming, unconditional, life-changing love, and they yearn to reciprocate that love upon their return. This depth of love doesn't permit petty elitism in the religious sweepstakes:

"I was raised a Mormon. I was raised thinking, maybe, that God loved certain individuals more than others. Or that he cared about certain individuals more than others depending upon how they lived. I didn't find that to be true.

"I found that his love was extended to everyone, all the time. And that he understood why we

*are what we are, and why we are going through
what we are going through...*

"*...too many times our priorities are mixed up.
We forget the teachings of the New Testament—
to love our neighbor, and to do all the other
positive things written there.*" (As quoted by
Arvin S. Gibson in Glimpses of Eternity,
pp. 188–90)

"*It is as though the unconditional love many
of them felt during their NDE swept away
the last vestiges of religious parochialism
and opened them up to a vision of humanity
united in a faith whose shared foundation is
God's limitless love for all.*" (Heading Toward
Omega, p. 163)

Upon their return, most near-death survivors can't look
at religion the same way they used to. This leads to many
having a difficult time relating to others. This shouldn't
come as a surprise, since the individual has experienced
a life-altering event while little has changed for everyone
else. He or she basked in the limelight of the grandest stage
in the universe, and while the changes are overwhelmingly
positive for these individuals, it isn't always easy for those
labouring "backstage" to adjust to the new celebrity. This
has the potential for conflict, doubly so if there are clergy
members in the family:

"Consider the case of a woman survivor in Alabama who is married to a fundamentalist Christian preacher. The two have been married many years, have three children and a busy, dedicated lifestyle. Since her experience, it has become increasingly difficult for her to attend her husband's church services:

"'He's wrong. I know now deep in my heart he's wrong. What he's preaching, that's not the way it is. I feel like he's telling everyone a lie and I don't know what to do about it. I love my husband and I love our children. I don't want to upset him or anyone else. I don't want a divorce or anything like that. But I can't listen anymore. I try to pretend I'm too busy to come.'" (Coming Back to Life, pp. 110–111)

A much more productive outcome resulted when it was a minister himself who had the NDE:

"One NDEer I spoke to had been a minister of the fire and brimstone variety. It wasn't infrequent, he said, for him to tell his congregation that if they didn't believe the Bible in a certain way, they would be condemned to burn eternally.

"When he went through his NDE, he said the being of light told him not to speak to his congregation like this anymore. But it was done

*in a non-demanding way. The being just
implied that what he was doing was making
the lives of his congregation miserable. When
this preacher returned to the pulpit, he did so
with a message of love, not fear."* (The Light
Beyond, p. 32)

These two examples illustrate beautifully the premise
and potential of *Death Therapy*. Here you have two ministers who were clearly sending the wrong message to
their congregants, a message based on fear and exclusivity
rather than on love and inclusion. It took an encounter
with death to convince the "fire and brimstone" minister
to change his ways. Now, imagine if the minister in the
first story were able to read and internalize the near-death
experience of the minister in the second. Perhaps it would
motivate him to institute some much-needed changes in
his life. It might also help him understand why his wife is
different (following her NDE) and why she doesn't seem
to want to listen to his sermons anymore!

That's what *Death Therapy* is all about, Bob: benefitting from the near-death experiences of others without
having to go through the ordeal yourself. All you have to
do is read and heed!

Let's get back to the quandary of Christianity's claim
that Jesus is the only way back to God. If Jesus really is the
literal Son of God and came to atone for the sins of all
mankind, isn't our acceptance of him the only thing that
really matters when it comes to our salvation? It's a valid
question, and one we would do well to consider. It's been

the subject of countless sermons, as well as many books and movies. One such example is the 2014 film *God's Not Dead*:[52]

Josh Wheaton is an evangelical college student who enrols in a philosophy class taught by an atheist professor, Jeffrey Radisson. On the first day of class, the professor tells his students that in order to pass the course they merely have to sign a declaration stating that "GOD IS DEAD." Josh is the only student who refuses to sign.

Radisson challenges Josh to debate the topic with him and agrees to let the class members choose the winner. Up against the ropes in the first two debates, Josh finally lands a haymaker on the wily professor in the third and final debate and gets the class to stand up and declare in unison: "GOD'S *NOT* DEAD!"

Chalk one up for the good guys: humble Christian student outwits arrogant unbelieving professor. Cue the applause.

At the end of the film, the professor is struck by a car and is lying in the street with a crushed chest and minutes to live. Fortuitously, a Christian happens to be passing by and he manages to elicit a confession of faith from the lifetime atheist as he gasps his last breath. Radisson accepts Jesus and (we are to assume) passes on to his eternal reward.

Another happy Hollywood ending...

...and typical Hollywood hogwash.

I'm not minimizing the importance of turning to God. I believe that's always a good thing, even if it happens on our deathbed. My personal belief is that someday, whether

---

[52] *God's Not Dead* is a 2014 drama by Pure Flix Productions, directed by Harold Cronk, starring Shane Harper, Kevin Sorbo, and others.

in life or in death, each of us will come face to face with the question of the reality of God.

But, are we supposed to believe that the serendipitous arrival of a missionary-minded Christian, seconds before the professor dies, is the single determining factor for where he ends up in eternity? Instant reassignment from hell to heaven ... simply because a Christian happened to be in the neighbourhood? That's the implication of the scene.

What if our Good Samaritan had arrived two minutes late?[53] What if the professor had been DOA?[54] What if he died before he could eke out those magic words? Does a confession under duress have any meaning anyway? What about the vast majority of nonbelievers who are denied such a fortuitous break? Is it an eternity of misery for them for the one simple reason that a concerned missionary wasn't handy?

So many "what ifs?"!

I know, I know, it's just a movie. I'm obsessing again over the salvation of a fictional character!

The problem is that this fictional scene is a reflection of some core Christian beliefs that are anything *but* fictional. First, is the notion that a confession of faith while we're still drawing breath is the *only* way we're going to make it to heaven. The second is the idea that a simple declaration of allegiance is sufficient *in itself* to ensure salvation

---

[53] The Good Samaritan refers to a parable given by Jesus, found in Luke, chapter 10, in the Bible. Ironically, given the context of the Good Samaritan Christian in the film who happened to be in the neighborhood, the Good Samaritan of the Bible was not actually a Christian (or even a Jew).

[54] DOA: Dead On Arrival

and that nothing else factors into the equation (including character and works of righteousness).

Some purveyors of the doctrine of "salvation by faith alone" even take it one step further: they view any attempt to impress God as somehow offensive to him. In their estimation, we are miserable sinners who can never come close to what God expects, so our feeble efforts at doing good amount to little more than an affront to his sensibilities.

"Salvation by faith alone" is a very permissive doctrine. It's a convenient excuse for not having to worry about the need to improve. It grants us license to indulge any character deficiency we see fit, secure in the belief that the slate will be instantly wiped clean the moment we die.

It's a capricious belief, and it's also one that doesn't mesh with the near-death experience. The impression I get from *all* NDEers is that we arrive on the other side toting the same baggage (and halos) we lugged around in life. To quote Jacob Marley in A Christmas Carol: *"I wear the chain I forged in life. I made it link by link, and yard by yard."*

(I know—I'm quoting fictional characters again. Worse, I'm quoting fiction to explain fiction! Time to get back to reality, Bob.)

The reality is that we won't be instantly fitted with angel's wings (and by the same token, neither will horns spontaneously sprout from our skull). The reality is that our standing will not be the least bit different one minute *after* we die than it was one minute *before* we died. There is no instant sainthood (and no instant demonhood for that matter, if there is such a word).

The first thing that will happen when we die is that we will be required to give an accounting for everything we've done while we were alive. This review of our life will occur in the presence of a loving, non-judgmental being of light, but while he or she will look upon the events of our life with profound love and compassion, we will likely find that we will not be able to dismiss our own deficiencies quite so easily. We are who we are, and we'll still have to live with ourselves, even in death.

Declarations of faith will surely fall on the "assets" side of the celestial balance sheet and will likely carry a lot of weight. Declarations of faith are far from the only thing, however, and will probably pale in significance next to the overwhelming evidence of deeds and actions. *Love, compassion, kindness, forgiveness, honesty, integrity...* these are the real watchwords of character, not confessions of faith. I suspect that loud declarations of devotion will be as pennies in the economy of heaven; quiet acts of kindness will be as gold bricks.

My intent here isn't to knock the grace of God. I believe it's real and that it will be the *very thing* that will bridge the chasm between us and God. No matter how hard we try, we will never measure up to God's standard of perfection. We are utterly dependent on his grace and at some point, we need to acknowledge that fact.

But we still do have to do our part! We can't leave it all up to God!

So, just where *does* Jesus fit in all this? If Jesus really is the only way back to God, and if our fictional faithful missionary *hadn't* come along in time to save our fictional atheist professor, what possible hope could Dr. Radisson have of redemption? This is the soul-searching question we Christians have to ask ourselves: What are we going to do with the billions of hapless souls who never have a real opportunity to learn about Jesus? Are we willing to condemn them to an eternity of misery for the one simple reason that they never accepted and followed Jesus?

There's only one answer to this dilemma unless you believe in a God who is capricious, plays favourites, and predestines just a few for salvation:

There still has to be the opportunity to learn saving truths... even in death.

It's the only way if God is to be equitable and fair.

What do near-death survivors have to say about it? Well, that's a little tricky. The problem is that the operative word is "survivors." As such, they are only privy to *near-*death knowledge, and not *final-*death certainty. Survivors are generally given a few pieces of the puzzle, but a knowledge of absolute truth (as it applies to religion) is generally not part of the package. To put it more simply, it seems to be an unwritten rule that near-death isn't the place to find out who's "right" in the religious sweepstakes.

Bottom line: don't look to NDEs to find the "truth" about religion. In this life, we are apparently required to live by faith.

What *do* we know?

One, is that our acceptance or nonacceptance of Christ doesn't seem to be a make-or-break proposition at the moment of our arrival in the afterlife. Apparently, it isn't even Christ who welcomes everyone. While many Christians are welcomed by a Christ-like being (or someone they assume to be Christ), non-Christians are more often met by a very different being, often someone they venerated in life:

> *"A Christian is apt to be greeted by Jesus, a Buddhist by Buddha, a Jew by Father Abraham, a Moslem by Mohammed, and an atheist by his or her next-door neighbor..."*
> (Coming Back to Life, p. 172)

> *"Any religious leaders and religious symbols encountered will always match the deep beliefs of the experiencer, yet the experience itself reflects all beliefs. We become as if gods and realize that our true identity is divine."*
> (Ibid, p. 166)

Unfortunately, we have to leave it at that. I personally believe that at some point, all will have the opportunity to learn the truth as it applies to religion, but what lies beyond the initial encounter is beyond the scope of the near-death experience. We are (at least as NDEs are concerned) left in the dark as to what comes next.

What *is* clear, is that there is hope for *everyone*, regardless of belief or religion. In death, every belief system (or lack thereof) will be treated with the utmost respect.

So, Bob, in conclusion, what can this chapter on religion contribute to our therapy? How can we benefit from what near-death survivors have told us about the state of religion on the other side?

First, if you're harbouring the delusion that God is going to save you, while condemning the rest of his children to hell, now might be a good time to discover some humility. *Everyone* is loved intensely by God: Muslims, Jews, Hindus, Buddhists, Christians, atheists, Manchester United fans (and yes, Man U *is* a religion... at least in Manchester). A Communist in China is as beloved as a Christian in Chile. *God has no favourites!* He wants all to partake of his love. *Unconditional love is unconditional!*

The depth of God's love is not dependent on what we believe. He is more interested in what's in our hearts than what's in our minds. He looks upon his children with a compassion that transcends religious differences. We are *all* of infinite worth to him. Isn't it time we started to see each other in that same light? What a difference it would make if we were to put aside our petty differences and simply accept one another for who we are.

Let us never, ever be found trying to tear down the fragile faith of another. However enlightened we may feel we are, we may someday learn that true enlightenment consists of being tolerant of those who don't think as we do. God apparently has a plan for everyone, and that plan may begin with whatever tiny kernel of truth they are capable of cultivating. Don't crush that seed before it has chance to take root.

Second, we would be foolish to assume that we've wrangled our way onto an escalator to heaven and that there's nothing left to do. There are always more truths to learn, deficiencies to correct, and burdens to lift.

Now would be a good time to relinquish our bigotry, since unresolved character flaws will not simply disappear when we die. We can either confront our prejudices now or we can deal with them later. Either way, they aren't going away by themselves, and all indications point to the fact that it is infinitely easier to correct problems in life than it will be in death. Here, we have the priceless gift of free will and it's only when we are free to choose that our choices really count.

In summary, religious devotion is a good thing if it teaches us to be loving, forgiving, tolerant, and kind. If, on the other hand, our religion imbues us with a sense of superiority and exclusivity, then it can quickly become a toxic disease.

But there's a cure... *Death Therapy!* The message of near-death survivors is that humility is the antidote to religious bigotry. Death will surely humble us if we arrive at that point filled with pride, conceit, and a sense of entitlement, simply because we think we've found a little nugget of truth a little shinier than the rest. Far better to discover some humility now, and what better way to demonstrate humility than by showing a willingness to learn from those who have died?

True religion is about love and tolerance, Bob. Anyone who learns that lesson can anticipate a warm welcome on the other side...

...and maybe even a nice bowl of grapes!

Chapter 15

Heaven and Hell

Heaven is where the police are British,
the chefs Italian,
the mechanics German,
the lovers French,
and it's all organized by the Swiss.

Hell is where the police are German,
the chefs are British,
the mechanics French,
the lovers Swiss,
and it's all organized by the Italians.

"The mind is its own place, and in itself
"Can make a Heav'n of Hell, A Hell of Heav'n."
—Satan in *Paradise Lost*[55]

The simplest answer is more often correct.
—Occam's Razor

---

[55] "Paradise Lost," published in 1667, is an epic poem by the seventeenth-century English poet John Milton.

WHILE AMERICAN AUDIENCES MAY NOT be familiar with him, Jimmy Savile was a larger-than-life celebrity for five decades in Britain. His eccentricity and flamboyance brought him immense fame and fortune, but he would be remembered as much for his prodigious charity fundraising as for his personality. When he died in October 2011, at the age of eighty-four, it was estimated that he had raised over 40 million pounds for various charities. The nation mourned the passing of a legend.

Jimmy Savile came from humble beginnings. He was conscripted to work in a colliery during the Second World War, but an injury to his spine put a quick end to his career as a coal miner. He decided to try his hand as a DJ and found his true calling.[56] He began playing records in dance halls, and his colourful, unconventional style quickly made him a celebrity. He claimed to have pioneered the art of using twin turntables, which eliminated the awkward pause between songs. He became a DJ for Radio Luxembourg in 1958, then turned his attention to television.

In 1964, Jimmy Savile became a household name when he hosted the first episode of Top of the Pops on the BBC. It was an instant hit. Every Thursday evening for the next four years, he became a fixture in millions of homes across the UK.

From 1975 to 1994, he hosted another popular television programme, Jim'll Fix It, in which he arranged for the wishes of viewers (mainly children) to come true.

He had many other gifts and passions: he became a professional wrestler (107 fights!), he participated in over

---

[56] DJ = "Disc Jockey" (for those born after the invention of the iPod).

three-hundred bike races, and he ran over two-hundred marathons.

His real passion, however, was charity. For over five decades, Savile devoted his life to raising money for charities, hospitals, and other worthy causes. He spent considerable time with mentally and physically disabled patients. He was such a regular visitor to hospitals and psychiatric facilities that a couple of them gave him his own room. He was frequently found in an all-girls' school in Surrey and a children's home on Jersey. He was described as a "prodigious philanthropist."

His charitable endeavours earned him many accolades: Order of the British Empire, Papal knighthood from John Paul II, and knighthood from the Queen. He was granted two honorary doctorates.

Flamboyant to the end, Sir Jimmy Savile's funeral was an elaborate affair. His satin gold coffin was displayed at the Queens Hotel in Leeds, attracting over four-thousand well-wishers. He was buried in Scarborough, with his coffin inclined at forty-five degrees to fulfil his wish to "see the sea."

A life well lived? It would seem so.

But there was a dark side to this *prodigious philanthropist*—a very dark side indeed.

In October 2012, a year after his death, allegations of sexual abuse at the hand of Jimmy Savile began to surface. It started as a trickle, but as the media latched on to the story, more and more victims came forward. Scotland Yard initiated an official investigation, and within ten weeks, 450 people had filed complaints of rape or sexual assault against Savile. The age of the victims (at the time of the assault) ranged from eight to forty-seven. They included ten eight-year-old boys and sixty-three girls under the age of sixteen. Three-quarters of his victims were under eighteen. The abuse spanned six decades.

How did Savile get away with it for so long? There were, of course, complaints along the way (some as early as 1964), but victims found themselves victimized a second time as they ran into the brick wall that protects the rich and famous. Some half-hearted investigations were started, but no one wanted to believe that the beloved celebrity who had done so much for children was, in fact, a vicious sexual predator.

It turned out that the many hours spent at the hospitals and schools were motivated by far more nefarious intent than simply comforting the ill. The fact that he was attracted to a psychiatric hospital, as well as a ward for teens with spinal cord injuries, made his actions all the more depraved. His interest in the all-girls' school and children's home clearly wasn't altruistic, either. For over sixty years, Savile's notoriety had allowed him unsupervised access to children and vulnerable adults (some of them mentally and physically disabled). Jimmy Savile inflicted incalculable damage on countless individuals.

As the truth of the allegations became undeniable, Savile's name was systematically removed from the places and organizations named after him. The charities connected to him were dismantled and their funds redistributed. His cottage in Scotland was sold. Even the headstone on Savile's grave was destroyed and sent to a landfill. His honorary degrees were rescinded. The only reason his OBE and knighthoods were not revoked was because there was no procedure to do so posthumously. Every effort was made to erase any trace of Jimmy Savile's life from the face of the Earth.

Fame and fortune protected Jimmy Savile from punishment in life...
But they wouldn't protect him in death.

Hell is real!
Hellish NDEs are only a small part of the near-death phenomenon (about 1 percent), but they do happen, and we ignore them at our peril. While hell is generally only a fleeting vision for some who suffer near-death, the fact that these stories exist tell us that hell is a real place and that we could end up there for such heinous acts as abusing children.

> *"You've got to tell people about hell. There is one. I know. I've been there. .... There's a hell, and people go there."* (Journal of Near-Death Studies, vol. 10, no. 3, spring 1992, p. 159)

So, let's deal with the burning question of hell (pardon the pun), and how to avoid it.
First of all, the fact that someone has a hellish NDE doesn't necessarily mean he or she is an evil person; even very good people are shown the dark side of the afterlife. We all arrive at the point of death with character deficiencies to overcome, and as we've already learned, those deficiencies aren't automatically erased when we die. This

regret for wasted opportunity must surely constitute a form of hell, but it doesn't automatically make us an evil person. If such is the case, we're all doomed!

Most creeds would have you believe that, at death, it's one way or the other, either heaven or hell—*forever*. As we'll find out in this chapter, however, hell seems to be less about retribution than it is about reclamation. Many NDEs have raised the possibility that hell may not be as final as it's often portrayed. Even a very negative NDE can have a positive effect on the individual:

> *"Let me tell you a very striking case. There was a young man who attempted to commit suicide. He had been a n'er-do-well all his life and wasn't really amounting to much. He took some kind of drug overdose and went into two different levels of experience. The first level was just physical pain and discomfort and horror as he sank into his near-death. He had a cardiac arrest in the presence of friends and turned blue.*

> *"Just by luck they were able to get medical personnel on the scene who resuscitated him. After he had entered into the critical death phase, he described to me the most nightmarish NDE that I had ever heard of.*

> *"He described images of some horrific beings clutching and clawing at him. It was something like descending into Dante's inferno. He*

had a claustrophobic, hostile, nightmarish NDE, without the slightest positive experience. No out-of-body episode, no being of light, nothing beautiful, nothing pleasant.

"But this experience totally transformed him. He was a different person and I felt it. He had a clarity about him. He had a wholesomeness and a sense of self-determination. He was not an unusually gifted or ambitious person, but he had such a firm sense of where he was going in life that it was remarkable." (The Light Beyond, p. 118)

This story was narrated by Dr. Raymond Moody. It was one of the only negative NDEs he ever heard and the incident had a curious twist to it. In what may just have been a serendipitous "accident," this interview was the only one in which Moody encountered technical difficulties:

"There is a very interesting twist on this story. I was delighted to have been able to tape-record his detailed account of his hellish NDE. But after he narrated the experience I tried to play it back on the tape recorder. The entire experience had been wiped out. The tape recorder that I had used for at least ten years had never failed me before and has never since. But when I tried to play back that experience, it was totally erased.

"I have no explanation for it." (The Light Beyond, p. 119)

Interesting!

We probably shouldn't read too much into this anecdotal anomaly, but the following story provides much food for thought (this incident was briefly introduced earlier): Dr. Maurice Rawlings, a cardiologist, was performing a stress test on a forty-eight-year-old mail carrier. During the procedure, the patient had a cardiac arrest and CPR was started. It was touch and go for several minutes—the patient teetering between life and death. While chest compressions were being performed, the mailman would be fully conscious and talking, but he would "die" again as soon as compressions were stopped:

> *"Each time he regained heartbeat and respiration, the patient screamed, 'I am in hell!' He was terrified and pleaded with me to help him. I was scared to death. In fact this episode literally scared the hell out of me! It terrified me enough to write this book.*

> *"He then issued a very strange plea: 'Don't stop!' You see, the first thing most patients I resuscitate tell me, as soon as they recover consciousness, is "Take your hands off my chest; you're hurting me!"...*

> *"Then I noticed a genuinely alarmed look on his face. He had a terrified look, worse than*

the expression seen in death! This patient had a grotesque grimace expressing sheer horror! His pupils were dilated, and he was perspiring and trembling—he looked as if his hair was 'on end.'

"Then still another strange thing happened. He said, 'Don't you understand? I am in hell. Each time you quit I go back to hell! Don't let me go back to hell!' ...

"After several death episodes he finally asked me, 'How do I stay out of hell?'" (Beyond Death's Door, p. 19)

The patient pleaded with Dr. Rawlings to pray for him, which he did. He was finally stabilized and was transported to the hospital.

"A couple of days later, I approached my patient with pad and pencil in hand for an interview. At his bedside I asked him to recall what he actually saw in hell. Were there any flames? Did the devil have a pitchfork? What did hell look like?

"He said, 'What hell? I don't recall any hell!' I recounted all of the details he had described two days earlier while he was on the floor next to the treadmill machine being resuscitated. He could recall none of the unpleasant events! ...

"He still does not recall the experiences that occurred in hell, but he does recall standing in the back of the room and watching us work on his body there on the floor.

"He also recalls meeting both his mother and stepmother during one of these subsequent death episodes. The meeting place was a gorge full of beautiful colours. He also saw other relatives who had died before. This experience was very pleasurable, occurring in a narrow valley with very lush vegetation and brilliant illumination by a huge beam of light." (Ibid, pp. 20–21)

This incident raises all kinds of questions which we'll get to in a minute, but first, we have to point out one very important inference: Dr. Rawlings' experience with the mail carrier suggests that we can't put too much stock in the "1 percent negative NDE" statistic. It raises the possibility that negative NDEs may be more common than we think, but for some reason they are often erased from the survivor's memory. Why this should be so is not clear.

Negative near-death accounts may be at a premium, but they can still add to our understanding of this most controversial and misunderstood place that we call hell. What can we learn from them?

First of all, you won't hear much in the near-death literature about the proverbial lake of fire and brimstone popular with nineteenth-century preachers. Hell sounds pretty miserable nonetheless:

"It's a dusky, dark, dreary area, and you realize that the area is filled with a lot of lost souls or beings that could go the same way I'm going [to the light] if they would just look up. The feeling I got was that they were all looking downward, and they were kind of shuffling, and there was a kind of moaning. There were hundreds of them, looking very dejected. The amount of confusion I felt coming off of it was tremendous. When I went through this, I felt there was a lot of pain, a lot of confusion and a lot of fear, all meshed into one. It was a very heavy feeling. They weren't turning toward the Light. In fact, they didn't even know the Light existed." (After the Beyond, pp. 82–83)

There doesn't appear to be a lot of physical punishment being inflicted in the nether regions: no slow-roasting on a spit or poking with pitchforks. The real battles seem to be waged in the mind of the individual. For the most part, we punish ourselves with remorse for the hurt we've done to others. This isn't to say that evil forces aren't present:

"An absolutely incredible malice displays itself. There are thousands of things that erupt from this malice, among them some things such that they are beyond description in the vocabulary of any language. ... I can bear solemn witness to the fact that they have so many forms of malice that scarcely one in a thousand can be described." (Heaven and Hell, p. 482)

"I felt an inner struggle going on between myself and some evil force. ... I found myself floating about six inches above my body. The next thing I remember is being sucked down a vast black vortex like a whirlpool and I found myself in a place that I can only describe like Dante's Inferno. I saw a lot of other people who seemed grey and dreary and there was a musty smell of decay. There was an overwhelming feeling of loneliness about the place." (Science and the Near-Death Experience, p. 134)

Hell seems to be a real place. The devil also appears to be real. Even children have encountered him. One little boy told his mother:

"'On the way back, I saw the devil. He said if I did what he wanted, I could have any-thing I want...

[He] said I could have anything I wanted, but I didn't want him bossing me around."' (The Return from Silence, pp. 111–12)

The devil's promise is always the same: we can have whatever we want, without cost or consequence. But there's a rule that is as incontrovertible in death as it is in life: nothing is free! Even a child knows that; adults are the ones who seem to struggle with the concept.

We talked about little Colton Burpo in Chapter 9. He died from complications of appendicitis at the age of three and had an extensive NDE. It was a thoroughly uplifting experience, with the exception of one moment:

> *"'Hey, Colton,' I said. 'Did you see Satan?'*
> *"'Yeah, I did,' he said solemnly.*
> *"'What did he look like?'*
>
> *"At this, Colton's body went rigid, he grimaced, and his eyes narrowed to a squint. He stopped talking. I mean, he absolutely shut down, and that was it for the night. ...*
>
> *"It became clear that in addition to rainbows, horses, and golden streets, he had seen something unpleasant. And he didn't want to talk about it."* (Heaven Is for Real, pp. 132–134)

One of my favourite "Far Side" cartoons depicts three rooms side by side in hell.[57] There are people in each room being tormented and each door has a label showing who's in the room. On the left are "Homicidal Maniacs," in the middle room are "Terrorists," and on the right are "People Who Drove Too Slow in the Fast Lane!"

(Admit it: you've been behind someone in the fast lane who's blocking your path, and just won't move over, even though the road is clear for miles ahead, and you've muttered those words: "There's a special place in hell...!")

---

[57] "The Far Side" is a single-panel cartoon series that was syndicated internationally to over 1,900 newspapers for fifteen years, by American Gary Larson (born August 14, 1950).

Just like heaven, hell appears to be a multifaceted place, and just as people congregate with those who are like-minded on Earth, so it seems to be in hell.

You'll recall Private George Ritchie's extensive encounter with death as he prepared to be shipped to Europe to join the war. He died and left his body for nine minutes. His was the "first," and perhaps most comprehensive, NDE of the modern era. He returned with detailed knowledge, not only of paradise, but also of the darker side of death. Few have witnessed as much as Ritchie did. It was almost as though someone wanted our first modern-day "ambassador" to the spirit world to have the complete tour, beginning in the basement.

George Ritchie's NDE began on Earth, or at least in the vicinity of Earth. One thing he quickly realized was that the spirit world (or *astral realm* as he called it) is right here, intermingled with our physical world:

> *"The astral realm has its own reality of sub-stance to it just as does our earthly realm with all our buildings and things man has con-structed. ... What made me feel as though my vision was out of focus was seeing another city superimposed on our physical city."* (My Life After Dying, p. 24)

If the realization that the dead are right here amongst us was not startling enough, Private Ritchie next found himself in a bar filled with both embodied and disembodied people, and quickly learned the full implications of that reality. What he witnessed shocked him to the core:

"The light drew me inside a dingy bar and grill near what looked like a large naval base. ... Though a few were drinking beer, most of them seemed to be belting whiskies as fast as the two perspiring bartenders could pour them.

"Then I noticed a striking thing. A number of the men standing at the bar seemed unable to lift their drinks to their lips. Over and over I watched them clutch at their shot glasses, hands passing through the solid tumblers, through the heavy wooden countertop, through the very arms and bodies of the drinkers around them.

"And these men, every one of them, lacked the aureole of light that surrounded the others...

"Furious quarrels were constantly breaking out among them over glasses that none could actually get to his lips...

"I watched one young sailor rise unsteadily from a stool, take two or three steps, and sag heavily to the floor ... the bright cocoon around the unconscious sailor simply opened up. It parted at the very crown of his head and began peeling away from his head, his shoulders. Instantly, quicker than I'd ever seen anyone move, one of the insubstantial beings who had been standing near him at

the bar was on top of him. He had been hovering like a thirsty shadow at the sailor's side, greedily following every swallow the young man made. Now he seemed to spring at him like a beast of prey.

"In the next instant, to my utter mystification, the springing figure had vanished. ...

"Twice more, as I stared, stupefied, the identical scene was repeated. A man passed out, a crack swiftly opening in the aureole round him, one of the non-solid people vanished as he hurled himself at that opening, almost as if he had scrambled inside the other man.

"Was that covering of light some kind of shield then? Was it protection against ... against disembodied beings like myself? Presumably, these substance-less creatures had once had solid bodies, as I myself had had. Suppose that when they had been in these bodies they had developed a dependence on alcohol that went beyond the physical. Spiritual, even. Then when they lost that body, except when they could briefly take possession of another one, they would be cut off for all eternity from the thing they could never stop craving...

"Surely that would be a form of hell. I had always thought of hell ... as a fiery place

somewhere beneath the Earth where evil men like Hitler would burn forever. But what if one level of hell existed right here on the surface—unseen and unsuspected by the living people occupying the same space. What if it meant remaining on Earth but never again able to make contact with it? ... to want most, to burn with most desire, where you were most powerless—that would be hell indeed.

"Not 'would be,' I realized with a start. Was. This was hell..." (Return from Tomorrow, pp. 59–62)

This experience left a profound impression on the young private, one that would carry over to his later work as a professional counselor:

"I gathered that these astral beings had become alcoholics when they were living on the Earth and had never been able to rid themselves of their addiction while they were human beings. They were still driven by this addiction and the only way they apparently could enjoy feeling intoxicated again was to enter a human's aura. This would profoundly affect my professional life, causing me to spend much time working with alcoholics and other substance-abuse cases.

"If only the people who are now calling for the legalization of these extremely addicting drugs could have seen what I saw, they would realize they need to have a better understanding of what happens to us after we pass through death. Human beings become addicted here and if they don't overcome the addiction while they are still alive, the Lord was showing me that this addiction does not stop just because they die." (My Life After Dying, p. 23)

Death Therapy in action, Bob! Take-home message from this chapter: overcome addictions while you still can. They won't just go away when you die.

Oh yes, and for those who are pushing for the legalization of marijuana: take a leaf out of Dr. Ritchie's book and consider the ramifications. They don't call potheads "stoners" for nothing. Sadly, however, this horse may have already bolted the stable: in a 2017 CBS News poll, the percentage of people in the United States who believe marijuana should be legalized is at 61 percent and climbing. A whole generation going to pot!

(Perhaps I'm being overly alarmist: maybe today's marijuana is less potent than it used to be. Maybe we really can keep it out of the hands of our youth. Maybe a truck stop is a good place to buy sushi.)

Back to the bar. The situation was not totally bereft of hope:

"But if this was hell, if there was no hope, then why was He [Jesus?] here beside me? Why did my heart leap for joy each time I turned to Him?" (Return from Tomorrow, p. 62)

Hope? In hell? Now there's a novel idea.

Maybe hell isn't quite as final as it's portrayed. Maybe there is hope for its inhabitants, even in death.

Before we get to hope, let's make sure we understand the depth of the problem. Private Ritchie hasn't yet seen the worst. There was more to come. As the tour progressed, he encountered another layer of hell, this even darker than the first:

"We ... were now standing ... on the edge of a wide, flat plain. ...

"Although we were apparently still somewhere on the surface of the Earth, I could see no living man or woman. The plain was crowded, even jammed with hordes of ghostly discarnate beings; nowhere was there a solid, light-surrounded person to be seen. ... And they were the most frustrated, the angriest, the most completely miserable beings I had ever laid eyes on. ...

At first I thought we were looking at some great battlefield: everywhere people were locked in what looked like fights to the death, writhing, punching, gouging. ... No one was apparently being injured...

"*They could not kill, though they clearly wanted to, because their intended victims were already dead, and so they hurled themselves at each other in a frenzy of impotent rage.*

"*If I suspected before that I was seeing hell, now I was sure of it. Up to this moment the misery I had watched consisted in being chained to a physical world of which we were no longer part. Now I saw that there were other kinds of chains. Here were no solid objects of people to enthrall the soul. These creatures seemed locked into habits of mind and emotion, into hatred, lust, destructive thought-patterns.*

"*Even more hideous than the bites and kicks they exchanged, were the sexual abuses many were performing in feverish pantomime. Perversions I had never dreamed of were being vainly attempted all around us...*

"*And the thoughts most frequently communicated had to do with the superior knowledge, or abilities, or background of the thinker. 'I told you so!' 'I always knew!' 'Didn't I warn you!' were shrieked into the echoing air over and over...*" (Return from Tomorrow, pp. 63–65)

It's difficult to picture a scene of such depravity, but why would we be surprised? Visit any modern prison and you'll find it filled with individuals who are quite capable of such behaviour. Now imagine the chaos that would ensue if there were no bars or guards to keep them in check!

As far gone and irretrievable as this company appeared to be, it seems that they were not totally lost. Private Ritchie began to notice other beings, hovering over the wretched creatures on the plain. They were similar in appearance to the being of light at his side, and none of them were rejoicing at the plight of the tragic mob. Quite the contrary:

> *"Once again, however, no condemnation came from the Presence at my side, only a compassion for these unhappy creatures that was breaking His heart. Clearly it was not His will that any one of them should be in this place.*

> *"Then what was keeping them here? ...*

> *"Unless there was a kind of consolation in finding others as loathsome as one's self, even if all we could do was hurl our venom at each other.*

> *"Perhaps this was the explanation for this hideous plain. Perhaps in the course of eons or of seconds, each creature here had sought out the company of others as pride-and-hate-filled as*

himself, until together they formed this society of the damned.

"Perhaps it was not Jesus who had abandoned them, but they who had fled from the Light that showed up their darkness. Or ... were they alone as at first it appeared? Gradually I was becoming aware that there was something else on that plain of grappling forms. Almost from the beginning I had sensed it, but for a long time I could not locate it. When I did it was with a shock that left me stunned.

"That entire unhappy plain was hovered over by beings seemingly made of light ... these immense presences were bending over the little creatures on the plain. Perhaps even conversing with them.

"Were these bright beings angels? Was the Light beside me also an angel? But the thought which had pressed itself so undeniably on my mind in that little hospital room had been: 'You are in the presence of the Son of God.' Could it be that each of these other human wraiths, wretched and unworthy like me, was also in His presence? In a realm where space and time no longer followed any rules I knew, could He be standing with each of them as He was with me?

I didn't know. All I clearly saw was that not one of these bickering beings on the plain had been abandoned. They were being attended, watched over, ministered to. And the equally observable fact was that not one of them knew it. If Jesus or his angels were speaking to them, they certainly did not hear. There was no pause in the stream of rancor coming from their own hearts; their eyes sought only some nearby figure to humiliate. It would have seemed to me impossible not to be aware of what were the hugest and most striking features of that whole landscape, except that I myself had stared at them unseeing.

"In fact, now that I had become aware of these bright presences, I realized with bewilderment that I'd been seeing them all along, without ever consciously registering the fact, as though Jesus could show me at any moment only so much as I was ready to see. Angels had crowded the living cities and towns we had visited. They had been present in the streets, the factories, the homes, even in that raucous bar, where nobody had been any more conscious of their existence than I myself had.

"And suddenly I realized that there was a common denominator to all these scenes so far. It was the failure to see Jesus. Whether it was a physical appetite, an earthly concern,

*an absorption with self—whatever got in the
way of His Light created the separation into
which we stepped at death.*" (Return from
Tomorrow, pp. 63–67)

Angels watch over us! Even in death.

George Ritchie's experience, as well as that of many
other NDEers, suggests that hell is not as final as we have
been led to believe. Perhaps hell is the final resting place
only of those who *choose* to remain there. It seems that the
work of angels is to encourage hell's inhabitants to choose
a better way. It's clearly not an easy way, but the very fact
that we're using the word *choose* in reference to death and
hell is a remarkable thing.

The near-death phenomenon seems to open the door
to the concept that hell has an exit as well as an entrance!
In truth, would a loving God want it any other way?

Whether hell has an exit or not, it's probably not a destination we want to put on our bucket list. On my drive
to work, a billboard was posted prominently on the side
of the road. In bold letters it proclaimed:

Where are you going? Heaven or Hell

I wanted to reply that I was just going to work, but
that's probably missing the point.

Just how *do* we avoid hell? The scripture on the sign
indicated that a simple expression of belief was all that
was required.

While I believe belief is important, I also maintain that more is required: like doing some good in the world.

For some, however, actions don't seem to count for much. Getting back to Dr. Rawlings's story of the mailman who pleaded not to be left in hell, there's an interesting follow-up to the story:

The mailman's cardiac arrest led to a diagnosis of coronary artery disease, which necessitated cardiac bypass surgery. The cardiologist (Dr. Rawlings) joined the surgical team in a consultant/observer role. Surgeons often chat during operations. This is Dr. Rawlings' summary of their conversation:

> *"'Isn't that interesting,' one doctor said to the others. 'This patient said he was in hell while he was being resuscitated! But that actually doesn't concern me too much. If there is a hell, I don't need to worry. I've led a respectable life and I've always taken care of my family. Other doctors may run out on their wives, but I never have. I also look after the children and I'm putting them through school. So I don't have to worry. If there is a heaven, I'll get there.'"*

Dr. Rawlings concludes:

> *"What this doctor said I knew was wrong, but I couldn't quote the Scriptures that might indicate the reasons. I looked them up later and discovered there were plenty. I just knew*

you couldn't get there by being good." (Beyond Death's Door, p. 23)

What? You can't get to heaven by being good? So just how do you get there?

Well, of course, we're back to a simple confession of faith and reliance on the grace of God. Forget the rest. Have a little fun, run around on your wife, drop the kid's college money on a Porsche.

I'm being facetious of course, and in the cardiologist's defence, a subsequent conversation indicated that the surgeon didn't believe in the existence of heaven or hell, or indeed, anything beyond the death of the body. Still, the surgeon sounds like a good man to me: he's faithful to his wife and is apparently a good father to his children. Aren't those at least steps in the right direction? Okay, so he isn't sure there's an afterlife, but is that enough to negate his efforts to live a moral life? Surely, he'll get credit for *something*?

The problem with starting down this "faith alone" road is that it leads to all sorts of erroneous conclusions, chief of which is that you have to condemn a lot of good people to an eternity of misery, simply because they didn't "believe" in the approved manner.

To illustrate: Dr. Rawlings was intrigued by the fact that the mailman could remember nothing of his terror but was only aware of a very pleasant near-death experience. He began to research the near-death phenomenon and discovered that a lot of other *non*-Christians had a similarly pleasant encounter with death. How could this be? Rather than reach the logical conclusion that "being

a Christian" isn't the only criterion for a pleasant NDE ...
there had to be another explanation:

> "*This experience of meeting a 'loving' or
> 'searching' being of light in a beautiful envi-
> ronment is commonly reported. Confessed
> atheists have told me of similar experiences,
> which, they say, proves there is no hell and
> that God, if he exists, loves everyone and
> therefore would punish no one.*

> "*In each account, however, the person is
> returned to his body before any decision is
> reached or any disposition is rendered. This
> initial encounter could conceivably repre-
> sent merely a sorting ground. It could also
> represent a deceivingly pleasant situation
> to imply security and sanctuary and to pre-
> vent a desire or need for changed lives. This
> could be a satanic deception according to
> Charles Ryrie, Billy Graham, Stephen Board
> and other Christian spokesmen who quote 2
> Corinthians 11:14 ['Satan himself is trans-
> formed into an angel of light'].*

> "*The following case involved a non-Chris-
> tian patient:*

> "*It was the third night I was in the coronary
> unit with a heart attack and I was awakened
> by the nurses. ...*

"[The patient:] *'All at once I started ascending upward rapidly through this huge tunnel. ... Then I was stopped by this brilliantly lighted person. He knew my thoughts and reviewed my life. He told me to go back—that my time would come later. I felt welcome. I don't remember getting back in my body, but I remember them waking me up and telling me my heart had stopped and they had just started it up again.'"* (Beyond Death's Door, pp. 88–89)

The implication, of course, is that since the patient was a non-Christian the *"brilliantly lighted person"* must have been Satan appearing as an angel of light. That's quite an extrapolation, but it's the only conclusion an inflexible Christian can reach. If Christians go to heaven and non-Christians go to hell, then there's no way this nonbeliever could have experienced anything other than a deceptive encounter with the devil. Right?

Never mind that he felt welcomed and looked back on the experience with fondness. I personally struggle with the concept of the Prince of Darkness knowing this man's thoughts and using that knowledge to comfort him and help him improve!

I also have a difficult time believing that the joyful, awe-inspiring, life-changing experiences of countless NDEers were just elaborate ruses of Beelzebub to lull them into complacency. I have no doubt that Satan is quite capable of turning on the charm when it's necessary, but to imply that any non-Christian having a good time in heaven is all part of a vast deception is a little beyond the pale.[58]

The argument that all these cases involved *near* death and not *final* death (and that *"the person is returned to his body before any decision is reached or any disposition is rendered"*), is a spurious one also. The implication is that if this *had* been final death, then the *"confessed atheist"* would have already been on his way to hell without passing GO and without receiving a GET OUT OF JAIL FREE card.[59]

Again, the capricious nature of a fickle God is on full display: granting the "near-death" atheist a second chance, while sending the hapless "really dead" atheist straight to hell!

Herein lies the biggest pitfall lying in the path of the near-death researcher: taking too many liberties with the facts. You absolutely have to approach the near-death phenomenon with an open mind. If you go into this thinking you already have all the answers, you run the risk of trying to manipulate the facts to fit your own preconceived assumptions. Rather than trying to squeeze the universe into the box our own intellect has constructed, we should, instead, be trying to understand where *we* fit in the universe.

Near-death survivors deal with facts. They simply try to describe what they've seen. They generally don't have their own agenda, because they've learned that there's

---

[58] The Pale was the part of Ireland directly under the control of the English government in the late Middle Ages. "Beyond the pale" simply means outside the bounds of reasonable or civilized behaviour (like where those wild Irish lived!).

[59] These are references to the board game "Monopoly," first published by Parker Brothers in 1935.

already an agenda, one much bigger and grander than anything they could come up with by themselves.

So, approach *Death Therapy* with caution, Bob. It's a powerful catalyst for change but you have to keep an open mind. You can't go into this thinking you already have all the answers and that you know more about death than those who've actually been there. It will send you down blind alleys (and it will also void the promise of a guaranteed cure!).

Heaven

Enough of hell. What about heaven?

The possibility that hell may not be the final destination of the wicked begs the question of whether the place NDEers are describing as *"heaven"* is not the final destination of the righteous, either. Could there be more to come for them also?

Most survivors seem to think they've visited "heaven." It's reflected in the titles of many of the books they've written:

My Journey to Heaven, Heaven Is for Real, To Heaven and Back, Waking Up in Heaven ...

And why not? They are describing a place of incomparable beauty and tranquillity. Shouldn't that be enough?

Glad you asked, Bob. More than one returnee has raised the tantalizing possibility that the stunning world encountered by NDEers is merely a way station on the path to something even grander. As far back as the eighteenth century, the scientist and inventor Emanuel Swedenborg described three "layers" of heaven:

"There are three heavens quite distinct from each other—an inmost or third heaven, an intermediate or second, and an outermost or first." (Heaven and Hell, p. 43)

And this from "the father of the NDE" himself, Dr. Raymond Moody:

> *"I state in 'Life After Life' that I had not found any cases in which a 'heaven'—at least in a certain traditional portrayal of that place— was described. However, I have talked with numerous individuals who tell with remarkable consistency of catching glimpses of other realms of being which might well be termed 'heavenly.' It is interesting to me that in several of these accounts a single phrase—'a city of light'—occurs."* (Reflections on Life After Life, p. 14)

Private George Ritchie was one of these individuals who was shown *"a city of light"*:

> *"We seemed to have left the Earth behind. ... We appeared to be in an immense void. ...*
>
> *And then I saw, infinitely far off, far too distant to be visible with any kind of sight I knew of ... a city. A glowing, seemingly endless city, bright enough to be seen over all the unimaginable distance between. The brightness*

seemed to shine from the very walls and streets of this place, and from beings which I could now discern moving about within it. In fact, the city and everything in it seemed to be made of light, even as the Figure at my side was made of light...

I could only gape in awe at this faraway spectacle, wondering how bright each building, each inhabitant, must be to be seen over so many light-years of distance...

"...two of the bright figures seemed to detach themselves from the city and start toward us, hurling themselves across that infinity with the speed of light.

"But as fast as they come toward us, we drew away still faster. The distance increased, the vision faded. Even as I cried out with loss, I knew that my imperfect sight could not now sustain more than an instant's glimpse of this real, this ultimate heaven. He had shown me all He could." (Return from Tomorrow, pp. 72–73)

Others have hinted at the same thing, but we'll leave it at that. Private Ritchie was only granted a glimpse of this "ultimate heaven" and it was clear that this was all he was going to get (*"He had shown me all He could"*). Clearly, we are not ready for more, either. Besides, if NDEers don't have the vocabulary to describe the place they *did* see, how in the world are they going to find the words to describe a layer of heaven *beyond* that?

Addictions

We'll close out this chapter on heaven and hell, appropriately enough, with a funeral.

A few years ago, I attended the funeral of a man who had become something of a recluse. Following his death, the contents of his house revealed that he had developed a crippling addiction which, in his later years, had probably consumed his every waking moment.

I don't know how much his pastor knew of his addiction, but the funeral service was hopeful and uplifting. This is as it should be, of course: you need to say nice things at funerals.

The message of the sermon was simple: several years prior to his death the man had confessed his faith in Christ to his pastor, and while he had rarely attended church, in the pastor's mind, this one act of contrition was all that was needed to earn him his place in heaven. He was now happily with the angels, already fitted with wings, his earthly struggles a thing of the past... instant sainthood.

My purpose is not to judge this man. He was meek and gentle and had probably never harmed a soul in his life. He wasn't blessed with many life skills and his terrible addiction had resulted in an existence that must have been a living hell. He'd already paid an awful price. I firmly believe that God will look upon him with profound compassion.

To suggest, however, that all his struggles and deficiencies are instantly wiped out at the time of death is not only naïve, but also disingenuous. It flies in the face of reason and contradicts everything near-death survivors teach us. When our spirit rises from the body, all the character traits, virtues, *and vices* that defined us in life rise with us. Sadly, for this man, I don't believe his addiction magically disappeared when he died. He will have to go through the same painful process of recovery that the living do, although he won't have the benefit of a physical body to validate his progress. This is why declarations of assured redemption based on faith alone, are, in my opinion, detrimental. They lull the hearer into believing that death short-circuits the process of repentance and grants instant sainthood. It doesn't. The truth is, that addictions and negative character traits have to be overcome, whether in life or in death. And it's infinitely better to work on them while we're alive because it doesn't get any easier in death.

The good news is that there is hope for this man. Not only is it likely that he'll seek out individuals who are meek and gentle like himself, but George Ritchie's vision of the angels hovering over lost souls implies that there may be a way out of his addiction even in death. Why else would angels work with "lost" souls unless there is real hope that they won't always remain lost?

Again we see the sublime fairness of God revealed by the NDE. The man whose funeral I attended could never have afforded a quality rehab program in life, and even if he could, I don't believe he had the will or the confidence to follow the process through. He was on his own and must have felt abandoned and incredibly lonely.

I'm convinced he's now participating in the most dynamic twelve-step addiction recovery programme in the universe. It's taught by angels, *and they will never give up on him!*

And you and I can sign up for this programme, Bob. Now, while we're still alive.

It's called *Death Therapy* ... but death isn't a requirement for enrolment!

Chapter 16

Death Therapy

"Get busy living or get busy dying."
—Stephen King, *Different Seasons* [60]

The Final Frontier

"Space: the final frontier. These are the voyages of the starship, Enterprise..." [61]

---

[60] *Different Seasons*, published in 1982, is a collection of four Stephen King novellas. One is entitled "Rita Hayworth and Shawshank Redemption: Hope Springs Eternal," which was subsequently made into a movie, *The Shawshank Redemption*, a 1994 crime/drama by Castle Rock Entertainment, directed by Frank Darabont, starring Tim Robbins, Morgan Freeman, and others. The quote was said by Ellis Boyd "Red" Redding (played by Morgan Freeman in the movie).

[61] This is from the opening title sequence of *Star Trek*, an American science fiction television series that ran from 1966 to 1969, created by Gene Roddenberry that follows the adventures of the starship *USS Enterprise* (NCC-1701) and its crew. A variation of the same opening title sequence was used for *Star Trek: The Next Generation*, also created by Gene Roddenberry, running from 1987 to 1994.

I'M NOT A TREKKIE, BUT THAT DRAMATIC introduction to "Star Trek" stirred my imagination when it debuted in 1966. I watched the first episodes in black and white, but it didn't matter. It was a provocative vision of the future. The universe was indeed full of strange new worlds, new life, and new civilizations, each one presenting a fresh challenge to the intrepid crew of the *Enterprise*. The show was so successful that it spawned several follow-ups, including: *Star Trek: The Next Generation*.

It was interesting to note the changes from the original Star Trek to The Next Generation. They were as much a reflection of the evolution of our own society as of theirs.

In a nod to the women's movement, a subtle modification was made to the introduction to The Next Generation. It was changed from: *"to boldly go where no* <u>man</u> *has gone before"* to: *"...where no* <u>one</u> *has gone before."* It took until the twenty-fourth century, but equality for women finally made its way into space.

Perhaps the reason equality was so long coming is that space apparently affected women differently than men. In the original Star Trek, a fascinating paradox manifested itself: space caused a distortion of the camera image when it was trained on a beautiful woman! Her face would become enveloped in a strange misty halo and seductive music would spontaneously erupt from nowhere. Inexplicably, the lens refocused itself and the music ceased when the camera panned back to the men! This troublesome anomaly plagued the female crew of the Enterprise during Captain Kirk's tenure. It wasn't just a "human" problem, since even alien beauties had the same mysterious effect on the camera.

It took almost a century to resolve the issue. Happily, by the time Jean-Luc Picard began his captaincy on The Next Generation, cameras were able to hone in on even the most sultry of women with laser-like focus. What changed, you ask? I have a few theories: either twenty-fourth century women were uglier than their forebears, *or* they had lost their strange allure, *or* (most likely) some technician figured out the glitch in the camera. In any event, one of the universe's more bizarre enigmas had been solved. The Enterprise was fulfilling its mission to *demystify* space (pardon the pun).

There were other marked differences between the original and the sequel. It was perhaps most noticeable in the evolution of the captains of the Enterprise: Kirk and Picard.

James Tiberius Kirk was the ultimate manly man (and with a middle name like *Tiberius* how could you be anything but!).[62] In stark contrast was the much more genteel Jean-Luc Picard: a man with a sensitive French name and a posh British accent. Picard relied on finesse and diplomacy. Kirk put his faith in phasers and photon torpedoes.

Captain Picard even had an "empathic counsellor" on his senior staff (Deanna Troi) on whom he regularly called to navigate delicate intergalactic negotiations. It would be hard to imagine Captain Kirk pausing an on-screen face-off with a Klingon warlord to ask the ship's counsellor what

---

[62] Actually, the middle name Tiberius was not revealed to be what the "T" stood for in James T. Kirk until it was mentioned in one of the cartoon episodes (*Star Trek: The Animated Series*, running from 1973 to 1974). No doubt it was still implicitly understood amongst the cast during *Star Trek* (TOS).

was causing his adversary to feel so conflicted. Better to use those precious seconds to arm the photon torpedoes.

That being said, it was nice to see women filling more prominent roles in Starfleet (other than being the out-of-focus love interest). By the time the twenty-fourth century rolled around, Starfleet was even commissioning female captains. Only five centuries had elapsed since the Suffragettes won the right to vote, so no one could complain that mankind wasn't evolving (sorry: "humankind").

But with all the social and technological advances made between the twenty-third and twenty-fourth centuries, the most glaring failure had to be the inability to solve the problem of male-pattern baldness. A bald captain on Starfleet's flagship in the twenty-fourth century doesn't bode well for the future of medical science. They'd figured out the secret to teleporting onto the Enterprise while traveling at warp speed and how to cure renal failure with a single pill, but they couldn't grow hair?! And if the cure for hair loss really is beyond the reach of mankind (sorry: "humankind"), surely there's an alien species out there somewhere that has the formula and would be willing to share it.

Perhaps, I'm not giving Captain Picard his due. Maybe they *had* solved the problem, but Jean-Luc chose not to avail himself of the cure. Maybe he felt secure in his manhood (sorry: "personhood") and was perfectly content with his shiny pate. Sadly, this is one mystery that remains unanswered—perhaps a sequel will address it.

Whatever the reason, consider investing in the Hair Club for Men—it apparently has a future![63]

---

[63] A purveyor of nonsurgical and surgical hair replacement and hair restoration options.

"Space: the final frontier..."

Space is *not* the final frontier. We've been to space. There are men and women living in space. Astronauts have returned from space and told us what's up there. The Hubble telescope has photographed galaxies billions of light-years away and peered back thirteen billion years into the universe's past. The Hubble has snapped images of galaxies spawned a mere 400 million years after the Big Bang—in cosmic terms, just about the time the new-born universe was getting its hiney slapped and taking its first breath. We know a lot about space.

Death is the *real* final frontier!

Death is final. Unlike space, death is a one-way ticket. You can't send someone to her death just to see what's there; the return rate is abysmal. You can't point a telescope at death. You can't photograph the afterlife.

For centuries, we knew very little about death. In fact, for most of the world's recorded history, we've had no hard data or eyewitnesses to tell us what death is all about. Religion was the only acknowledged authority on the subject, but even then, the information available was spotty at best: just some vague assurances that it was something to look forward to, as long as you were good. There wasn't a lot more to say.

All that changed dramatically in the middle of the twentieth century with the onset of the near-death revolution. It began in December 1943, when Private George Ritchie succumbed to pneumonia and embarked on the most comprehensive tour of the afterlife ever granted a human being. In nine minutes, he learned more about death than mankind had gleaned in thousands of years.

It would be another decade and a half before the CPR movement would begin in earnest, but when it did, all those last-minute rescues from the brink of death proved to be fertile ground for NDEs. The near-death revolution grew exponentially. Fully one in twenty people you meet can now claim first-hand knowledge of what happens to us when we die.[64] The wealth of information we've amassed in the last seventy years is staggering. We've advanced from a state of grave ignorance about death to being buried under an avalanche of information (please pardon the death puns).

So, maybe space really *is* the last frontier after all!

Think for a moment about the implications of the phenomenon we've come to know as the near-death experience. There are now literally millions of people who claim to have first-hand knowledge of the place that will be our home for eternity.

Serendipitously, by unlocking the mysteries of death, they've also unlocked many of the mysteries of life. The beauty of coming to an understanding of what counts in *death* is that it teaches us what's really important in *life*.

Further, while this knowledge is precious from a purely educational standpoint, it also has the potential to be highly transformative in a behavioural sense.

This is an important point: as valuable as this knowledge is in its own right, its true value lies in its ability to change behaviour. As one author put it:

---

[64] This poll was mentioned in the Introduction of *Coming Back to Life: The After-Effects of the Near-Death Experience* by P. M. H. Atwater.

"In talking to all of these near-death experiencers, I had come to believe something: they are all transformed by this experience of light...

"Some researchers have gone so far as to state that one cannot have had a 'real' NDE unless one is transformed by it. Phyllis Atwater, for instance, says that the aftereffects of the NDE are the yardstick for its authenticity."
(Transformed by the Light, p. 6)

In other words, the real proof in the near-death pudding is whether the experience changes lives.

Here are a few testimonials from NDEers themselves about the transformative power of the near-death experience:

"I'm no longer afraid of death because I'll never forget what happened to me there. Now I'm certain that life goes on. Over the years I've undergone a number of changes. I feel a strong connection with nature. The garden now plays an important role in my life. I've become much more emotional. I've acquired a great sense of justice. I've become more patient and peaceful. I can see things in perspective now. My aggression is a thing of the past. I feel a strong inner urge to never lie again. I'd rather keep silent than tell a little white lie...

"I enjoy life immensely." (Consciousness Beyond Life, pp. 47–48)

Loss of the fear of death is an almost universal theme among survivors. Some even remark that the very word "death" is frowned upon by those in the know. To them, the process of dying is more of a beginning than an ending. "Rebirth" may be a more accurate term. Death is really just a new start.

> *"Although this event occurred a long time ago, it marked a very crucial point in my life. I began a new chapter; a chapter which was to continue for the rest of my life. This moment and the following minutes and hours changed my life entirely. I was transformed from a man who was lost and wandering aimlessly, with no goal in life other than a desire for material wealth, to someone who had a deep motivation, a purpose in life, a definite direction, and an overpowering conviction that there would be a reward at the end of life...*

> *"The changes in my life were completely positive. My interest in material wealth and greed for possessions were replaced by a thirst for spiritual understanding and a passionate desire to see world conditions improve."* (Heading Toward Omega, p. 99)

Again, common themes: motivation, purpose, direction, conviction. The knowledge that we have a purpose on Earth often leads to a radically new perspective on our relationships and interactions with others:

> *"Before my accident, the behavior of some of my colleagues deeply aggravated and irritated me. Afterward, while I still didn't like the behavior, I realized that I do not know their purpose on Earth, nor why they are in my life. As difficult as it sometimes to accept, I do know that God loves each one of them every bit as much as He loves me. Rather than being irritated by their behavior, I now take joy in the knowledge that their behavior is teaching me patience and I give thanks for this. I also began to pray for them, which has changed my perspective significantly."* (To Heaven and Back, p. 101)

Barbara:

> *"The only emotion I feel is love. ... I don't get caught up much anymore in anger with my kids or my husband. ... Jealousy and all those other things have been gone for years."* (Heading Toward Omega, p. 128)

> *"Well, I think it makes you more tolerant of other people, a little bit more understanding. ... I don't think I judge people quite as harshly as I once did. ... Maybe I have a better sense*

of humor than I once had." (Heading Toward Omega, p. 129)

Love, patience, tolerance, understanding, compassion—these are all the virtues this world could use in greater abundance.

NDEers learn that it's okay to be happy. They also want others to be happy:

> *"My joy comes from another's smile. I also notice that I reach out and touch people more. ... I seem to make people feel better. I know this— that when there's a family problem, everyone turns to me. ... I have more insight into other people. ... It's very difficult for me to lose my temper anymore. I can see the pain in other people's eyes. That's why they hurt other people because they really don't understand. ... The most important thing that we have are our relationships with other people. ... It all comes down to caring and compassion and love for your fellow man. ... Love is the answer. It's the answer to everything."* (The Return from Silence, pp. 195–96)

You'll struggle to find an NDEer who isn't changed by the experience, but the benefits aren't exclusive to the protagonist. The passive observer is also affected. This is what happened to Raymond Moody, the author of Life After Life. He listened to George Ritchie's tale and felt a stirring in his soul. After interviewing more than two hundred near-death survivors, Moody realized that his own life could never be the same again.

The same can be said of the many doctors who were inspired by their patients' experiences. Many of the books on NDEs are written by medical doctors (which is not unexpected, since doctors are on the front lines of the battle with death).

That being said, the average doctor tends to get uncomfortable when patients come to us with bizarre metaphysical claims. We're scientists and pragmatists at heart. We're trained to stack our patients' stories up against the monolith of established medical science, and NDEs don't stack up well.

When patients provide proof, however, it's harder to ignore.

The "proof" comes in two parts: first, patients often cite details of their resuscitation which they couldn't possibly have witnessed with mortal eyes, and second, it becomes increasingly difficult to deny the remarkable changes in the life of the near-death survivor.

Dr. Melvin Morse, a paediatrician, noticed significant changes in the later lives of his young near-death patients:

> *"People who have had NDEs exercise more than the 'normal' population, eat more fruits and vegetables, use fewer medications like aspirin and other over-the-counter remedies. They also have fewer psychosomatic complaints, miss less time from work, and have fewer years of unemployment than the control groups.*

"Also, they have fewer hidden symptoms of depression and anxiety than any of the control groups. They spend more time alone in solitary pursuits or in meditation or quiet contemplation...

"Those touched by the light at an early age give more of themselves to the community by performing volunteer work. They also give more of their income to charities and are often in helping professions like nursing or special education.

Apparently there is some quality in their experience of light that makes them gravitate toward those professions." (Transformed by the Light, pp. 189–190)

Dr. Morse quickly realized that his young patients' stories were more than just the products of overactive imaginations. Children don't prevaricate, they just tell the truth. And the proof was in the form of changed lives—including the life of the paediatrician who listened to them.

All these benefits have been well documented in the growing body of near-death literature, but there is one more layer of the NDE that the literature has largely ignored: the phenomenon's potential effect on those who are not connected with it in any way.

That's where *Death Therapy* comes in. *Death Therapy* peels back one more layer of the near-death onion and speaks to the vast majority of the population (95 percent) who have neither had a near-death experience, nor met someone who has. That would be you and me, Bob!

We are ignorant, naïve, and uninformed! But we do have one thing going for us:

We can read!

Just by reading a lot of near-death accounts, a subtle but real transformation can occur in your life and mine. It won't be the epiphany of the experiencer, nor the awe of the interviewer, but it can be an enduring change nonetheless. At the very least, these principles will be on our minds and will surely influence the way we live our lives.

This is how it has affected me:

When I run into someone who's difficult to love, I find myself thinking about the love that emanates from the being of light—and empathy comes a little easier.

When my first inclination is to lash out at someone who's ruffled my pride, I can't help but think of that life review—and compassion wells up to displace wrath.

When I'm tempted to make decisions that could harm another, I try to think how my actions will affect *them*— and the scales tip toward altruism.

When I start allowing myself the luxury of bad behaviour, I find my thoughts drifting to that place where self-delusion isn't possible.

And on and on. You get the picture.

I'm not ready for sainthood, but I do like to think I'm a better person for having studied the phenomenon of near-death. At the very least, these principles are frequently in my thoughts and have become something of a guiding light to me.

With all that in mind, and as I contemplate the inevitable review of my own life someday, I should probably practice what I preach and apologise to anyone I may have offended during the course of this book. I don't want to come to that life review haunted by a long list of individuals who took offence to my words. This list of those to whom I owe an apology is presented in the order in which they appear in the book; the order does not necessarily reflect the depth of remorse I feel toward each group.

My heartfelt apologies to:

Chicken McNugget connoisseurs, British chefs, French chefs, bikers, baseball fans, the British press, Hillary supporters, cat lovers, supermodels, religious fanatics and elitists, mega-pastors, Hollywood scriptwriters, and last but not least: people who drive too slow in the fast lane.

Glad I got that out of the way. I feel much better.

Getting back to the beneficial effects of NDEs on the reader: Wouldn't this world be a much happier place if everyone were to understand what's expected of us in the afterlife? Wouldn't our society be better if we were all a little kinder to each other, kinder to animals and to the environment? Wouldn't it be more peaceful if we were more tolerant of religious differences, more willing to look for the good in every religion? What if we were to turn our intolerance for others into intolerance for our own failings? What if we all tried to make our corner of this world a little microcosm of the idyllic world to come?

NDEs affirm that life has meaning. They teach us that every soul is precious, that everyone has worth, that we should give up on no one. They teach us that there is good in everyone, even if it's sometimes difficult to find. They teach that love conquers all. Above all, they teach that every soul is loved by God, more than we can possibly fathom.

As precious as this knowledge has become to me, I still have to confess to being a little jealous of near-death survivors. They've enjoyed a vision of such majesty that nothing I experience could even begin to compare. I would love to know what it feels like to be loved unconditionally. I'd love to have unrestricted access to the secrets of the universe. I'd love to know what it's like to actually look forward to dying!

All those things would be nice, but the problem is that the price is just too high—the price is death.[65]

And dying is definitely not on my agenda today!

But here's the wonderful thing: we can still benefit from the near-death experience without having to go through the decided inconvenience of dying! All we have to do is consider the words of those who *have* died.

True it is that reading about it will never be the same as being there, but the stark reality, Bob, is that you and I are not going to be there until it's too late to do much about it. So, the only question remaining is whether it's worth investing our time *now* to learn about death, *before* it's at our doorstep.

For me, there are three very good reasons for learning about death:

---

[65] This is reminiscent of the 1965 Loretta Lynn song, "Everybody Wants to Go to Heaven, But Nobody Wants to Die."

One: death is where we will be spending the balance of eternity. This mortal life is a mere blip in the timeline of our existence. Wouldn't it be nice to know something about our permanent home?

Two: how we live *now* determines what sort of life we can expect to live *then*. This is an incontrovertible fact. Our actions determine what we *become*, and what we *become* determines where we will *end up*. The last thing we want to do is arrive at that life review with a heart filled with malice and a long list of offences to answer for. It will make for a *very* long and painful movie, (maybe even longer and more painful than Gone with the Wind, although that's a stretch).[66]

And three: the knowledge we gain about death won't just become useful when we get there. It can help us lead happy, productive lives *now*. Where else can you find a greater source of practical life skills?

This is the whole premise of *Death Therapy*: living better lives by learning from the experiences of those who've died and come back.

While there isn't a lot written about the impact of NDEs on those who haven't been personally exposed to it, a few authors have commented on the possibilities:

> *"Human beings have the ability to be inspired
> by a light which has the power to transform*

---

[66] *Gone with the Wind* is a 1939 drama/history/romance by Selznick International Pictures, directed by Victor Fleming, George Cukor, and Sam Wood, starring Clark Gable, Vivien Leigh, and others. It runs for three hours and fifty-eight minutes, not including the intermission time.

them. We do not have to die to learn from this experience. We only have to be open to its message." (Transformed by the Light, p. 218)

"It's not just those who experience NDEs whose lives change—those who study NDEs are impacted as well. A survey of those studying NDEs on the university level found the students reporting increased compassion, increased self-worth, a stronger conviction of life after death, a strengthened view of God, a stronger spiritual orientation, and a stronger conviction of the purposefulness of life." (Near-Death Experiences, p. 151)

"Those who believe that these are real brushes with eternity might aspire to live as if they'd experienced an NDE, since NDEers typically claim that their lives are fuller and richer as a result. Many of those who study NDEs report that their lives change as a result of their research. I believe this study has impacted my own life." (Near-Death Experiences, p. 83)

"From the study of the NDE, we have learned to see death in a new way, not as something to be dreaded but, on the contrary, as an encounter with the Beloved. Those who can come to understand death in this way, as NDEers are compelled to, need never fear death again. And liberated from this primary fear, they too,

*like NDEers, become free to experience life as
the gift it is and to live naturally, as a child
does, with delight. Not everyone can have
or needs to have an NDE, but everyone can
learn to assimilate these lessons of the NDE
into his own life if he chooses to."* (Heading
Toward Omega, p. 268)

*"More than academic and professional issues
are involved. It involves deeply personal issues,
for what we learn about death may make an
important difference in the way we live our
lives. If experiences of the type which I have
discussed are real, they have very profound
implications for what every one of us is doing
with his life. For, then it would be true that
we cannot fully understand this life until we
catch a glimpse of what lies beyond it."* (Life
After Life, p. 184)

In his book, Heading Toward Omega (again, *Omega*
being the last letter of the Greek alphabet and therefore
the *end*), Kenneth Ring postulates the fascinating possibility that the NDE is part of a grand evolutionary movement in humanity's progression:

*"May it be that NDEers—and others who
have had similar awakenings—collectively
represent an evolutionary thrust toward
higher consciousness for humanity at large?
Could it be that the NDE itself is an evolutionary mechanism that has the effect of*

*jump-stepping individuals into the next stage
of human development by unlocking spiritual potentials previously dormant? Indeed,
are we seeing in such people—as they mutate
from their pre-NDE personalities into more
loving and compassionate individuals—the
prototype of a new, more advanced strain
of the human species striving to come into
manifestation?*

*"...Why are so many people having NDEs and
other transformative spiritual experiences at
this time in our history?"* (Heading Toward
Omega, pp. 255 and 259)

Why, indeed? Private George Ritchie also believed
that it wasn't just coincidence that the near-death phenomenon had arrived at this particular time in history. He
was of the opinion that the NDE was a necessary coun-
terbalance to the extreme troubles the world would soon
face. He believed, however, that it is not evolution, but
God, who is in the driver's seat:

*"God is busy building a race of men who know
how to love. I believe that the fate of the Earth
itself depends on the progress we make—and
that time now is very short. As for what we'll
find in the next world, here too I believe that
what we'll discover there depends on how well
we get on with the business of loving, here and
now."* (Return from Tomorrow, p. 12)

Evolution or God? Or both? It doesn't matter. If the near-death phenomenon is helping to improve our society, that can only be a good thing. If it helps you and me *"get on with the business of loving,"* that's even better. It isn't much more complicated than that.

Death Therapy works, Bob. It's simple, it's cheap, and it's guaranteed.

Conclusion

I WAS GIVEN A JIGSAW PUZZLE FOR MY birthday a couple of years ago. It was a landscape featuring beautiful Neuschwanstein Castle in Bavaria, Germany. Neuschwanstein is a gorgeous castle in a picturesque setting. It's been featured in many prominent films and was the inspiration for Disneyland's Sleeping Beauty Castle.

This was a two-thousand-piece jigsaw, by far the biggest I've done. There was a lot of homogeneous sky, a lot of homogeneous mountains, and an *awful* lot of *very* homogeneous forest. The castle was the "easy" part.

Each piece had to be painstakingly found by sifting through the mass of possibilities. It took several weeks to complete and became a labour of love.

I constructed the jigsaw on a large whiteboard with a raised border. I kept the project atop a high bar, beyond the reach of our grandchildren. Miraculously, it survived to completion, and one glorious afternoon I triumphantly dropped the last piece in place and stood back to admire my handiwork.

It was difficult to view horizontally on the countertop, so I had the bright idea of tilting it vertically, the theory being that the rim of the whiteboard would keep the whole thing in place.

(You can probably guess where this is going.)

I carefully raised the board to an angle of about seventy-five degrees and propped it up against the wall. So far, so good.

The countertop was smooth, and I knew it was too much of a risk to leave the board unsupported. The problem was that there was nothing at hand to brace it. I remembered there was a heavy metal weight outside the back door, a mere twenty feet away. The board seemed to be holding in place, so I raced outside, retrieved the weight, and raced back in as fast as I could. The picture was facing me as I entered the house. It looked stunning.

As I got within a few feet of the jigsaw, the board began to slide off the slick countertop. I wasn't fast enough: the jigsaw hit the ground and shattered into a thousand pieces (two thousand pieces, to be precise!).

Actually, the puzzle didn't completely break up—large portions of it were still intact. For a moment, I wondered if it could still be salvaged.

Sadly not. Murphy's Law states that "anything that can go wrong, will go wrong." The dog's water bowl just happened to be on the floor by the bar and it took a direct hit from the whiteboard. Naturally, the bowl was full of water.

So, now my jigsaw is sitting in a pool of water, and if it was difficult to fit all those little pieces together when they were dry, imagine trying to do it when they're a mass of soggy cardboard! My masterpiece was toast (pulp, actually). I got to enjoy it for all of five minutes.

So, what's the moral of the story (apart from the obvious: DON'T DO STUPID STUFF!)?

Remember Viktor Frankl's, Man's Search for Meaning? I've tried to find meaning in my jigsaw fiasco. It wasn't easy, but this is what I came up with:

The sum total of our existence will be the aggregate of everything we've said and done while we lived. Words and actions combine to create a vibrant portrait of the person we really are. Every kind word or action adds to the beauty of the landscape; every unkind word or selfish act detracts from it. The end result can be either a work of art—or a soggy mess—or something in between. We choose every moment of every day what the final product will look like.

Near-death survivors teach us that life is a precious gift, an invitation to make something beautiful of our lives, a chance to create a masterpiece. They teach us that life endures, that consciousness continues, that *everything* we say and do has consequences, and that the effects will ripple through the eternities. They teach us that death is not to be feared, that it's something to be anticipated with joy, that a glorious future awaits us. They teach us that life has meaning.

We began this book with Bob Wiley alone in the woods, contemplating his fate. He was tied up, canisters of black powder around his neck, timer ticking. In his sweet naïveté, Bob believed the bombs were fake—just another brainchild of his innovative psychiatrist.

As for Dr. Marvin, he made no pretence of subtlety. He just wanted to get rid of Bob, and if that required twenty pounds of gunpowder, so be it. This cure was going to be permanent.

Dr. Marvin was right, but not in the way he intended. Unwittingly, his twisted scheme untwisted Bob's emotional knots and cured him of a lifetime of phobias. Where all others had failed, Dr. Marvin succeeded. Bob was inspired to embark on a new career as a psychologist and to write a book about his experience: *Death Therapy*. It became a bestseller and jump-started a new school of therapeutic ideology.

But *Death Therapy* never got written, because the movie is fiction, and that's a shame because it's a great title.

If Bob *had* written the book, what would he have said? I believe he would have said that by forcing him to face his own mortality, Dr. Marvin gave him the motivation to make some needed and lasting changes in his life. Gunpowder gave Bob a *reason* to change.

And when you think about it, that's exactly what near-death experiences do. They remind us that we are mortal beings and that one day this life will end. NDEs cause us to confront the truth of what life is really all about and to reflect on the pressing question of what comes next.

Learning about death changes you! It's my belief that study of the near-death experience is one of the most beneficial exercises that we, the living, can engage in. This phenomenon has the potential to change lives like no other. The NDE is a gift to mankind, given at a moment in time when it's needed the most. Our society is on life support and desperately needs a shot in the arm. *Death Therapy* may be just the tonic we need.

So, thanks for taking this journey with me, Bob. Those bombs around your neck—they really are phony. You have no reason to fear death. Just embrace it and learn from it.

It's Death Therapy, Bob. And it really is a guaranteed cure!

Afterword

I'VE TRIED TO KEEP MY RELIGIOUS CON-
victions out of this book. My reasons are threefold:

First, I believe the near-death experience transcends
religion. It's as pertinent to an atheist as it is to a Buddhist,
a Hindu, or a carpet salesman. Labels mean little in death.
Character and integrity are everything. If there's a take-
home message from the NDE, it's that religion is most
helpful if it teaches us to be tolerant and kind toward
those not of our faith.

Second, much of the criticism levelled against people
of faith is brought on by those who *do* put stock in labels
and use them to justify claims to salvational exclusivity.
It really is naïve, when you think about it, to believe that
any of us has a monopoly on truth and that everyone else
is deluded and lost. Near-death survivors teach us that
anyone who lives up to the best principles of humanity
can anticipate a glorious afterlife. I believe this applies
to believers and nonbelievers alike. My atheist friends
are some of the most charitable people I know, and since
they believe there is no afterlife (and therefore no hope
of eternal reward), this makes their altruism all the more

impressive. Every good thing *I* do is done in expectation of a payoff!

Third, anyone with strong religious convictions is unfortunately exposed to the ever-present danger of manipulating the near-death literature to fit their own particular version of the truth. The antidote to this is to just let NDEers speak for themselves, but even then one has to avoid the trap of "cherry-picking" the NDE accounts to fit the narrative. Some bias inevitably creeps in, and for that I apologise. In the end, each of us has to decide for ourselves what to accept as truth and what to reject.

I don't know whether my particular interpretation of the NDE is entirely accurate. What I *do* know is that studying near-death has changed me for the better. My hope is that *Death Therapy* might encourage you to look deeper into this most fascinating of subjects, and that doing so will enrich your life, as it has mine.

Thanks for listening.

Bibliography

Alexander, Eben. *Proof of Heaven: A Neurosurgeon's Journey into the Afterlife*. New York: Simon & Schuster, 2013

Atwater, P. M. H. *Coming Back to Life: The After-Effects of the Near-Death Experience*. New York: HarperCollins, 1988

Atwater, P. M. H. "Is There a Hell? Surprising Observations About the Near-Death Experience," *Journal of Near-Death Studies* 10, no. 3 (spring 1992)

Atwater, P. M. H. *Near-Death Experiences, The Rest of the Story: What They Teach Us About Living and Dying and Our True Purpose*. New York: Hampton Roads, 2011

Bennett, R. William. *Jacob T. Marley*. New York: Shadow Mountain, 2011

Besteman, Marvin J. and Lorilee Craker. *My Journey to Heaven: What I Saw and How It Changed My Life*. New York: Revell, 2012

Brinkley, Dannion and Paul Perry. *Saved by the Light: The True Story of a Man Who Died Twice and the Profound Revelations He Received.* New York: HarperCollins, 1994

Burke, John. *Imagine Heaven: Near-Death Experiences, God's Promises, and the Exhilarating Future That Awaits You.* Grand Rapids, MI, 2015

Burpo, Todd and Sonja. *Heaven Changes Everything: Living Every Day with Eternity in Mind.* Nashville, TN: Thomas Nelson, 2012

Burpo, Todd and Lynn Vincent. *Heaven Is for Real: A Little Boy's Astounding Story of His Trip to Heaven and Back.* New York: Nelson, 2010

Carter, Chris. *Science and the Near-Death Experience: How Consciousness Survives Death.* New York: Inner Traditions, 2010

Dickens, Charles. *A Christmas Carol.* New York: Chapman & Hall, 1843

Flynn, Charles P. *After the Beyond: Human Transformation and the Near-Death Experience.* New York: Prentice Hall, 1985

Frankl, Viktor E. *Man's Search for Meaning.* New York: Beacon Press, 1946

Gibson, Arvin S. *Glimpses of Eternity: New Near-Death Experiences.* New York: Horizon Publishers & Distributors, 1992

Grey, Margot. *Return from Death: An Exploration of the Near-Death Experience.* New York: Arkana, 1985

Grosso, Michael. *Experiencing the Next World Now.* New York: Simon & Schuster, 2004

Heinerman, Joseph. *Spirit World Manifestations.* Salt Lake City: Magazine Printing, 1978

McVea, Crystal and Alex Tresniowski. *Waking Up in Heaven: A True Story of Brokenness, Heaven, and Life Again.* New York: Simon & Schuster, 2013

Miller, Steve J. *Near-Death Experiences: As Evidence for the Existence of God and Heaven.* Acworth, GA: Wisdom Creek Press, 2012

Milton, John. *Paradise Lost: A Poem Written in Ten Books.* London: Samuel Simmons, 1667

Moody, Jr., Raymond A. *Life After Life.* New York: Mockingbird Books, 1975

Moody, Jr., Raymond A. *Reflections on Life After Life: More Important Discoveries in the Ongoing Investigation of Survival of Life After Bodily Death.* New York: Random House, 1977

Moody, Jr., Raymond A. and Paul Perry. *Glimpses of Eternity: Sharing a Loved One's Passage from This Life to the Next.* New York: Guideposts, 2010

Moody, Jr., Raymond A. and Paul Perry. *Reunions: Visionary Encounters with Departed Loved Ones.* New York: Random House, 1993

Moody, Jr., Raymond A. and Paul Perry. *The Light Beyond: New Explorations by the Author of Life After Life.* New York: Sobel Weber Associates, 1988

Morse, Melvin L. and Paul Perry. *Closer to the Light: Learning from Children's Near-Death Experiences.* New York: Villard, 1990

Morse, Melvin L. and Paul Perry. *Transformed by the Light: The Powerful Effect Of Near-Death Experiences on People's Lives.* New York: Piatkus Books, 1992

Neal, Mary C. *To Heaven and Back: A Doctor's Extraordinary Account of Her Death, Heaven, Angels, and Life Again: A True Story.* New York: Crown Publishing Group, 2011

Rawlings, Maurice. *Beyond Death's Door.* New York: Random House, 1978

Ring, Kenneth. *Heading Toward Omega: In Search of the Meaning of the Near-Death Experience.* New York: Harper Perennial, 1984

Ring, Kenneth. *Life at Death: A Scientific Investigation of the Near-Death Experience.* New York: William Morrow and Company, 1980

Ritchie, George G. *My Life After Dying: Becoming Alive to Universal Love.* New York: Hampton Roads, 1991

Ritchie, George G. *Ordered to Return.* New York: Hampton Roads, 1991

Ritchie, George G. and Elizabeth Sherrill. *Return from Tomorrow.* New York: Baker Publishing Group, 1978

Rogo, D. Scott. *The Return from Silence: A Study of Near-Death Experiences.* New York: Aquarian Press, 1989

Sabom, Michael B. *Recollections of Death: A Medical Investigation.* New York: HarperCollins, 1982

Sartori, Penny. *The Wisdom of Near-Death Experiences.* London: Watkins Publishing, 2014

Serdahely, William J. and Barbara A Walker. "The Near-Death Experience of a Nonverbal Person with Congenital Quadriplegia," *Journal of Near-Death Studies* 9, no. 2 (winter 1990)

Swedenborg, Emanuel. *Heaven and Hell.* New York: Simon & Schuster, 1758

Top, Brent L. and Top, Wendy C. *Glimpses Beyond Death's Door: Gospel Insights into Near-Death Experiences.* New York: Covenant Communications, 2010 van Lommel, Pim. *Consciousness Beyond Life: The Science of Near-Death Experience.* New York: Harper Collins, 2010

Zalesky, Carol. *Otherworld Journeys: Accounts of Near-Death Experience in Medieval and Modern Times.* New York: Oxford University Press, 1987